PRAISE FOR *UNDERSTANDING RADICALISM:*
HOW IT AFFECTS WHAT'S HAPPENING IN
EDUCATION AND ITS IMPACT ON STUDENTS

"It is a well-known fact, that public education in America has been sowing the seeds of secularization for over half a century. In recent years the intolerant fruit of radical progressive ideologies is being reaped in public schools. Unsurprisingly, this has led many who hold to traditional Christian values to homeschool and private education. Dr. Zarra brilliantly exposes the harmful secular indoctrination and woke ideology that is radicalizing public schools and grooming children across America. This impressive work underscores the desperate need for truth in education. Dr. Zarra rightly appeals to wisdom in the pages of this book to address the challenges. It is a fight that requires us to heed the warning of scripture, 'that no one takes you captive by philosophy and empty deceit, according to human tradition, according to the elemental spirits of the world, and not according to Christ' (Colossians 2:8). This is a battle for the young people in America. And I dare say a battle for the souls of this generation that is worth fighting. I'm grateful to have this tremendous resource!"

—Wes Carpenter, author, *Woke Religion: Unmasking*
the False Gospel of Social Justice

"Dr. Ernie Zarra is an indispensable watchman on the wall who keeps the faithful apprised about the ever-worsening, nightmarish, and declining path of academia. Furthermore, he helps to equip readers by warning them and responding to the troublesome direction of education. I consider it a great honor and privilege to feature Ernie on my daily live broadcast, *Iron Sharpens Iron Radio*, and know of no other author who is his equal on shedding light upon and into the darkness of radical, leftist, scholastic elitism. I look forward to additional interviews to introduce his invaluable new work, *Understanding Radicalism*, to my global audience. I pray that this exposure leads many concerned parents, students, and educators to add this vital book to their arsenal in repudiating cultural lies, preserving truth, and empowering minds."

—Chris Arnzen, host, *IronSharpensIronRadio.com*

Understanding Radicalism

How It Affects What's Happening in Education and Its Impact on Students

Ernest J. Zarra III

ROWMAN & LITTLEFIELD
Lanham • Boulder • New York • London

Published by Rowman & Littlefield
An imprint of The Rowman & Littlefield Publishing Group, Inc.
4501 Forbes Boulevard, Suite 200, Lanham, Maryland 20706
www.rowman.com

86-90 Paul Street, London EC2A 4NE, United Kingdom

British Library Cataloguing in Publication Information Available

Library of Congress Cataloging-in-Publication Data

Names: Zarra, Ernest J., 1955- author.
Title: Understanding radicalism : how it affects what's happening in education and its
    impact on students / Ernest J. Zarra III.
Description: Lanham, Maryland : Rowman & Littlefield, [2023] | Includes
    bibliographical references and index. | Summary: "Understanding Radicalism explains
    the approaches taken by teachers and influencers whose end-game is the creation of
    ideological activists through indoctrination of students. These students eventually take
    to the streets as activists, cancel those on school and college campuses, and attack
    dissenting parents as domestic terrorists"—Provided by publisher.
Identifiers: LCCN 2023007692 (print) | LCCN 2023007693 (ebook) | ISBN
    9781475869484 (cloth) | ISBN 9781475869491 (paperback: acid-free paper) | ISBN
    9781475869507 (epub)
Subjects: LCSH: Education—Political aspects—United States. | Education—Philosophy.
    | Public schools—United States. | Education, Humanistic—United States. | Teachers—
    Political activity—United States. | Radicalization—United States. | Online social
    networks—Political aspects—United States. | Internet and activism—United States. |
    Radicalism—United States—21st century. | United States—Social conditions—2020-
Classification: LCC LC89 .Z3 2023 (print) | LCC LC89 (ebook) | DDC 379.73—dc23/
    eng/20230324
LC record available at https://lccn.loc.gov/2023007692
LC ebook record available at https://lccn.loc.gov/2023007693

This book is dedicated to parents who understand the signs of the times and who are stepping in to rescue their children from the dangers of radicalism. Their job is enormous and they need all the support they can get.

I also dedicate this book to Generation Z. My prayer is that the indoctrination that your generation is experiencing is overtaken by a spiritual awakening to truth, logic, and biological reality.

Last, I dedicate this book to the physicians and counselors who understand exactly what is taking place in American culture under the guise of a pseudo-identity movement. Please continue to hold the line against the insidious trend to alter minor children's bodily integrity.

Contents

List of Tables

Foreword

If you care about dark trends in educational philosophy and policy in America and how these ideas are disseminated from the philosophers into the classroom, the boardroom, the legislature, and even the pulpit, then *Understanding Radicalism: How It Affects What's Happening in Education and Its Impact on Students* is for you.

If you think that critical thinking is better than indoctrination, that reason is a better guide to reality than emotion, and that the Judeo-Christian tradition has more wisdom than Marxism and its spin-offs, then you will cheer, as I did, when you read *Understanding Radicalism*. This book is written by a well-published scholar who is knowledgeable in educational theory, political ideology, American history, and worldviews. Therefore, Dr. Ernest J. Zarra's treatment of how American radicalism has shaped our institutions through indoctrination and activism is highly valuable. It shines light into the darkness and the darkness cannot hold out against it.

The word "radical" may mean many things. Most basically, it means "to get to the root." As such, it is descriptively neutral or, as we say, we want to "get to the bottom of things." Similarly, if I claim that a book is "radically biblical," I mean that it is *rooted* in the Bible and is *biblical in its essence*. I wanted my own academic contribution, *Fire in the Streets*,[1] to expose critical race theory (CRT), and to be *radical* in the sense of getting to the philosophical roots of CRT, and to offer a better alternative.

The desire to be radical is philosophically commendable, since we should avoid smokescreens, obfuscations, misinformation, disinformation, and confusions about the meanings of terms as well as about social, political, and religious movements. We ought to "cut to the chase" in our evaluations, as I tried to do in *Fire in the Streets*—especially given all the confusion and misdirection being spouted about "social justice." Dr. Zarra's ambition is the same as mine—to get to the root of current issues through rigorous investigation historically, politically, and philosophically. By being radical in his assessment of radicalism, he reveals how radically wrong and radically dangerous radicalism is!

But people hijack words all the time, and *radical* is one of them. Today, to be *radical* means to be a leftist or leftwing politically. Radicals, in this sense, do not want to get to the root of America's greatness by rediscovering and implementing our founding principles.[2] Rather, they yearn to uproot American order and replace it with an un-American, statist, and socialist system, out-of-sync with the vision of our brilliant (although flawed) Founders. We saw that ideology at work in flames of the race riots in the summer of 2020. And, of course, this radicalism must be indoctrinated at the earliest possible age in state schools, the engines of a secular agenda. Everything from the old order—religion, traditional sexual morality, the traditional family—must be delegitimized and replaced—each of which is chronicled in *Understanding Radicalism*.

But the left is not radical in the positive sense, since it fails to understand the roots of human nature, sexuality, the basis of morality, the nature of the state and civil society, the secret of human flourishing, and our true standing in God's world as made in his image, although fallen. Because the left misses the roots of reality, its fruits are rotten, corrupt, and corrupting of others, as Dr. Zarra so astutely demonstrates in this clearly-written, deeply-researched, and timely book.

Dr. Douglas Groothuis,
professor of Philosophy at Denver Seminary

NOTES

1. Douglas Groothuis. *Fire in the streets: How you can confidently respond to incendiary cultural topics*. 2022. Washington, DC: Salem Books.
2. Ibid.

Preface

It has been said that a person is radicalized when (1) an ideology takes shape in his or her mind, (2) critical thinking has been neutralized or suspended by emotions, and (3) actions promoting an ideology manifest themselves by him or her. The process of radicalization includes the mind, the heart, and the body. While this is generally true of young adults, this same process cannot be assumed to occur in the same fashion in the hearts and minds of younger children. Make no mistake about it. Children are being indoctrinated and this indoctrination will mature over time. But the key to radicalization of young children is the building of relational empathy and playing on the sense of uninformed right and wrong.

This book is written to expose the indoctrination that is taking place in American public education. Students as young as kindergarten come home from school questioning their feelings and their bodies. Because children have natural innate trust in their teachers, competing ideologies from home and school may cause confusion. Children are being confused as to what is true and what is error, and their confusion has become a family matter.[1]

THE PROBLEMS DEFINED

Can a person be radicalized and not become an activist? The answer depends on whether or not one's mind is sold on an ideology and whether one's emotions are truly invested in what is believed. It can be argued that an activist has indeed been indoctrinated by an ideology toward a cause but lacks the initiative to act upon it. This can occur with students favoring the political, religious, or moral right or the left. There is difficulty in trying to prove that one's ideological beliefs will always lead to activism. What is clear in both, however, is that indoctrination has had to have occurred in minds in both instances. This remains truly a present concern throughout K–12 education in America.[2]

In previous books, I have chronicled changes in education policy and practice (*The Wrong Direction for Today's Schools*), examined the changes in the nature and behaviors of students (*The Entitled Generation*), and demonstrated how the conversion from *e pluribus unum* to self-deification and racial separation (*When the Secular becomes Sacred*) have led us to the current station of education in the United States.

There are problems between warring political and religious factions in American culture, as one side sees progress while the other sees indoctrination. Both sides would agree that what is at stake are the minds and hearts of the next generation. Many parents sense this battle but are not certain how to move forward. One of the reasons is, "Today's militants are already a great deal more pragmatic than their parents' or grandparents' were in their youth. In mobilizing for things such as universal health care, a Green New Deal, debt cancellation . . . the . . . left thinks in terms of institutions and an expansion of democratic state power."[3] Not everyone agrees with this pragmatism.

Schools across America have shown signs of radicalization. The classical meaning and purpose of education in the United States has been undermined by a conscious effort to create a system that evokes compliance and signifies obedience to an ideology that subverts the pursuit of knowledge. This effort is not unlike those of the past in the United States.

The decades through which I have taught are evidence enough of the changes that have taken place. The creation of radical activists, instead of math scholars, does not bode well for the nation. Students are keen on protesting in the streets and causing disruption to the lives of average Americans, yet have little to no idea about the history of their own nation.

Literacy and reading scores continue to plummet, particularly in urban areas. In some areas there are less than 10 percent of graduating high school seniors who can read at grade level. Yet, these same students seem to understand how to riot and blame the riots on a nation that is assumed to be reeling from the radical systemic oppression of people.

Understanding Radicalism provides parents excellent advice and elaborates on what is currently ongoing in America's schools. The problems are defined for the reader throughout the chapters of this book.

As a different matter, teachers today operate under the assumption that every class now has students who are either quiet about their sexuality or confused about their gender. The argument presented by LGBTQ+ advocates is that addressing these issues in class helps provide a safe and secure place in which students can safely be themselves.

Much of what transpires at school happens out of the sight of parents, so as not to generate any controversies. In fact, schools are being told that they are not allowed to inform parents if their child claims he or she is a homosexual or feels like the opposite gender. These are important concerns for parents and children, both of which may be drowning amidst the chaos of their confusion.

THE IMPORTANCE OF THIS BOOK

This book is immensely important for three fundamental reasons. *First*, schools have become places where direct indoctrination of children occurs. Public education seems to have lost touch with accountability, discipline, and academics. This book will argue for a return to classical education so as to prepare public education students for the world they will eventually face upon graduation from high school and/or college.

Second, public education is a system where the claim is made that any and all ideologies are accepted. This claim is not true. Traditional Americanism and Judeo-Christian values are unwelcome in public schools. Public schools are now centers of intolerance and this intolerance leaves out a large number of parents and students that lack advocacy in their struggle against the rising tide of educational currents that besiege them.

Public schools do not exist only for the leftist radicals and activists. However, reports from families indicate that students are being silenced, bullied, and made to feel unwelcome in their own classrooms because they hold to traditional values and do not wish to submit to teacher bias and one-sided propaganda.

Third, this book is vital because public education has become a place for people to brainwash children into believing non-scientific and even anti-scientific opinions. In so doing, teachers indoctrinate children to question their own biological makeup. This is accomplished by the addition of supportive curriculum and outside groups that may be intent on grooming children.

Such grooming is meant to introduce children to an alternative set of values and practices and reduce challenges to their moral filters. For example, a well-crafted book for younger students can make children empathetic to a character. This empathy may be the first step in softening emotions, through the heart and mind, which ultimately plays on a natural sense of fairness that most students possess.

Older students may be brainwashed into thinking that loving someone of the same sex is the same as loving someone of the opposite sex. They might also be led to believe that their moral upbringing should be questioned. The fact is, children deriving pleasure from sex with a person of the same sex is sometimes directly encouraged by radicals. This may be because the one doing the encouragement has had similar experiences. Graphic materials are sometimes sneaked onto school library shelves by librarians who are part of the LGBTQ+ movement by these teachers.

Taking things one step further, mental illness aside, no one wakes up one day and, without influence, decides to remove their sex organs, or realizes that their birth gender and sex are wrong. Adjacently, it takes more than melanin to create a racist of any color. The importance of this book cannot be overstated. In summation, *Understanding Radicalism* is an important book for our time, for very specific reasons. Foremost among these reasons is the connection between indoctrination and radicalization of Gen Z.

HISTORICAL AND CONTEXTUAL OVERVIEW

Radicals seek sudden and widespread change. The greater the call for radical change, the greater the efforts and the extremes necessary to initiate and expedite these changes. Most dictionaries generally define radicalism as *shifting a person or group's opinions and actions* toward either end of the political spectrum. For example, if leftist radicals on a college campus *believe* the positions of conservatives on social issues are hate-filled, then canceling and protesting conservative speakers on college campuses may become the norm.

Emotions play a significant role in developing students into radical activists. The focus on social-emotional learning and personal identity exploration are not random ideas emerging from nothing. Teacher-training programs across the nation began to introduce methods based in emotional learning. These training programs instructed teachers-in-training to be certain to tie emotional learning to the content being taught. This was a panacea for those seeking student disciples. After the harmful COVID-19 school lockdowns, and the general failure of subsequent online learning, students were ripe for the picking.

Emboldened leftist teachers were rallying around the defeat of Donald Trump in his 2020 reelection bid. They were not shy in using tactics to shut out any positive discourse related to the former president's administration. Teachers began to feel free to demonstrate their inner makeup and parents began to see just exactly what their children's teachers stood for and how they were affecting their students.

Imagine the shock of parents as they discovered, during the summer of 2020, that some teachers were burning down buildings and were involved in Antifa. Imagine the surprise of others, when school administrators and teachers were discovered to be drag queens, or have adult web sites and Only Fans pornography accounts. Parents began to see radicalism in real time. Sometimes it was from the teaching or the assignments. Other times, it was the material on the walls in the classrooms and the flags hanging in support of fringe groups that were revealed on camera. In many ways, Gen Z and the propaganda that came their way in schools was the ideal environment in which to capture the attention of a willing-to-be-captured group.

Radicalism in the United States is nothing new. Radicals dating back to the Boston Tea Party, and even earlier, have been part of American history. Terence Renaud writes,

"The origins of neoleftism as a distinct organizational phenomenon date to the two decades following the end of World War I, when Western Europeans or particularly Germans developed a radical left politics on the margins of mainstream Social Democratic and Communist parties."[4]

There seems little debate historically as to the impact of Karl Marx's ideology upon the current neo-leftists in the United States. German philosophy "had produced Karl Marx and inspired so-called Western Marxism, which provided the theoretical impetus behind so many new lefts."[5] However, according to Renaud, "Neo-leftist-style formations such as Occupy always end up in entropy and decline, much like neoliberalism has atomized social communities and decimated public services around the world. Every radical magazine, study group, and encampment devolves into its own idiosyncratic new left, much as neoliberalism lionizes the solitary, entrepreneurial self. Sooner or later, every new left succumbs to the assimilatory new spirit of capitalism."[6]

Renaud describes why history is important *to learn* and, of greater importance, *to learn from*. For example, on college campuses[7] the leftists do not hide their radical aspirations any longer. Neither do they hide their methods to crush conservative voices.[8] This century's new leftists "will undoubtedly combine party forms and nonparty forms. For all of them, a popular slogan and graffiti from the 1960s may serve as an inspiration: The struggle continues."[9]

REASONS FOR WRITING THIS BOOK

Readers will come to understand that states' departments of education have become themselves radicalized and that academic standards and curriculum frameworks have been changed to reflect this radicalization. Two good examples of this are the newer civics programs and sex education curriculum. The fuel behind these programs is LGBTQ+ advocacy and acceptance and woke culture.

Student activism has become of greater importance in the 2020s, in terms of social justice, than knowing the history of the nation, the rights found in the Constitution, and the branches of governmental power established by the shared branches of the federal and state governments. Learning the

Constitution is secondary to taking up a tribalistic ideological cause and fighting for it.

There is a direct push to forgo constitutional knowledge in favor of action civics, which usually amounts to a teacher suggesting ways to fight systemic racism, seek social justice, and to dismantle white supremacy as an antiracist. According to critics of the Civics Secures Democracy Act, learning about citizenship and the Constitution is placed alongside developing a diverse teaching force and implementing political ideology through group activism.[10]

Sexual education that far exceeds the maturity of children is a form of exposure to desensitize them to carnality, and to introduce sex as an attempt to imprint graphic adult and aberrant behaviors into the psyches of the children. Why else would a teacher invite a drag queen into his or her classroom of young children? There is no positive, redeeming academic or social value in such exposure.

Furthermore, in what world is the radicalization of children to sex and gender allowed as curriculum and education programs—more often than not—backed up by purchases by librarians of controversial and highly questionable library materials? What could possibly be wrong with these types of materials, since a librarian was in charge of acquiring them?

Some of the books contain clear graphic sexual acts, with drawings and caricatures, so that students/children may be encouraged to be touched by others, to touch their friends' privates in private, and to grow toward openness with same-sex relationships, as well as explore their gender.

American students are becoming more exposed to sex and gender information outside of their homes. Pornographic literature is in their school libraries. Teachers bring in special guest speakers who have no business presenting sex and gender ideology to students, especially without parents' permission. Social studies classes as far down as kindergarten now incorporate the expectations of students acting on select political and cultural issues to bring about change. Students are to question their very gender and are told that a doctor and their parents made a guess about their gender at their birth.

In some school districts, teachers dress up as drag queens in adult performer's clothing, and solicit money from children, encouraging them to place the money into the performers' undergarments. During Pride Month, some schools celebrate mandatory drag-queen performances and LGBTQ+ practices, while reading books to illustrate a form of normalization of behaviors. State standards are already being changed to reflect these. Several of these states are presented in the research for this book (see appendix).

Political elections have consequences. One of these consequences is pushing agenda. From Virginia to California, from Florida to Utah—and everywhere in between—families are being affected by the confusing voices and vices of Gen Z and LGBTQ+ sex, gender, and race activists.

One thing is certain, that there are concerted efforts by leftist radicals to change learning and knowledge to obedience and activism. From teacher-training institutions to K–12 classes, the push for social change by indoctrinating students and subverting classical education is alive and well.

SCOPE OF THE BOOK

Understanding Radicalism examines and explores the ever-growing trend to use education, outside groups, and social media as agencies of indoctrination and moral suasion to capture students' emotions. Indoctrination of children is more blatant today, and leftists do not even hide the fact they intend to capture the psyches of American children through the schools.[11] Within the scope of this book, there are explanations of approaches taken by influencers whose end-game is threefold:

- the indoctrination and radicalization of sex, gender, and race activists who take to the streets to provide life to a radical narrative;
- the bullying and canceling of those on school and college campuses who dissent and go against the radical narrative; and
- the spread far-left political ideologies that are grounded in Marxism, fluidity of personhood, and the absence of truth.

Understanding Radicalism serves as a warning about why it is a bad idea to allow extremism to flourish in mainstream American society. This pertains to both leftist socialist groups and right-wing nationalist groups. When students are radicalized, there is a certain *we-they* ideology established and the only thing that matters is power to control, even with violence if necessary. This book will explain this empowerment by examining the major tenets of the modern movements to radicalize students.

For example, one of the tenets of those radicalizing students includes: *science yields to emotions*. In battling against dissent, the actions stemming from these tenets can be summed up in *marginalize, ostracize*, and *radicalize*. Other tenets include (1) *cancel those with whom you disagree*, (2) *punish dissent in the name of protecting democracy*, and (3) *shame detractors in public*. The reader will come to understand that the battle for the hearts and minds—and even the souls—of children is real.

The more radicalized a person becomes, the greater his or her emotional bias is. Arguing with such a person yields a greater chance of being attacked by a larger group that is enlisted to support the fray online, at one's place of study, at work, or at home. Radicals do not find compromise a virtuous thing to behold, especially in politics, and even more fervently as politics play out across the American social landscape. Radicals actually find uprooting and dismantling as virtuous.[12] As a result, the tactics, rules, and strategies employed by radicals, as they seek to gain control in schools, politics, and society in general, are examined and critiqued in this book.

The advent of specialized movements and identity groups has flipped the classic notion of tolerance on its head. For example, it used to belong to the radical left to fight for acceptance, rights, and freedom. While that is still the case in some measure, the political, conservative right is now battling to be heard.

The Swing of the Pendulum

The political pendulum has swung quite far to the left in the areas of politics, K–16 education, churches, inner cities, and coastal wealthy enclaves. Once clamoring for power, the radicals now expect others to cower to their power. These radicals have enlisted a generation of disciples to their causes. As the pendulum has moved, it has swept up a gullible Generation Z. What about this generation is found to be so attractive and ripe for the picking?

Issues that have taken center stage are demarcated along social, cultural, sex\gender, and economic lines. One demarcation pertains to the rise of the transgender movement in America. Gen Z is the largest generation to claim they are not the identities that physicians, parents, family members, and others claim them to be. They claim they can create their own. Influencers have somehow convinced Gen Z to look at themselves as fluid, which has resulted in nearly seventy gender choice expressions defined by sociologists and psychologists.

Gender critical theory asserts that people make guesses as to what children are at birth. As they grow, the theory states, they can decide in their own minds and hearts whether they are boys or girls, neither, or some variant expression that is added to an ever-burgeoning list.

STRUCTURE OF THE BOOK

Understanding Radicalism is six chapters in length. The layout of the chapters is meant to walk the reader into his or her understanding of indoctrination of students, the propaganda tactics and methods used to gain support, as well as how and why students are radicalized to act on behalf of an ideology or cause.

Chapter 1 is titled, "Indoctrination and Education." This chapter takes the reader into the differences between indoctrination and education. It examines belief systems and answers the question as to whether all indoctrination is bad or harmful to children. In addition, the chapter addresses some of the types of indoctrination that occurs in schools and why ideologues in education today seek to make converts to their causes. A table of information is provided for the reader to understand fundamental differences between indoctrination and education.

Chapter 2 is titled "Ideologies and Radicalization." This chapter takes a dive into how ideologies play into students being radicalized. World views are examined and characteristics of radicals are included. A table of examples of radical ideologies on the extreme left and the extreme right is included in the chapter. Radicalization occurs on the left and the right. Much has been written about the religion of woke-ism and its Marxist tenets. Chapter 2 is also the queering of religion, as LGBTQ+ pastors seek to theologize gender and sex into normalcy biblically. Contending for truth is now more important than ever. The differences between sociological assumptions and fact are presented.

Chapter 3 scrutinizes "Radicals and Their Radicalism." A brief history of radicalism is presented and this history is contrasted with the present. Characteristics of radicals are explained and several of the theories that comprise a package of radicalism in America today are presented. The chapter delves into how education has been radicalized and the ideologies that have taken hold in schools across America.

Chapter 4 is an analysis of "Gen Z as the New Radicals." It lays out the case as to why this generation is the target of social influencers and radical race, sex, and gender advocates. A series of four comparative tables assists toward that end. The implications for affecting a generation with error will have serious outcomes. Issues of race and skin color, the planet, and the environment, or one's sexuality are part of the foundation of ideologies that are followed by Gen Z today. This chapter also addresses Gen Z and the concept of grooming, in relation to indoctrination into sex and gender awareness.

Chapter 5 takes aim at elected government officials and bureaucracy, in general. It presents the case as to why "Top-Down Radicalism" is real in America. Included also are challenges for school administrators and school principals. This chapter explains how radicalism emerges from the tops of ivory towers of some of our nation's supposed elite universities and colleges. Also included is a table of several notorious historical figures who became political leaders and how their tenures ended.

The final chapter of this book, chapter 6, is titled "The Battle against Radicalism." This chapter compares and contrasts disinformation and radicalism. There is a push by some well-heeled radicals to say that children do not really belong to their parents and that schools and teachers know what is best for them. This chapter examines efforts to fight back against usurpation of parental authority. A strategy is offered for parents to battle against the indoctrination of their children into thinking about ideas generated by adults for the sole purpose of turning children away from their parents' values.

The final section of this book contains a helpful appendix. The title of the appendix is "Excerpts of Equity and Social Justice Policies Adopted by School Boards." This tabular data provides parents with exact quotes as excerpts, to provide a sense of what is taking place in public schools under the guise of social justice.

INSPIRATION FOR THE BOOK

The explosion of homeschooling and the overwhelming numbers of students on waiting lists at private schools signal that something is wrong in public education. As an advocate for school choice, it is agreed that parents should be free to select the education system and processes that work best for their children and families. That being said, trust has eroded for public education in this nation. There is no longer any hiding of the fact that a very secular, progressive ideology exists in America's public schools. When one digs down more deeply, some of the ugly aspects of this ideology emerge. It is these things that drive parents away from public education.

The inspiration of this book rests squarely on the shoulders of those who stand against the indoctrination and radicalization of America's children. This includes parents and grandparents who take to school board meetings to stand with each other against indoctrination. This also includes teachers who risk their careers on behalf of families and the truth. Last, and certainly not least, students who defend truth in the classrooms also inspire me. May this book be as inspiring to you all, as you all are to me.

NOTES

1. Jeremy S. Adams. *Hollowed out*. 2021. Washington, DC: Regnery Publishers.

2. Will Flanders and Dylan Palmer. "From the top." Wisconsin Institute for Law & Liberty (WILL). July 2022. Retrieved September 20, 2022, from https://will-law .org/wp-content/uploads/2022/07/FromTheTop2.pdf. Cf. Parker Bono. "Indoctrinated America. How the left influence education at every level." Association of Mature American Citizens (AMAC). May 25, 2022. Retrieved June 2, 2022, from https:// amac.us/indoctrinated-america-how-the-left-influences-education-at-every-level/.

3. Terence Renaud. *New lefts: The making of a radical tradition*. 2021. Princeton, NJ: Princeton University Press, p. 293.

4. Ibid., p. 3.

5. Ibid.

6. Ibid., p. 14.

7. Staff. "The state of American colleges." *Upward*. July 29, 2021. Retrieved September 22, 2022, from https://www.upward.news/us-colleges-indoctrination/.

8. Rainer Zitelmann. "Anti-capitalism on US university campuses: The culture war is fought dirty." *Forbes*. February 16, 2020. Retrieved September 22, 2022, from https://www.forbes.com/sites/rainerzitelmann/2020/02/16/anti-capitalism-on-us-university-campuses-the-culture-war-is-fought-dirty/?sh=269596235c4b. Cf. Toby Young. "The neo-Marxist takeover of our universities." *The Spectator*. September 8, 2018. Retrieved August 3, 2022, from https://www.spectator.co.uk/article/the-neo-marxist-takeover-of-our-universities.

9. Renaud. *New lefts*, p. 294.

10. Staff. "Civics secures democracy act." *CivXNow*. 2022. Retrieved September 3, 2022, from https://civxnow.org/our-work/federal/.

11. Scott Walker. "2021: The left's radical indoctrination of students." *The Washington Times*. December 31, 2021. Retrieved Jun 15, 2022, from https://www.washingtontimes.com/news/2021/dec/31/2021-the-lefts-radical-indoctrination-of-students/. Cf. Joseph P. Lorio. "Guest column: Conservatives aren't overreaching on left-wing indoctrination in schools." *The Ledger*. July 6, 2021. Retrieved June 17, 2022, from https://www.theledger.com/story/opinion/columns/guest/2021/07/06/conservatives-arent-overreacting-left-wing-indoctrination-schools/7864810002/. Cf. also, Virginia Allen. "This teacher says left has turned public schools into indoctrination centers." *The Daily Signal*. April 5, 2021. Retrieved June 12, 2022, from https://www.dailysignal.com/2021/04/05/this-teacher-says-left-has-turned-public-schools-into-indoctrination-centers/.

12. Bobby Jindal. "Republicans must learn to compromise like Democrats." *Newsweek*. July 11, 2022. Retrieved September 4, 2022, from https://www.newsweek.com/republicans-must-learn-compromise-like-democrats-opinion-1722608.

Acknowledgments

I am deeply grateful to my publisher Rowman & Littlefield for providing a platform to address what some would call highly contentious issues. We live at a time when social media and large technology companies have the capacities to control narratives. On the flip side, these same companies can be of great service in reaching out to wider audiences. I acknowledge that being able to share ideas through various online media—with both like-minded people and detractors—has helped to refine this book.

There is no doubt that indoctrination and radicalization are important concerns for today. Compulsory public education holds children hostage to radical ideas. However, not all teachers and certainly not all schools have delved into the woke culture of sex, gender, and race. My thanks go out to those institutions and teachers who believe there are vast differences between education and indoctrination and practice excellence in teaching students.

Many thanks go out to the numbers of Gen Z students and their families who helped to shape this book and to colleagues and former colleagues whose opinions are always welcome. Extra-special thanks to Coach Prasek, Chris Arnzen, and Heike Braun for the hours of interview time addressing a host of topics that definitely made a difference in the lives of listeners and readers.

Last, I would be remiss if I did not send a shout out of appreciation to the person I call the C. S. Lewis of today, Dr. Douglas Groothuis. Seldom do we find such unity of spirit and focus of work between a philosophy and theology scholar and an education researcher. Sufficient to say, I am always blessed to read Doug's books and have Doug's input and wisdom, as a brother-in-Christ and an expert on various cultures and ideologies. In addition to this, I am blessed to also call him *friend*.

Chapter 1

Indoctrination and Education

Without Revolutionary theory, there can be no Revolutionary Movement.

—Vladimir Lenin

The left is very adept at the art of projection. Often when they accuse their opponents of being something evil, they are actually describing themselves.[1]

Educators would be mistaken to refer to indoctrination by the term *education*. Certainly, indoctrination comes by way of some sort of education process and appears intentional, but there are serious side-effects and at least four implications result from it. *First*, education and indoctrination are not synonymous and they certainly should not be considered equivalent. Granted, in this era of rapidly changing culture, the ability to separate the two entities is as difficult as it is problematic.

Second, indoctrination is not education because it does not require critical thinking. Critical thinking is the ability that develops from the training of one's mind and thoughts to consider alternatives and multiple sides of arguments, and from the presentation of facts and opinions that are tempered and validated by reason and evidence. Above all, critical thinking enables the pursuit of truth. Critical thinking is not a hallmark of indoctrination. In fact, to the indoctrinated, obedience to an ideology is valued more greatly than one's individual thoughts.

Third, in school settings, indoctrination does not provide students options to remove themselves from its impact in their classrooms. The reason is because dissent is an expression of power against the narratives espoused by those in power. *Fourth*, classroom indoctrination amounts to selective and biased instruction by a teacher. Usually, a biased presentation revolves around a slanted worldview on issues. Some of these issues include (1) people in power, (2) race, (3) politics, (4) worldview and ideology, (5) sex, (6) gender, and (7) religion. When indoctrination is successful, students are moved from

1

belief into unquestioned obedience. The next step is motivational with the final goal being activism.

INDOCTRINATION

Teachers around the nation are implementing social-emotional learning (SEL). This is the system through which teachers are instructed to organize, execute, and manage their classrooms. However, SEL focuses on engaging emotions as a guide to instructing social relationships in classrooms, understanding conflict, and accepting all students.[2] Often, what students recognize as right or wrong is the result of instruction by the teacher, who operates as the facilitator of a predetermined outcome. As a result, a dogmatic system of teaching occurs. When there is a demand for "unyielding obedience . . . [this] can lead to the invocation of extreme measures to enforce allegiance."[3]

Students who are indoctrinated learn through their emotional centers. These students are more likely to act on what they are taught. This is not a subtle point. Teachers who are not willing to allow students to criticize what they are taught, or to reconsider ideas based on additional merits, are slighting children in their education. When this happens, according to Bonnie Kerrigan Snyder, students—as well as teachers—"are effectively trapped in a small structure they should outgrow."[4]

If students are guided by a teacher's bias on an issue, there may arise a two-fold concern—both of which may run afoul of parents. *First*, many parents do not want a teacher's personal life, political bias, or instruction in sex (etc.) woven into their children's education. Such actions on the part of the teacher could be viewed as indoctrination and substituting emotion-shaping in the place of education.

Second, much of what indoctrinated students may have been taught may be based on erroneous material, and since students are generally not allowed to question what they have been taught, the validity of the information could be in question. For true education to occur, students must be allowed to develop and mature in critical thinking, and not be led as a group-think experiment in teacher-driven biases.

Basic Questions

One must ask basic questions if indoctrination of students is suspected. These questions are pertinent to K–12, as well as to college-level students. These questions include: (1) What is the philosophy and purpose behind the indoctrination? (2) Who is being indoctrinated and who is orchestrating it? (3)

What is the endgame of the indoctrination? and (4) To what extent does the indoctrination lead to radicalism and expectations of activism?

These questions must be answered only after there are clear definitions of both indoctrination and radicalism. On their face, the terms, whether used by the progressive left or the radical right, evoke certain biases and partisan conclusions. The terms themselves are neutral, but their meanings and implications are further shaped by the ways in which they are derived and applied in school settings.

Any teacher who does not allow students to question what is taught should arouse suspicions. One must be wary about doctrine that is above questioning. This goes especially for adults watching out for their children. The practice that disallows academic questions is defined as *doctrinaire*, where people are "stubbornly or excessively devoted to a doctrine or theory without regard to practical considerations."[5] This is the ultimate goal. That is not to say that all doctrine is bad, or sordid. Radicalism, on the other hand, is the result of indoctrination with something less than good doctrine. (See chapter 3.)

Types of Reasoning

There are two basic types of reasoning that qualify as pensive activity, in regards to sorting through what is taught as doctrine. These are important as students analyze information for truth and fact, and weigh out opinion and bias. Depending on the content area being studied, the application of a reasoning method could change. It is important to note that with indoctrination a teacher guides the information students hear and instructs them through the process of what to think about that information. Students, therefore, must be able to battle through the teachers' indoctrination tactics.

1. *How to Think.* Generally, good critical thinking applied in the proper ways to academic disciplines—and doctrine within those disciplines—should result in *how to think*. This should not result in students being taught what to think. On this note, Snyder explains the differences between two types of applied thinking methods: *deductive reasoning* and *inductive reasoning*. She writes:

> The differences between inductive and deductive reasoning matter. Deduction is a form of valid reasoning. It is considered to be top-down (or big to little), where you start with a general premise and then follow logical steps to collect evidence and reach a specific conclusion. The scientific method, for example, uses deduction to test hypotheses or theories. Inductive reasoning is the opposite: making broad generalizations from specific examples. . . . Inductive reasoning allows for the conclusion to be false, whereas proper deductive reasoning does not. Inductive reasoning can be a way to begin to uncover questions worth

investigating, but it insufficient to settle arguments because it is potentially flawed; deductive reasoning is considered to be the standard for scientific research and empirical proof or evidence.[6]

American students are typically not instructed on how to think. Most students exit public school classrooms having worked in groups or with partners and have not had to struggle over material for themselves. When asked to do so, they may give up or claim to not know how to manage the task independently. Snyder explains a concern that arises from such a myopic classroom methodology: "Rather than looking at multiple points of view to form a circumspect analysis or conclusion, we are to look at everything the same way, with this ubiquitous, inescapable power lens. This is precisely the way in which oversights, blind spots, and groupthink occur."[7]

2. *Cognitive Development.* William Perry's stages of cognitive development inform us that there are multiple levels of learning about complex ideas. He asserts that the lowest level applied to understand is that of *dualism.* Dualism is where "people simplistically believe that everything is binary, which means there is an absolute right or wrong answer to everything. People who think dualistically tend to believe there is a correct list of answers engraved on golden tablets in the sky, and that these are known by authority figures."[8] Perry also concludes, "The role of the student is to learn (memorize) the right answers, so that then s/he will know them too. Other ways to describe dualistic/binary thinking: either or, black-white, good-bad (evil), all-or-nothing, with-us or against-us thinking. This type of low-level thinking can lead to tribalism, which equates to an *us-them* mentality. Such a mentality sees an in-group/out-group dichotomy and can lead to the persecution of those not in the right group."[9] Examples of this type of entrenchment may include whether a person claims to be politically liberal or conservative. Another example are the pro-life and pro-abortion positions.

Those that indoctrinate generally do not care about balanced logic or common sense. They do care about pressing one-sided biases. This is accomplished by playing on emotions. For example, in a recent political debate, a progressive candidate criticized his opponent, who was pro-life. He was branded as a radical by the progressive because of an answer he gave to a question on abortion. The question was how the pro-life advocate could be both for life in the womb and against life when it came to capital punishment. This is an example of a radical's myopic, binary thinking.

Unfortunately, the pro-life candidate did not reply properly to the charge. What he should have said in response was, "How can you, my opponent, be in favor of killing by abortion and not capital punishment? Shouldn't you be consistent? On the one hand, you favor killing the innocent. On the other hand, you favor allowing murderers to live. Which one of us has our values and ethics backward? I favor punishing criminals for their actions. What crime did a baby in the womb commit to merit being at the mercy of someone's choice to execute it?"

The ability to think critically is an enemy of indoctrination. Critical thinking is "self-directed, self-disciplined, self-monitored, and self-corrective thinking."[10] R. C. Murray adds, "Socialist and atheist John Dewey called it cooperative intelligence. Other like-minded deconstructionists, including Piaget, Vygotsky, and Erikson, called it *discovery* or *student-centered learning.*[11]

INDOCTRINATION AND BELIEF SYSTEMS

Michael Metarko notes:

> I have seen firsthand the issues we face. I know the results of taking our focus off educating children as individuals created in the image of God with unique talents and gifts. I have witnessed how special interests promote their own agendas and obstruct efforts to improve our schools. . . . I do not doubt that teachers, parents, administrators, and school board members are often sincere in their desire to educate children. But anyone reading the news will quickly note that there is a growing culture of corruption and the sacrifice of ethics for self-interest and personal gain in public education.[12]

Metarko goes farther and warns parents, "Don't be fooled; our public schools do teach religion.. . . . Public schools are deeply entrenched in the religion of secular humanism . . . [On] March 4, 1987, US District Judge W. Brevard Hand, in *Smith v. Board of School Commissioners of Mobile County, Ala.*, ruled that secular humanism is a religion."[13]

Metarko is correct. According to the First Amendment, "secular humanism is a religious belief system, entitled to the protections of, and subject to the prohibitions of, the religious clauses."[14] According to Samuel Blumenfeld, "what we have in our public schools and state colleges and universities are government-supported establishments of religion, which are patently unconstitutional and therefore illegal."[15]

Metarko names a "few of the effects of indoctrination in secular humanism through public education: abortion, divorce, single-parent families, euthanasia, gay marriage, condoning homosexual behavior, pornography, racism, and no nativity scenes or the Ten Commandments."[16] Bruce Shortt extends the matter by addressing Christian education. He realizes that "the situation for Christian teachers and administrators is even worse. Your faith has been virtually criminalized within government schools. For many of you, even the slightest affirmation of your Christian beliefs at school would lead to discipline or termination if found out."[17] Secular religion is allowed in schools, but the belief system of Judeo-Christianity—the very system that helped to form America's laws and culture—is not.

WHAT QUALIFIES AS EDUCATION?

What qualifies as education has been debated for centuries. Plato wrote, "The untrained mind keeps up a running commentary, labelling everything, judging everything. Best to ignore that commentary. Don't argue or resist, just ignore. Deprived of attention and interest, this voice gets quieter and quieter and eventually just shuts up."[18] However, with compulsory education and a system intent on not shutting up, many assume that this is just the way of education.

There are certain elements that have proven themselves to be the foundation of a good education. Evidence of such has been associated with civic outcomes, each of which may prove beneficial to the development of students in preparation for competition in the real world. But civic education is not enough. Civics alone, without normative character components, comes across as less concerned about individual students' academic and intellectual growth and more concerned about the accomplishment of a set of predetermined educational goals. Without knowledge and understanding, based in a context of character, student preparation toward employment success may fall short of what is best for students out in the real world.

Ideology and Outcomes

Jason Stanley, the Jacob Urowsky Professor of Philosophy at Yale University, weighs in on the difference between indoctrination and education, and the results each produces. He contends that education has been at the forefront of all ideological battles throughout the better part of American history. He states that ideologies come quite directly from education.[19] What happens when this occurs?

America's students have once again demonstrated their overall inability to compete academically on the world's stage. The 2022 National Assessment of Educational Progress (NAEP) reports reading scores and math scores of American students, age nine, in comparison to other nations' students of the same age.

The National Center for Education Statistics (NCES) conducted the special assessment to measure pre-pandemic and post-pandemic scores. Academically, American students fell farther behind other nations after the pandemic. The assessment demonstrated that "In 2022 . . . average scores for age 9 students in 2022 declined 5 points in reading and 7 points in mathematics compared to 2020. This is the largest average score decline in reading since 1990, and the first ever score decline in mathematics."[20]

In states where political ideology enforced school closures during the COVID-19 pandemic, the negative impacts on student scores were dramatically greater. The sad reality is that students in lower income brackets suffered the most. Was it the pandemic or radical ideologies—or both—that found its way into America's schools by way of political agreements between teachers' unions and their members?[21]

One of the untested, yet important, features of the two-year COVID-19 restrictions is that students became more aware of gender ideology and also learned about transitioning from one gender to another. Nowhere in the NAEP battery of tests is there an assessment category on implicit bias or racism, or on whether transgender students see mathematics as repressive, or whether students should become activists. So, where then did this radicalization of students come from?

Generation Zoomer

Some teachers who used distance learning management systems were observed by parents, as they patently indoctrinated their students. Teachers were observed indoctrinating students toward ideologies and personal social causes, all of which affected students' minds and emotions. Could this exposure be partly responsible for the recent explosion of Gen Z's interest in personal gender and sexual issues, as well as dysphoria?[22] The number of hours the average Gen Z student spent online during the pandemic is astounding.[23]

Students spent many hours online and out of their parents' and teachers' view. One of the leading factors for indoctrination and eventual radicalization is infiltration to gain control of what students see and hear. Enter social media, its influences, and how it has changed the psychology of a generation.[24]

Some of the changes in younger students resulted in borderline narcissism, among Generation Z. Worship of self is not a new practice. Such worship has taken many forms throughout history. In a sobering historical parallel, American culture and politics have spawned rapidly growing cults of personality. This is the reason the book *Detoxing American Schools* was written and published. In the book, facts are presented to show that school districts are evolving and now appear more like cults in the ways they manipulate children. This conclusion is drawn by examination of both woke ideology to which school districts subscribe and observations of the praxis and curriculum. The cult in question has been fueled by those claiming to ascribe to woke ideology.[25] In particular, Gen Z, "the Zoomers," are often looking inward for their identities, in working out their religion of self and identity.[26]

Some *woke folk* piously celebrate their own personal and social awareness.[27] Woke leaders have now adopted their own personalized claims of self-worship, and often demonstrate them by making changes to their external features as signs of their conversion.[28] Mary Eberstadt agrees, "Self-worship has become the ultimate expression of sacrifice on the altar of emotional identity and feelings."

In her book *Primal Screams*, Eberstadt elaborates:

> One thing that seems to happen is some people, deprived of recognition in the traditional ways, will regress to a state in which their demand for recognition becomes ever more insistent and childlike. This brings us to one of the most revealing features of identity politics: its infantilized expression and vernacular. . . . What critics of identity politics have missed is that the manifest panic behind cries of cultural appropriation is real—as real as the tantrum of a toddler. It's as real as the developmental regression seen in the retreat to safe spaces on campus, those tiny ersatz treehouses stuffed with candy, coloring books, and Care Bears. It's as suggestive as the pacifiers that were all the rage as campus accoutrement in the 1990s.[29]

EDUCATION AND DEMOCRACY

Stanley argues that "education is the foundation of any democracy,"[30] and yet education has also been labeled as a system that indoctrinates students. There are differences in meaning and implication to consider when addressing such a label. Since "education is compulsory, students are subject to whatever the education narrative is in the schools. Unlike churches, where indoctrination can also occur, students are held hostage"[31] to whatever ideology is being taught. If the narrative does not include all aspects of history, then Stanley thinks students are being indoctrinated to a uniform narrative. This can occur in schools, churches, on the left and the right, and is certainly an underlying part of the motivation of influencers on social media.

If Stanley is correct in his assessment of American public education, the shift among marginalized groups, coupled with compulsory education, presents several layers of concerns. When indoctrination into a worldview emphasizes a select ideology, which aligns with one or more biases, a uniform narrative quickly becomes status quo. This status quo becomes a narrative that is then parroted by like-minded affinity groups to feed followers a consistent message. This, then, is known as "a law of propaganda, often attributed to the Nazi Joseph Goebbels,"[32] who believed that the repetition of a lie "often enough . . . becomes the truth."[33]

Critics of public education today claim that schools do not emphasize student assimilation. Instead, under the guise of diversity, equity, and inclusion students themselves are taught to view their world through a predetermined ideological lens. For example, teachers have abandoned the nation's accumulated "inherited cultural wisdom and shared enlightenment values . . . replacing them with activism and newer identity-based departments."[34] Departments such as these reject open debate and dialogue, often detesting any notion of political neutrality. Therein lies some of the major problems associated with indoctrination within a compulsory environment.

Divisions in Schools

Unchecked, public education is a fertile environment for red-flag concerns. Parents have every right to be suspicious of what is being taught to students, if they begin to hear and see things from their children that are concerning. However, parents are often caught between their children's compulsory attendance at school and how much they should object. There is a fear of retribution toward students, if parents speak up.[35] There is also a fear for teachers if they speak out against parents, or the radicalism and indoctrination they see taking place in the schools in which they are employed.[36] But the good news is that not all students will be deeply indoctrinated or will hopelessly fall prey to teacher biases.

Realistically, the reason that not all students are inclined to buy in to a narrative is because some students are natural skeptics. Other students pretend well, keep quiet, and *go along to get along*. The fact remains that all students are *exposed* to indoctrination in classrooms where teachers are bent on such exposure. Indoctrination does not fall away merely because some students refuse to accept the doctrinal bias. The probability of an effect upon those who hear the persistent drumbeat of these ideologies is greater than it is on those who are never exposed.

Take, for example, a classroom where all of its students were exposed to the smell and taste of burgers and fries made from plant-based ingredients. The probability that some would be hungry for the food, and some not hungry for the same food, does not negate the statistical probability that some students will indeed refuse plant-based foods, no matter how hungry they are. The same is true with similar ideas, including those that sound pleasant but come with more radical and distasteful implications.

It is a fallacy, for example, of critical race theory to state that whites are more inclined to help students of color if the white students get something out of it for themselves. The reality is that not all students will be radicalized toward seeing all white students as self-serving and helpful only to them-selves. The same is true about woke ideology and gender theory. Not all students will accept these radical ideologies. Those that do not buy into them are neither racist nor anti-gender. Those that believe the opposite have already succumbed to indoctrination.

All Indoctrination Is Not Identical

The reader should take note that a person would be hard-pressed to find a group of public schools that spend their time radicalizing students in the direction of *conservative* philosophies and causes. Why is this? The fact is that nearly every student favoring conservative causes is considered *persona non grata* in most public schools. Such persons are viciously labeled as anti-American and as haters of BIPOC (black, indigenous, and people of color), anti-LGBTQ+ (lesbian, gay, bisexual, transgender, intersex, queer/questioning, asexual, and many other terms), or somehow despisers of democracy. This reaction demonstrates how unwelcome challenges to the status quo are. This is quite apparent at postsecondary institutions, where "disparaging comments about political conservatives are common."[37]

There is great indoctrination and control where in-class challenges are neither encouraged nor allowed. The problems on college campuses are best summed up by political science professor Matthew Woessner, at the University of Arkansas. He writes: "Regarding teaching, conservative students often have their views challenged by leftist professors, while liberal students rarely face corresponding challenges from the right. Because left-leaning students rarely have professors who provide them with thoughtful conservative perspectives, their education is often incomplete. Since leftist faculty are especially dominant at elite colleges and universities, we are particularly concerned about how a one-sided worldview might arrest the intellectual development of America's best students."[38]

Education critics could make the claim that private Christian schools indoctrinate their students with religion, morality, and theology. That may be true. However, as was mentioned earlier in the chapter, not all indoctrination is of the sordid type. Parents are not beholden, in a compulsory sense, to keep students in private schools or even private colleges with which they disagree. Specifically, at the K–12 level, removal of students from public education is not possible for the majority of American parents, especially during times of economic difficulty.

An issue that education critics overlook is also one major difference between private schools and public schools. Particularly, Christian schools set out a doctrinal statement and/or educational philosophy that is presented to parents. Parents generally know in advance what their children are being taught and must sign documents attesting to this fact. Public schools have no such transparency requirement.

When indoctrination at school manifests itself within the compulsory setting, then the groundwork of indoctrination has been established. Across the public education spectrum, parents are now realizing they have been kept in the dark about what is taught in their children's schools.[39] Parents are speaking out.

Progressive Ideologies

Progressive ideologies have built-in assumptions that conservatives are the real radicals. Much like BLM (Black Lives Matter) and CRT (critical race theory) claim that all non-BIPOC are racists, progressives claim that all conservatives are truly dangerous to America. President Biden illustrated this very thing in a 2022 speech in Philadelphia, where he labeled all persons supportive of former President Trump as violently dangerous and disrespectful of the US Constitution, and that the "make America great again" (MAGA) slogan was a radical ideology dangerous to America democracy.[40]

Irony meets reality in odd ways. Within three weeks after the speech given by President Biden, where he condemned "MAGA" Republicans and labeling them as a violent threat to the United States, forty-one-year-old Shannon Brandt intentionally ran down eighteen-year-old Caylor Ellingson in an alley after a town street dance. Brandt called 9/11 to report the intentional act and indicated he did it because Ellingson was an extremist.[41] If words are violence, as progressive politicians state often, then the probability of violence by radical progressives whose goal is to "burn down"[42] capitalist America should rank highly on the list of domestic terrorists.

One of the more progressive ideologies that has made its way into schools is called *queer ideology*, or *queering*. It undergirds much of LGBTQ+ politics, transgenderism, and even queer theology.[43] The main goal is to bomb psyches with information and twisted logic, to make it seem that something queer is as normal as heterosexuality or as religious as evangelical Christianity—the very norms they wish to overthrow. Indoctrination concerning sex and gender is uncompromising. If students dare to object or express dissent to sex or gender indoctrination, they run up against ridicule and bullying, property damage, along with threats of violence and death.[44] Those on the radical right are also resorting to threats of all sorts, including toward hospitals and surgeons practicing gender transition surgeries.[45]

Snyder pins indoctrination of children on teachers and school leaders, as she writes: "Our nation has a problem. Recently, in both urban and rural communities, young children are being indoctrinated, bullied, and harassed by their fellow students and teachers for not falling into line on various topics."[46]

The concerns are real because "children who are too young to have developed solid or informed opinions on these and other topics are being forced into premature ideological conformity with some teachers and administrators who seem intent on pushing their own particular worldviews in K–12 classrooms."[47]

Snyder goes on the say that "I've noticed that liberal parents are—in some ways—even more alarmed over the rapid transformation of their children's schools and surprised to find themselves opposed to it. If it ever was once a partisan issue, the problem of school indoctrination has steadily worsened to the point that people across the political spectrum have found themselves allied against it."[48] When it comes to censorship and totalitarian control in schools over ideology, far too many people just do not want to spend time thinking about the changes that have occurred in American schools, let alone the education issues across the national cultural landscape. Many of these people would opt to send their kids "to school and trust implicitly in the system. . . . However, ignoring the problem won't make it go away. This fight will come to you, whether or not you want it."[49]

As with most ideologies, there is a certain faddishness about them that is appealing. This appeal is also found in woke activism. Woke activists "are unique in that they view these experiences as sacred and unquestionable. While most recognize that experiences are useful as illustrative tools, lived experiences take on the status of quasi-divine revelation for the woke. . . . Just because one experiences racism does not show that racism is widespread or deeply ingrained."[50] Add to this the fact that while some Americans support LGBTQ+ issues, queering remains a radical ideology for, and outside the normal experience of, most Americans.

IS ALL INDOCTRINATION HARMFUL TO CHILDREN?

Education is critical for the development of healthy children, not only for their bodies but also for their brains, emotions, and ability to think more broadly on issues. Where any one of these suffers compromise, is controlled, neglected, or otherwise disregarded, student development suffers. The cost is great for America's students where compulsory indoctrination occurs. Yet, for indoctrination to be effective, an ideology must stand unchallenged and its dissenters must be silenced and even viewed as enemies to the messaging.

R. Roderick Palmer wrote a prescient explanation of indoctrination during the time of the Cold War between the United States and the Soviet Union. His explanation rings true nearly seven decades later. Palmer wrote: "Usually indoctrination refers to the molding of children in somewhat the same way that propaganda refers to the molding of adults, but within this limitation, indoctrination may refer to several things. Sometimes it simply means influencing the immature; sometimes it means influencing them in a particular way, as by a play upon their feelings; and sometimes it means dealing with them in such a manner as to hinder their freedom of thought in a certain area."[51]

Influences Supersede Truth

At what point do students actually conclude that they are a different gender and want to change their bodies medically and surgically? The influences upon children supersede truth and replace it with squishy theory that can be dangerously life-altering if followed to its illogical end. But there must be pushback. The truth is, "In liberal science, no one gets special say simply on the basis of who he happens to be. . . . Every assertion must be subjected to the same method of checking and double-checking—subjected to doubt—regardless of the identity of the checker and the source of the assertion."[52] But woke ideology has become pervasive in American culture.

Instead of studying the fundamentals of a good education, during the pandemic, students spent a lot of time on social media. This was certainly the case with university students who, now, are battling a new form of addiction.[53] The ideologies and influences emerging from social media have significant impacts upon still-developing hearts, minds, and emotions of young people. Snyder agrees: "A public school, of course, is not a voluntary community: it is compulsory. In our pluralistic, secularized society, no one has the right or authority to compel a system of belief on another. Therein lies the rub."[54] In terms of political persuasion, "public schools . . . should not be directing our children on . . . political issues at all. They are supposed to practice viewpoint neutrality, so that young people, eager to fit in and please those who formally evaluate them, won't feel the need to conform and yield to the clear dictates of the messaging."[55]

Schools are captive places for children. The indoctrination of children with radical ideas affects the moral compass of their captive young minds. This should not be allowed to occur. But this is not the first time in history when this has occurred.[56] For more than three decades, educators have been duped into thinking that telling students they are wrong, or that their efforts do not meet certain standards, is a hurtful attack on students' self-esteem. It remains true that the influences of psychology supersede truth.

Equity

By providing for every need and even most desires of their students, often without accountability, educators have yielded material and emotional

expectancies exacted upon the rest of society. Hence, there are severe reper-
cussions now that a generation feels entitled. Entitlement is just a small step
away from what we now understand as *equity*,[57] a radical concept that allows
people with power to provide guaranteed unmerited outcomes for those
deemed economically or socially oppressed.

Equity has become a value that is placed on others, rather than one that
allows people to place on themselves. Giving people things without accountability is somehow supposed to lift their self-esteem. It does just the opposite. Someone, or some group, has determined the worth of a degree, or of a
person, or of a job.

Values such as hard work and sacrifice are lost on many young people in
America today. Some simply do not *feel* their best efforts are necessary to be
assured opportunities that are granted to others. For example, the University
of California recently agreed to do away with the SAT and ACT as requirements for admission. The University of California system is not alone in this
decision.[58]

Equity is not a new educational concept. Equity is to guarantee-of-
outcomes as self-esteem is to everyone-receives-a-trophy. When students
are polled, they agree on people having similar outcomes guaranteed.[59]
Practices of equity are also found among corporate America's hiring policies.
Outcomes of the hiring process can now be based on immutable characteristics that supersede any form of merit-based achievement.

The children of the 1970s and 1980s self-esteem movement are now
professors in our colleges. These professors are shaping the next generation
into the radicals they could not become but to which they had aspired. Along
with the current reduction of education requirements and the vestiges of the
self-esteem movement, our nation has produced more than one generation of
entitled narcissists. These narcissists are primed for action and seeking dissenters whom they may vanquish. They take their cues from the influencers
who hide behind their cushy college positions, or meld anonymously into the
social media mayhem that grants them a modicum of pseudo-privacy.

Drilling Down on the Differences

Regarding the reasons American culture has experienced such a lurch to the
left, it has been determined that "Several cultural trends coalesced to bring
us to this current tipping point. First . . . look at what's been happening to the
curriculum in American colleges and universities, where the current crop of
incoming teachers is prepared."[60] Teacher education programs need overhaul-
ing and reform.[61]

The main differences between indoctrination and education rest in (1) the
development of healthy questioning brains and critical thinking abilities,

and (2) the development of healthy emotions and emotional responses to those with whom student and teachers agree and with whom they disagree. Students of all ages must be free to question and to challenge any and all ideas in classrooms. (See table 1.1 below)

IDEOLOGICAL EXPOSURE COMES IN MANY FORMS

Interesting methodologies are used by ideologues in pursuit of the persuasion of young minds. Young adults are exposed to every type of message, such as the sky is falling, climate disaster awaits within a decade, moral suasion, and economic disparity. Politics is no exception, and exposure to political indoctrination is commonplace these days. Indoctrination with extreme ideologies tends to produce more extreme radicalization. This is the current state of America.

Specifically, ideologues rely on exposure to social and ideological ideas. For example, the Chinese described their "cultural revolution"[62] by way of Mao Tse-tung as a "Great Leap Forward."[63] In this forward movement, an estimated 20 to 40 million Chinese perished due to a government-imposed, massive famine. Only a radical could claim this was an improvement.

Other terms that have been radicalized by current oppositional political forces in the United States include: *build back better, make American great again, democracy, socialist, semi-fascist, leftist,* and *insurrectionist,* among others. From politicians to pundits, from influencers to preachers, ideas are used in the persuasion of young minds.

Political Indoctrination and Radicalism

On any given day, students pop online and succumb to influence. Their minds can be pushed and pulled, resulting in conviction, confliction, and confusion. Influencers seize these moments and inject ideas into compliant psyches. That is what influencers are paid to do. But indoctrination is multifaceted and does not merely settle for perpetual mental bombardment of error or disinformation.

Several of the facets of indoctrination include a steady diet of social media under the guises of several platforms bent on questioning cultural norms. For example, LGBTQ+ youth utilize "a range of digital media platforms to explore identity, find support and manage boundaries. Less well understood, however, is how they navigate risk and rewards across the different social media platforms that are part of their everyday lives."[64]

Revelations about major social media and their impacts upon certain demographics come to the forefront each day. Organizations like Project Veritas,

Table 1.1 Five Differences between Indoctrination and Education*

INDOCTRINATION	EDUCATION
1. Students are led to believe facts and the truth as told by a truth teller who influences the student. There is an inability to back up the facts with anything other than ideology and opinion.	1. Students and teachers seek facts and truth, examining and analyzing both the facts and truth to assess validity and accuracy. There is objective truth and observation of universal facts.
2. Can occur as a result of belonging to a political party, a cult, or a belief system that is assumed to be true. The evidence is just how open and willing people are to welcome differences and those who are not part of their chosen group. One ideology is elevated over all other systems of belief and only the selected ideology is considered as truth.	2. Grows with the addition of more facts, through trial and error and reassessment. These assist in the maturation of a belief system that has been arrived at by a process based on critical thinking and not a mandate by an influencer.
3. Uses universal language that is applied to groups and individuals and meant to shape thinking rather than a language of possibilities. Examples include: "all Christians believe myths"; "Democrats are dishonest"; and "MAGA proponents are violent."	3. Often supported by data that bolsters fact-finding. Confidence levels rise with each corresponding evidential set of facts. Reasoning develops maturity and understanding of deeper concepts.
4. There is only one way of rightful thinking and solutions to problem are crafted by ideology. Dissent or secondary thoughts are those of troublemakers, bigots, or racists. Examples include: "America is a racist nation and must be dismantled"; "Whites are oppressors and BIPOC are the oppressed, and power must be seized by any means"; "Evolution is a fact and there is no other explanation for all that exists"; and "the COVID-19 vaccine will prevent you from getting COVID."	4. Allows for different, thought-out solutions to problems and the insertion of dissenting opinions as conclusions. Students develop their own beliefs after a wide-range of exposure to positions and experts, always free to modify and accept another viewpoint.
5. Has an agenda, and that agenda is to drive students to believe their teacher, become social group advocates, and develop a blind belief that spurs actions on behalf of the accepted agenda. Particularly found in tribal, or group dynamics as activists.	5. Strives to be unbiased, and is best demonstrated by the neutrality of the teacher in class toward any political party or controversial social cause and avoids influencing students to a predetermined end or ideology.

*Information summarized and assembled from the following sources: Manisha Kumar. "Difference between education and indoctrination." *Difference Between (DB)*. July 28, 2011. Retrieved September 2, 2022, from http://www.differencebetween.net/miscellaneous/difference-between-education-and-indoctrination/. Cf. Staff. "What's the difference between education and indoctrination?" *American Center for Law and Justice*. 2022. Retrieved September 21, 2022, from https://aclj.org/whats-the-difference-between-education-and-indoctrination.

individuals like comedian and talk show host Bill Maher, and entrepreneur Elon Musk have publicly exposed the politically based underbelly of major print and social media. Along with Facebook's admission of content restrictions, Twitter's use of misinformation bots and the corporation's decision to remove any negative attribution to Joe Biden—especially by allegations of covering up his son's dealings and the supposed "laptop from hell"—helped to avoid political fallout just weeks prior to the presidential election of 2020.[65] The media had taken a politically biased, protectionary approach, proving that political ideology comes before honesty, accountability, and truth.

When it comes to schools and institutions of learning, "There are several moral and legal objections to leveraging a public educational institution to advance a political purpose. First of all, public schools are agencies of the government. As such, when they use their position and resources to keep themselves in power, they injure democracy and undermine their own integrity."[66] Next, depending on the party in power, "A state legislature would never approve public funding to promote one party over another without immediate outcry."[67] So, moving about politically through complicit media platforms helps to radicalize social media by controlling the messaging. The longevity of any media message is often short-lived, and outcries die down with the next information/disinformation cycle. Politicians count on such cycles to rebrand their messages after scandals break.

During the 2020 and 2022 elections, teachers and professors branded political opponents with pejorative labels. The rhetoric became so heated at the time that radicals in the media and institutions of higher education began to disallow even the mention of Donald Trump support or the wearing of his campaign merchandise. Violence was found to occur at the mere mention of the name Trump, dating back to his first presidential campaign.[68] Violence occurred by those claiming to be Trump supporters,[69] with talk of even overthrowing democracy and the US government.[70]

Parents Become Aware

When parents are convinced that teachers are indoctrinating their children, many become angry and begin speaking out. In order to alleviate parental concerns and avoid confrontations with parents, some school districts have been told not to mention certain buzz-words. Teachers have also been told not to admit to teaching gender theory or critical race theory.

Other school districts have chosen to combine one controversial program with another. Social-emotional learning, for example, has become a segue for a raft of ideas to fall under the radar of the parents. Along with this, any controversies have become the responsibility of new offices of diversity, equity, inclusion, and opportunity (DEIO).

If parents learn that their children are being indoctrinated, they will react. Indoctrination of children means that parents will react. In fact, they will react similarly if they are not informed that their children are learning about issues through a conservative lens, which is certain to be called indoctrination by more liberal parents. Indoctrination claims can be made from the left and the right. And yet, the issue-at-stake is that parents are not being informed about what their children will be learning. When parents sense that a school is hiding something from them about what their children will experience, these same parents, understandably, become upset.

In most private schools, the curriculum is on display and their educational philosophy and even statements of faith are posted for all to see. Public schools do not usually feel compelled to let parents know there is a day when teachers will promote transgenderism or drag queen days. School faculty are sometimes told not to inform parents of some of the more controversial events, activities, assemblies, or in-class speakers. They are not even likely to inform parents of their reading of graphic sexual or gender materials made available in their children's classrooms or school libraries. School unions and school boards somehow think that what the schools teach is not parents' business.[71] This is certainly radical and must be corrected.

Indoctrination Embedded

Specialists are now regularly hired to oversee the incorporation of and alignment with radical and controversial practices in curriculum, daily instruction, faculty and staff training, and academic standards. Major universities are offering questionable majors in their business schools and management programs.[72] For example, at the University of Washington, hiring for the DEIO Office includes the following breakdown of core responsibilities.[73] From these offices comes indoctrination often based on race, sex, and gender. Professors whom I have interviewed have confirmed that professional development often takes place under the specter of social engineering. The same practice exists in the corporate business sectors[74] and is captured below.

- diversity blueprint planning and implementation support (25 percent)
- diversity council membership and meeting coordination (25 percent)
- staff recruitment and retention (25 percent)
- diversity resources coordination (25 percent)

In taking matters even further, school librarians at public schools around the nation began to come out as advocates for supporting the sexualization of young children. The selection of LGBTQ+ books with graphic content placed school librarians front-and-center in the dispute about exposure of children to sex and gender issues beyond their years.[75] Once parents discovered what was actually on the library shelves for students and that, in some cases, was procured by the librarians, a tidal wave of reaction was set off by public school parents and activists.[76] What could be the purpose of supporting such graphic library resources?

SEEKING CONVERTS TO RADICALIZE

Those seeking converts to their radical ideologies definitely do have an agenda. Political officials often convince union leaders and state bureaucrats of their intentions and positions by pressuring them and offering financial incentives. Support trickles down from the top and finds its way to the general masses. For example, this is the way it is for sex, race, and gender groups that have pressured politicians and education policymakers.[77]

The battle to convert the minds and wills of children is fought daily in America's public learning institutions. The essence of this battle has, at its core, the challenge to what it means to be male and female. An example of this battle is found in the book recommended for high school students' sex education. The book is titled *S.E.X.: The All-You-Need-to-Know Sexuality Guide to Get You through Your Teens and Twenties* and is brimming "with descriptions of anal sex, bondage and other sexual activity."[78] Students in public schools today are being indoctrinated with a perverse adult sexual ideology,[79] with the intention of generating sympathetic conversion toward aberrant sexual ideology.

Sexual Indoctrination Leads to Radicalism

According to anecdotes shared with me during the pandemic, Zoom-bombers caused great disruptions to online classes, posting pornographic videos and even masturbating on camera. Exposure to sexual ideology comes in many forms and, unfortunately, so too do sexual harassment and activism.

Consider my recollection of an encounter with a very outspoken, self-proclaimed lesbian teacher-in-training. When asked why she wanted to be a teacher, she replied, "So I can become a proud vocal activist for children who are emerging LGBTQ+ or who are curious." When challenged about what sixty-or-so parents may say about her goal, she replied, "Who cares? They need to deal with their bigotry and homophobia."

Along with race and gender ideologies, sex is consciously being pushed by some into the psyches of today's younger students. Some would argue that students are going to find out anyway. Is the content of current sex education curricula one of the reasons why teachers are pressing for parents to sign agreements not to watch what goes on in their children's online classes? Regardless, parents should request to view the materials in advance. If they are not allowed, then such restrictions should present great concerns.

Teachers are instructed by the National Education Association, and through the support of LGBTQ+ advocacy groups, that children as young as ten should learn how to use condoms. Such activities are within the practice sections that come along with the newer sexual education programs that are supported by groups who aim to expose children to a variety of sexual choices,[80] which American sex culture has enabled to become part of a new sexual norm.[81]

Sexually graphic books have appeared on shelves in libraries. Some teachers have gone ahead and developed their own in-class libraries, exclusive to sex and gender ideologies. This type of literature has posed problems for parents across the nation. Those for whom such sexual exposure to their children is problematic are labeled by the ideology that favors such exposure as radicals, bigots, and trans-phobic, among others. However, it is not the parents' ideologies that are taking away the innocence of children.

In addition to common-sense conflicts over science, there is continued jamming of secular sexuality and popular gender ideologies into the minds of students of all ages.[82] Scientific data, along with detailed genetics information and neuroscience, contradicts the emotional, sociological, and psychological theory that drives so much of social culture today.[83] Radicalism is based on ideology and avoids any true comparison to science and scientific fact. Radicals also do not consider the element of trauma in regards to the lives of students who have suffered or are suffering severe sexual abuse.

The Battle over Innocence

The battle for sexual innocence is now being fought by parents. Children as young as four are being told that their parents did not know their gender when they were born, "so they assigned"[84] them genders; the children are encouraged to figure themselves out over time. Gender activists have recruited strategically oriented teachers, and their influences on children are used as tools to prompt children to question their genders and sexual beliefs while at school. So, is it any small wonder that a child becomes confused about his or her place and role in the family, relationships, the school, and society at large?

Could early sexual experimentation and the confusion about gender and sexuality be contributing factors to the skyrocketing rates of suicides and attempted suicides among teenagers? The evidence indicates the answer is yes.[85] Ben Shapiro addresses this confusion. He maintains, in order to stem the perceived risk of suicide resulting from the complacency of physicians regarding the assistance of gender-dysphoric patients, surgeons give in to demands. But, as Shapiro argues, "Surgery doesn't militate against suicide."[86]

Shapiro intimates that a better way to capture the egregiousness of medical castration may be by the phrase "to mutilate doesn't militate against suicide." This raises two serious questions that require additional research: (1) Why is suicide ideation and suicide on the rise among the younger generations in America, and (2) What is the extent of the correlation or causation of student indoctrination and radicalization to the increase of mental health issues among the younger generations?

Control of the Message

All is not lost in the battle against indoctrination over race, sex, and gender that has America's students confused. But the onslaught upon the minds and hearts of children is a very real human and societal struggle. According to Rebecca Friedrichs, "America's . . . teachers have been silenced and bullied by the very organization that is pushing the sexualization of children: That is, labor unions."[87] This sexualization is supported by the National Education Association (NEA), which works in partnership with the Southern Poverty Law Center (SPLC), the National Association for the Advancement of Colored People (NAACP), the American Civil Liberties Union (ACLU), the Gay, Lesbian, and Straight Education Network (GLSEN; formerly called Gay and Lesbian Independent School Teachers Network), and the National Center for Trans-Equality, Human Rights Campaign (NCTEHRC), among others.[88]

America's children are being sexually sacrificed and exposed to materials that are not age or emotionally appropriate. An example of this is the exposure of younger children to genitalia by way of handing out lifelike models of erect penises for them to fondle. Some teachers, along with concerned parent groups, are unwittingly caught by the inclusion of tactical, adult-like exposure to sex toys and a cavalier approach to sexuality. In fact, a growing number of teachers, as well as parents, are highly disturbed by this sexualization of children.[89]

When teachers and administrators are not comfortable with having to defend their own ideologies inside their classrooms, they frequently enlist outside advocacy groups to intercede on their behalf. Some of the topics that have been presented by outside groups include: (1) adult sexual practices; (2) ways to experience sex pleasurably and safely; and (3) being open to having sex with students of the same biological sex and gender. With these propositions in mind, it is obvious why the majority of parents are often not allowed to attend these sex education meetings with their own children.[90] Children are being intentionally victimized.

SEXUAL VICTIMIZATION OF CHILDREN

Children's sexuality is the last phase of human innocence. To sacrifice this innocence on some humanistic, philosophical altar constructed by adults is wrong. Some teachers' own universes are scarred by their personal sexual confusion, and in some cases they are victims of child sexual abuse themselves. Gaining entrance to the doorways of the minds of children eventually affects those children's emotions and plants within them the curiosities of adult pleasures.

The trauma experienced by some teachers should not be relived at the expense of children and their exploitation. The door to victimization of generations of children should never be opened. The fact is that exposing children to early sexual knowledge is a dream scenario for pedophiles, pederasts, and korephiles.

There are some encouraging signs. Recently a "veteran California teacher explained that most teachers are disturbed by the decades-long push to indoctrinate and oversexualize school children by teachers' unions dedicated to far-left cultural and political causes and not the well-being of kids."[91] Anyone arguing that early sexual exposure makes kids safer, and that the more knowledge the better, demonstrates that the sacrifice of the last bastion of childhood innocence is best accomplished in tandem with schools and sexual and gender groups, many of which may be comprised by victims of sexual abuse themselves.[92] One has to question why exposure to sexuality is so important to bureaucrats and those lobbying for this exposure.

Types of sex education programs mandated by states, such as California, leave little room for focusing on abstinence. The programs certainly elevate alternate sex and gender expressions over heterosexual relationships in importance. The fact is, the more options students think they have at their disposal, the greater the opportunity for sexual experimentation and encounters. However, this is adult-level thinking that is pushed into the minds of children. Therefore, this is not information; this amounts to indoctrination. What follows is a prime example of this indoctrination from the State of California.

A California sex education program includes: All instruction and materials in grades K–12 must be inclusive of LGBTQ+ students. Instruction shall *affirmatively recognize* that people have different sexual orientations and, when discussing or providing examples of relationships and couples, must be *inclusive of same-sex relationships*. [EC § 51933(d)(5)]. It must also teach students about gender, gender expression, gender identity, and explore the harm of negative gender stereotypes. [EC § 51933(d)(6)]. This means *that schools must teach about all sexual orientations* and what being LGBTQ+ means. The California Healthy Youth Act requires that sexual health education be appropriate for use with students of all genders and sexual orientations [EC §51933(d)] and clearly states that part of the intent of the law is "to provide pupils with the knowledge and skills they need to develop healthy attitudes concerning adolescent growth and development, body image, gender, sexual orientation, relationships, marriage, and family." [EC § 51933(d)(2)]. The California Healthy Youth Act also prohibits sexual health education classes from promoting bias against anyone on the basis of any category protected by Education Code §220, which includes actual or perceived gender and sexual orientation. (Emphases are mine)[93]

The California sex education framework informs teachers that students in kindergarten can identify themselves as transgender and offers tips for how to talk about that, adding that "the goal is not to cause confusion about the gender of the child but to develop an awareness that other expressions exist."[94] For the sake of logic, presenting math that is outside the scope of a child's understanding is not understandable with the addition of more confusing mathematics. This is called exposure and planting seeds of doubt in the minds of children. Adults who think that other adults cannot claim their children's genders and sexual identities are exercising the same authority they claim that birth parents and physicians are violating.

A NEW SEXUAL REVOLUTION

Mary Eberstadt views the sexual indoctrination of children as the beginning of a new sexual revolution. The new sexual revolution among children will lead to more curiosity about sexual pleasure with members of the same and opposite sex. As children reach the teenage years, and then young adulthood, there will be an "overabundance of available sexual partners,"[95] which will then pressure relationships by making it more difficult "to hold the attention of any one of them."[96] Certainly, childhood innocence is in the crosshairs as a target for early sexual exposure.

Despite the goal of self-autonomy, it comes far too early in the lives of children. Children do not think like adults, and they should not be expected to reach conclusions as such. Such expectations only confuse children. But this is exactly what one can expect when children are indoctrinated. Such pressure is direct manipulation of minds and hearts and is tantamount to deception and indoctrination by confusion.

The California framework, quoted earlier, also advises teachers that the real issue is to press people to see LGBTQ+ community issues as civil rights issues. Attaching the message to a storied civil rights era is a bait-and-switch method used to lull citizens into thinking that historically recent protests based on sexuality and gender are somewhat equivalent to the hundreds of years of slavery, Jim Crow cultural racism, and horrid restrictions experienced by Black Americans. This is a false equivalency.

But Stephanie Gregson disagrees. Gregson is the director of the Curriculum Frameworks and Instructional Resources Division at the California Department of Education. She relates, "I think that people hear the word 'transgender' or 'gender identity' in guidance for kindergarten through grade three and they think the worst. . . . It's really about civil rights issues."[97] But who will ever argue about issues regarding civil rights and risk being called phobic or a racist? California parents are justified in their concerns. Parents from all states should be equally concerned. This is headed their way.

The sex education frameworks give "tips for discussing masturbation with middle-schoolers, including telling them it is not physically harmful, and for discussing puberty with transgender teens that creates 'an environment that is inclusive and challenges binary concepts about gender.'"[98] The nation must end the glorification of psychological sex experimentation and gender expression among our children.

Teachers and parents who disagree with the direction that culture is heading and the trend of exposing children to sex and gender knowledge must stand together and speak up. Teens are already turning to social media for their sex education.[99] This has been a disaster. It is difficult to believe that adults are just fine with sexualizing children, earlier and earlier, as a growing number of states' sex education frameworks are doing just that. Make no mistake about it: ideologies create radicals and radicals express their ideologies radically.

NOTES

1. Benjamin Bosman. *Leftist tactics, conservative solutions: A conservative analysis of Alinsky's rules and other tactics*. 2022. Monee, IL: self-published, p. 42.

2. Staff. "Fundamentals of SEL." Collaborative for Academic, Social, and Emotional Learning. 2022. Retrieved October 30, 2022, from https://casel.org/fundamentals-of-sel/.

3. Bonnie Kerrigan Snyder. *Undoctrinate: How politicized classrooms harm kids and ruin our schools—and what we can do about it*. 2021. Nashville, TN: Post Hill Press, p. 130.

4. Ibid., p. 129.

5. *Merriam-Webster Dictionary*, s.v. "doctrinaire." Retrieved August 28, 2022, from https://www.merriam-webster.com/dictionary/doctrinaire.

6. Snyder. *Undoctrinate*, p. 169.

7. Ibid., p. 126.

8. Ibid., p. 167.

9. Ibid.

10. Ibid., p. 125.

11. R. C. Murray. "Dumbing them down," in Colin Gunn and Joaquin Fernandez (eds.). *Indoctrination: Public schools and the decline of Christianity.* 2012. Green Forest, AR: Master Books, p. 79.

12. Michael Metarko. "America's Trojan horse: Public education," in Colin Gunn and Joaquin Fernandez (eds.). *Indoctrination: Public schools and the decline of Christianity.* 2012. Green Forest, AR: Master Books, pp. 28–29.

13. Ibid., p. 30. Cf. Ernest J. Zarra. *When the secular becomes sacred: Religious secular humanism and its effects upon America's public learning institutions.* 2021. Lanham, MD: Rowman & Littlefield Publishers, p. xiv, 4, 19–21, 42.

14. Samuel Blumenfeld. "Is humanism a religion?" *The New American.* February 23, 2010. Retrieved September 4, 2022, from https://thenewamerican.com/is-humanism-a-religion/.

15. Ibid.

16. Metarko. "America's Trojan horse," p. 31.

17. Bruce Shortt. "Appendix A: Postscript to teachers and administrators," in Colin Gunn and Joaquin Fernandez (eds.). *Indoctrination: Public schools and the decline of Christianity.* 2012. Green Forest, AR: Master Books, p. 350. Cf. Snyder. *Undoctrinate,* p. 129.

18. Quoted in Sharika S. Nair. "29 quotes from Plato, the father of western philosophy." *YourStory.* March 2, 2017. Retrieved October 30, 2022, from https://yourstory.com/2017/03/29-quotes-by-plato#:~:text=%E2%80%9CIf%20a%20man%20neglects%20education,the%20end%20of%20his%20life.%E2%80%9D.

19. Jason Stanley. "Education vs. indoctrination." *The Brainwaves—A Video Anthology.* Posted September 16, 2016. YouTube video. Retrieved September 1, 2022, from https://www.youtube.com/watch?v=HQy4yDx01bA.

20. Staff. "NAEP long-term trend assessment result: reading and mathematics." National Center for Education Statistics. 2022. Retrieved October 4, 2022, from https://www.nationsreportcard.gov/highlights/ltt/2022/.

21. Christopher Tremoglie. "Another radical leftist teacher caught trying to brainwash students in California." *Washington Examiner.* November 11, 2021. Retrieved November 25, 2021, from https://www.washingtonexaminer.com/opinion/another-radical-leftist-teacher-caught-trying-to-brainwash-students-in-california.

22. Betsy McCaughey. "Why schools won't tell parents what their kids are being taught." *New York Post.* September 6, 2022. Retrieved September 8, 2022, from https://nypost.com/2022/09/06/why-schools-wont-tell-parents-what-their-kids-are-being-taught/,) https://www.ncbi.nlm.nih.gov/pmc/articles/PMC9350299/.

23. Melinda Wenner Moyer. "Kids as young as 8 are using social media more than ever, study finds." *The New York Times.* March 24, 2022. Retrieved, September 3, 2022, from https://www.nytimes.com/2022/03/24/well/family/child-social-media-use.html.

24. Staff. "ExpressVPN survey reveals the extent of Gen Z's social media fixation." *ExpressVPN.* December 1, 2021. Retrieved June 3, 2022, from https://www.expressvpn.com/blog/gen-z-social-media-survey/#:~:text=For%20Gen%20Z%2C%20'likes%2C,image%2C%20anxiety%2C%20and%20more. Cf. Julie Jargon. "When teens question their gender, social media can provide support—and

pressure." *Wall Street Journal*. October 23, 2021. Retrieved June 3, 2022, from https://www.wsj.com/articles/when-teens-question-their-gender-social-media-can-provide-supportand-pressure-11634994000.

25. John McWhorter. *Woke racism: How a new religion has betrayed black America.* 2021. New York: Penguin Books. Cf. Michael Barone. "The new religion of woke anti-racism." *American Enterprise Institute*. June 11, 2020. Retrieved October 30, 2022, from https://www.aei.org/op-eds/the-new-religion-of-woke-anti-racism/.

26. Connor O'Neal. "Why are millennials and Gen Z shying away from religion? Twin cities leaders weigh in." *KARE*. July 28, 2022. Retrieved October 30, 2022, from https://www.kare11.com/article/news/community/why-millennials-and-gen-z-are-not-religious/89-dd12340e-d5b2-4087-a41a-46b8c0088529.

27. Ernest J. Zarra, III. *Detoxing American schools. From social agency to academic urgency.* 2020. Lanham, Maryland, Rowman & Littlefield Publishers.

28. Rachel Holt. "Generation Z: The woke generation." *GALE: The Chronicle of Higher Education*. 2020. Retrieved October 30, 2022, from https://sponsored.chronicle.com/Generation-Z-The-Woke-Generation/index.html.

29. Mary Eberstadt. *Primal screams: How the sexual revolution created identity politics*. 2019. Conshohocken, PA: Templeton Press, pp. 64, 66.

30. Stanley. "Education vs. indoctrination."

31. Ibid.

32. Tom Stafford. "How liars create the illusion of truth." British Broadcasting Company (BBC). October 26, 2016. Retrieved October 30, 2022, from https://www.bbc.com/future/article/20161026-how-liars-create-the-illusion-of-truth.

33. Tom Stafford. "How liars create the illusion of truth." British Broadcasting Company (BBC). October 26, 2016. Retrieved October 30, 2022, from https://www.bbc.com/future/article/20161026-how-liars-create-the-illusion-of-truth.

34. Snyder. *Undoctrinate*, p. 89.

35. Staff. "Schools activist says parents, teachers afraid of retribution if they speak out." National Public Radio (NPR). January 23, 2017. Retrieved October 30, 2022, from https://www.ualrpublicradio.org/local-regional-news/2017-01-23/schools-activist-says-parents-teachers-afraid-of-retribution-if-they-speak-out.

36. Laura Meckler and Hannah Natanson. "New critical race theory laws have teachers scared, confused and self-censoring." *The Washington Post*. February 14, 2022. Retrieved October 30 2022, from https://www.washingtonpost.com/education/2022/02/14/critical-race-theory-teachers-fear-laws/.

37. Conor Friedersdorf. "Evidence that conservative students really do self-censor." *The Atlantic*. February 16, 2020. Retrieved September 7, 2020, from https://www.theatlantic.com/ideas/archive/2020/02/evidence-conservative-students-really-do-self-censor/606559/.

38. Matthew Woessner. "Campus conservatives aren't under siege—but there's more to the story." *THINK*. August 14, 2019. Retrieved September 6, 2022, from https://www.nbcnews.com/think/opinion/right-says-campus-conservatives-are-under-siege-left-dismissive-both-ncna1042051.

39. James Varney. "Parents say they are kept in the dark about schools' use of critical race theory." *The Washington Times*. June 12, 2021. Retrieved October 30,

2022, from https://www.washingtontimes.com/news/2021/jun/12/parents-say-kept
-dark-use-critical-race-theory/. Cf. Jeremiah Poff. "Texas school told teachers to
keep parents in dark if students came out as transgender." *Washington Examiner*.
January 4, 2022. Retrieved October 30, 2022, from https://www.washingtonexaminer
.com/policy/texas-school-told-teachers-to-keep-parents-in-dark-if-students-came-out
-as-transgender.

40. President Joseph Biden. "President Biden's full speech on democracy." You-
Tube. September 1, 2022. Retrieved September 3, 2022, from https://www.youtube
.com/watch?v=JemWkV2Vcic.

41. David Zimmer. "Man killed teen he believed was a republican extremist."
American Experiment. September 21, 2022. Retrieved September 23, 2022, from
https://www.americanexperiment.org/man-killed-teen-he-believed-was-a-republican
-extremist/.

42. George Washington University. "Anarchist/left-wing violent extremism in
America." National Counterterrorism, Innovation, Technology, and Education Center.
November 2021, pp. 17–19. Retrieved September 8, 2022, from https://extremism
.gwu.edu/sites/g/files/zaxdzs2191/f/Anarchist%20-%20Left-Wing%20Violent
%20Extremism%20in%20America.pdf.

43. Ernest J. Zarra, III. "Straight talk about radical love." *Minding the Campus*.
National Association of Scholars. October 7, 2022. Retrieved October 8, 2022,
from https://www.mindingthecampus.org/2022/10/07/straight-talk-about-radical-love
/?fbclid=IwAR143tS7lJEcYyrCo00-JHMQL3jbnqikI3jJj4y7_uIi7apF8mgIXrOQIe8.

44. Grant Braaten. "Christian school receives death threats over its traditional
Christian views on sexuality and marriage." *The Lion*. August 24, 2022. Retrieved
October 30, 2022, from https://readlion.com/2022/08/24/christian-school-receives
-death-threats-over-its-traditional-christian-views-on-sexuality-and-marriage/.

45. D'Anne Witkowski. "The latest fad in radical right harassment campaigns?
Children's hospitals, of course." *Pride Source*. August 31, 2022. Retrieved October 30, 2022, from https://pridesource.com/article/the-latest-fad-in-radical-right
-harassment-campaigns-childrens-hospitals-of-course/.

46. Snyder. *Undoctrinate*, p. 5.

47. Ibid., p. 9.

48. Ibid., p.11.

49. Ibid., pp. 12–13.

50. Timothy Hsiao. "The lived experience fallacy." *Academic Questions*. 35(2):
n.p. National Association of Scholars. Retrieved August 20, 2022, from https://www
.nas.org/academic-questions/35/2/the-lived-experience-fallacy.

51. R. Roderick Palmer. "Education and Indoctrination." *Peabody Journal of Education*. 34(4): pp. 224–228. January 1957. Retrieved September 23, 2022, from https:
//www.jstor.org/stable/1490797.

52. Snyder. *Undoctrinate*, p. 115.

53. Hilal Parlak Sert and Hatice Baskale. "Students' increased time spent on social
media, and their level of coronoavirus anxiety during the pandemic increased social
media addiction." National Library of Medicine. July 7, 2022. Retrieved August 24,
2022. Cf. Peter Sociu. "American spent on average more than 1300 hours on social

media last year." *Forbes.* June 24, 2021. Retrieved July 18, 2022, from https://www
.forbes.com/sites/petersuciu/2021/06/24/americans-spent-more-than-1300-hours-on
-social-media/?sh=52ac38012547.

54. Snyder. *Undoctrinate*, p. 121.

55. Snyder. *Undoctrinate*, p. 61.

56. Douglas Blair. "I'm a former teacher. Here's how your children are getting indoctrinated by leftist ideology." The Heritage Foundation. August 17, 2020. Retrieved June 16, 2022, from https://www.heritage.org/education/commentary/im
-former-teacher-heres-how-your-children-are-getting-indoctrinated-leftist.

57. Ernest J. Zarra, III. "From self-esteem to equity." National Association of Scholars. May 25, 2021. Retrieved June 17, 2022, from https://www.nas.org/blogs
/article/from-self-esteem-to-equity. Cf. Ernest J. Zarra, III. *The entitled generation: Helping teachers teach and reach the minds and hearts of Generation Z.* 2017. Lanham, MD: Rowman & Littlefield Publishers.

58. Nanette Asimov. "UC settles student lawsuit, agrees not to use SAT, ACT scores in admission." *San Francisco Chronicle.* May 14, 2021. Retrieved May 15, 2021, from https://www.sfchronicle.com/local/article/UC-settles-student-lawsuit
-agrees-not-to-use-16178677.php.

59. Staff. "Meet the students pushing for more equity in public schools." This Changes Everything (podcast). Season 3, Episode 5. March 23, 2022. Retrieved June 16, 2022, from https://crosscut.com/podcast/changes-everything/3/5/podcast-meet
-students-pushing-more-equity-public-schools.

60. Snyder. *Undoctrinate*, p. 89.

61. Daniel Buck. "Yes, teacher-prep programs are that woke." *National Review.* March 27, 2022. Retrieved October 30, 2022, from https://www.nationalreview.com
/2022/03/yes-teacher-prep-programs-are-that-woke/.

62. Lance Izumi, Cassidy Syftestad, and Christie Syftestad. *The corrupt classroom: Bias, indoctrination, violence, and social engineering show why America needs school choice.* 2017. San Francisco, CA: Pacific Research Institute, p. 27.

63. Ibid.

64. Benjamin Hanckel, Son Vivienne, and Brendan Churchill. "That's not necessarily for them: LGBTQ+IQ+ young people, social media platforms affordances and identity curation." *Media, Culture, & Society.* 41(8). May 13, 2019. Retrieved October 30, 2022, from https://journals.sagepub.com/doi/10.1177/0163443719846612.

65. Miranda Devine. *Laptop from hell: Hunter Biden, big tech, and the dirty secrets the president tried to hide.* 2021. Nashville, TN: Post Hill Press.

66. Snyder. *Undoctrinate*, p. 142.

67. Ibid.

68. Staff. "Parents say Peninsula teen attacked at school for support of Donald Trump." ABC7 News. November 10, 2016. Retrieved October 30, 2022, from https:
//abc7news.com/donald-trump-protest-oakland-protests/1599714/.

69. Mike Levine. "No blame? ABS News finds 54 cases invoking 'Trump' in connection with violence, threats, alleged assaults." ABC News. May 30, 2020. Retrieved October 30, 2022, from https://abcnews.go.com/Politics/blame-abc-news-finds-17
-cases-invoking-trump/story?id=58912889.

70. Staff. "Oath Keepers called for violent overthrow of US government, trial hears." *The Guardian*. November 18. 2022. Retrieved November 19, 2022, from https://www.theguardian.com/us-news/2022/nov/18/oath-keepers-trial-closing -arguments-capitol-attack.

71. Jack Schneider and Jennifer Berkshire. "Parents claim they have the right to shape their kids' school curriculum. They don't." *The Washington Post*. October 21, 2021. Retrieved October 20, 2022, from https://www.washingtonpost.com/outlook /parents-rights-protests-kids/2021/10/21/5cf4920a-31d4-11ec-9241-aad8e48f01ff _story.html. Cf. Ben Johnson. "Parents aren't necessary for students to learn." *Edutopia*. July 23, 2013. Retrieved October 30, 2022, from https://www.edutopia.org/blog/ parents-not-necessary-for-students-to-learn-ben-johnson.

72. Wharton Management Department. "MBA Diversity, Equity & Inclusion Major." University of Pennsylvania. 2023–2024. Retrieved October 31, 2022, from https://mgmt.wharton.upenn.edu/programs/mba/dei-major/.

73. Human Resources Staff. "Diversity, equity, and inclusion." The University of Washington. 2022. Retrieved October 30, 2022, from https://hr.uw.edu/diversity/ hiring/sample-position-description-and-tips/.

74. Frank Dobbin and Alexandra Kalev. "Why diversity programs fail." *Harvard Business Review*. July-August 2016. Retrieved October 30, 2022, from https://hbr.org /2016/07/why-diversity-programs-fail.

75. Ernest J. Zarra, III. "Graphic content restrictions are not books bans." *Minding the Campus*. National Association of Scholars. February 2, 2022. Retrieved October 30, 2022, from https://www.mindingthecampus.org/2022/02/02/graphic-content -restrictions-are-not-book-bans/.

76. Jeff Johnston. "Sexualizing schoolchildren: Classroom and library books." *The Daily Citizen*. May 5, 2022. Retrieved June 14, 2022, from https://dailycitizen .focusonthefamily.com/sexualizing-schoolchildren-classroom-and-library-books/.

77. Ernest J. Zarra, III. *When the secular becomes sacred*. 2021. Lanham, MD: Rowman & Littlefield Publishers, pp. 129–136.

78. Staff. "California votes to overhaul sex ed guidelines for public schools to include LGBTQ+ issues." CBS News. May 8, 2019. Retrieved September 16, 2022, from https://www.cbsnews.com/news/california-sex-ed-curriculum-overhaul-sexual -education-guidelines-today-2019-05-08/.

79. Marilyn Quigley. "The legalized sexualization of America's young children." Independent Women's Forum. January 5, 2022. Retrieved October 30, 2022, from https://www.iwf.org/2022/01/05/the-legalized-sexualization-of-americas-young -children/. Lois M. Collins and Sara Lenz. "The end of innocence: The cost of sexualizing kids." *Deseret News*. September 17, 2011. Retrieved October 30, 2022, from https://www.deseret.com/2011/9/18/20216829/the-end-of-innocence-the-cost -of-sexualizing-kids.

80. Ernest J. Zarra, III. *America's sex culture: Its impact on teacher student relationships today*. Second edition. 2020. Lanham, MD: Rowman & Littlefield, Publishers.

81. Doug Mainwaring. "Most teachers quite disturbed about their unions' push for sexualization and indoctrination of school children." *Life Site News*. October 10,

2019. Retrieved July 18, 2020, from https://www.forkidsandcountry.org/news/life
-site-news-most-teachers-quite-disturbed-about-their-unions-push-for-sexualization
-and-indoctrination-of-school-children/#none.

82. Ken Ham. "Gone in only one generation: The battle for kids' minds."
Christian Heritage. April 28, 2014. Retrieved September 22, 2022, from https://
christianheritagewa.org/gone-in-only-one-generation-the-battle-for-kids-minds/.

83. Paul Stevens-Fullbrook. "15 learning theories in education (a complete summary)." Education Corner. *Teachers of Sci*. April 18, 2019. Retrieved September 29,
2022, from https://www.educationcorner.com/learning-theories-in-education/.

84. Mainwaring. "Most teachers quite disturbed about their unions' push for sexualization and indoctrination of school children."

85. Ann P. Haas and Jack Drescher. "Impact of sexual orientation and gender
identity on suicide risk: Implications for assessment and treatment." *Psychiatric Times*. 31(12). December 31, 2014. Retrieved August 10, 2022, from https:
//www.psychiatrictimes.com/view/impact-sexual-orientation-and-gender-identity
-suicide-risk-implications-assessment-and-treatment. Cf. Russell B. Toomey, Amy
K Syvertsen, and Mauro Shramko. "Transgender adolescent suicide behavior."
Pediatrics. 142(4). October 2018. Retrieved July 3, 2022, from https://publications
.aap.org/pediatrics/article/142/4/e20174218/76767/Transgender-Adolescent-Suicide
-Behavior.

86. Ben Shapiro. "The insanity of the left's child gender-confusion agenda." *Facts
don't care about your feelings*. 2019. Hermosa Beach, CA: Creators Publishing, pp.
156–157.

87. Mainwaring. "Most teachers quite disturbed about their unions' push for sexualization and indoctrination of school children."

88. Ibid.

89. Cameron Sheppard. "Parents express concerns over sex education legislation."
Peninsula Daily News. February 25, 2020. Retrieved July 15, 2022 from https://www
.peninsuladailynews.com/news/parents-express-concerns-over-sex-ed-legislation/.

90. Brook Pessin-Whedbee. *Who are you? The kids guide to gender identity*. 2016.
Philadelphia, PA: Jessica Kingsley Publishers.

91. Mainwaring. "Most teachers quite disturbed about their unions' push for sexualization and indoctrination of school children."

92. Andrea Roberts, M. Maria Glymour, and Karestan C. Koenen. "Does maltreat-
ment in childhood affect sexual orientation?" *Archives of Sexual Behavior*. 42(2): pp.
161–171. February 2013. Retrieved July 15, 2022, from https://www.ncbi.nlm.nih
.gov/pmc/articles/PMC3535560/.

93. Emphasis throughout is mine. Staff. "FAQ for sexual education. HIV/AIDS,
and STDs." California Department of Education. August 30, 2019. Retrieved August
3, 2022 from https://www.cde.ca.gov/ls/he/se/faq.asp.

94. Staff. "California votes to overhaul sex ed guidelines for public schools to
include LGBTQ+ issues."

95. Eberstadt. *Primal screams*, p. 75.

96. Ibid.

97. Staff. "California votes to overhaul sex ed guidelines for public schools to include LGBTQ+ issues."

98. Ibid.

99. Tayler Adlgun and Kerry Justich. "Teens are turning to TikTok for sex ed. Here's what they're learning." *Yahoo!Life*. November 11, 2022. Retrieved November 12, 2022, from https://www.yahoo.com/lifestyle/teens-turning-to-tik-tok-for-sex-ed -154352813.html.

Chapter 2

Ideologies and Radicalization

Values are a guiding star by which to evaluate competing ideas and ideologies.

— Bonnie Kerrigan Snyder, *Undoctrinate*[1]

Tactics means doing what you can with what you have. Tactics are those consciously deliberate acts by which human beings live with each other and deal with the world around them . . . the first rule of power tactics: Power is not only what you have but what the enemy thinks you have.

— Saul Alinsky, *Rules for Radicals*[2]

The existence of radicals begs the question as to how these radicals developed. Exposure to ideologies in the processes of indoctrination and questions about motivation toward actions are keys to understanding radicalization. Are radicals born as feisty spirits, naturally inclined toward being radicalized? Are radicals on the left and right considered comparable, as some would say "a radical is a radical"?

What ideologies go into the creation of radicals? Are radicals exposed to indoctrination and radical ideas at home, outside the home, or both? How do worldviews on race, religion, sex, and gender play into the creation and development of radicals and their ideologies?

IDEOLOGIES AND RADICALIZATION

When the term radical is used, it usually refers to people, ideas, and/or actions. When it comes to radicalized persons, there is usually the expectation of actions. For radicals, there are often plans to generate some sort of sudden change—a radical change!

Ideologies are worldviews that espouse major tenets, doctrines, or statements of belief. Some ideologies can be philosophical, while others are political, religious, or a combination of other culturally appropriated beliefs. In terms of race, examples such as those associated with radical social justice warriors, include fundamentals of critical race theory. One can expect that people who ascribe to the LGBTQ+ ideas about sex and gender have an ideology that matches.

Some general examples of philosophical ideologies today are found in woke-ism, secularism, religion, progressive politics, socialism, Marxism, liberation, and, in some aspects, queer theology. Each ideology, then, has its foundation in a worldview and reveals fundamental beliefs. Aside from dissimilarities among ideologies, there is one aspect that is common to all. Each ideology eventually calls for some sort of action on the part of its adherents.

On a larger geographic scale, adherents to radical views are labeled anti-Israel, pro-jihadist, anti-American, and so on. Others proclaim their radical label on a more localized level. Oath Keepers, Proud Boys, Christian Nationalists, Antifa, Ku Klux Klan (KKK), Black Lives Matter (BLM), Neo-Nazis, and Communists are examples, to name a few. Sometimes violence accompanies the radicalism of groups and their members. The following cases illustrate recent occurrences of violence or threats of violence.

- Violence against both pro-life and pro-abortion facilities.[3]
- Burning and firebombing of pro-life clinics by pro-abortionist radicals.[4]
- Threats of violence toward Supreme Court justices and conservative politicians by pro-abortion radicals.[5]
- Threats against the US government by the Oath Keepers.[6]
- Domestic terrorism concerns through radicalized Islamists in the United States.[7]

Education and Ideology

In terms of the worldviews that pertain to the discipline of education, Rousas Rushdoony states, "This total war is one which must be recognized, and education is at present perhaps the central theater of war. Van Til is right. There are two, and only two, mutually exclusive philosophies of education."[8] These are "theistic and humanistic,"[9] and "attempts to fuse the two [philosophies of education] are untenable (Matthew 6:24). . . . This means that the teacher cannot be neutral nor subscribe to humanistic philosophies with respect to his field of study. Either there is a neutral void behind every fact, or the living

God. In our teaching, we will always consciously or unconsciously acknowledge one or the other."[10]

Rushdoony points to something quite significant for education. That is, there is the fact of objective truth. At the same time, by contrast, he also points out that "the idea that there exists a common value system known as Americanism no longer prevails in American public schools."[11] Blumenfeld agrees with Rushdoony but adds, "there is a deeply spiritual aspect to the concept of Americanism, which our secular, anti-God education system rejects."[12] Thus, "Humanistic education is the institutionalized love of death."[13]

Modern philosophers of education hold to premises that are dissimilar to Rushdoony's, as they are "often emphatic in declaring there are no final answers. . . . As a result, modern humanism is hostile to the idea of answers."[14] Additionally, "students can easily anticipate and apply the repetitive narrative, rather than thinking spontaneously and originally. In other words: it's easy and requires little to no original thought. Mouthing slogans is effortless, fast, and instantly gratifying."[15]

When it comes down to parents watching over their children, the conflict is not about the parents. The conflict is with the public school system, over the children. The system is actually set up to parent the students, out of the sight of the actual parents and caretakers.

Parents must be on guard against hidden agendas that are part of their local schools. As Snyder validates, "Hidden agendas and deceptive practices have absolutely no place in an educational institution, and concealed motives, once exposed, inevitably erode trust. Parents have a right to be properly and fully informed, so that they can make responsible decisions about what, if any, actions to take, and must be allowed to transfer children out of lessons or classrooms where a teacher has renounced non-partisanship and undertaken openly activist aims in opposition to their family's values and educational aims."[16]

Radicalization and Change

Radicals are often defined by advocating for things that are "(1) very different from the usual or traditional, (2) favoring extreme changes in existing views, habits, conditions, or institutions, (3) associated with political views, practices, and policies of extreme change, and (4) advocating extreme measures to retain or restore a political state of affairs."[17] Some of these persons are intentionally radicalized at home and are mentored into activists.[18] Others are taught early in schools and spend time online with radical influencers, and later either form or join like-minded groups. There is no generic, transferable profile that suffices as a model for the production of a radical.

Given that the apparent educational status quo is grounded in political progressivism, the reality is that radicals that hold the power in American politics also control the schools. Although labeled as dangerous radicals by the National Education Association, concerned parent groups are popping up all over the nation to fight back against the one-sided power structure found in public education.[19] Parents have at least as much distrust in public education as teachers' unions have in parents.

Under the Biden presidency, radical progressives maintain power, while those seeking to regain a conservative power base are viewed as radicals and haters of democracy. In fact, anyone wearing a red hat is labeled as a potential terrorist favoring violence. A common tactic by radicals is to project onto their opponents the very things they are doing themselves. This will be examined in greater detail later in this chapter, and also in chapter 3. This tactic is used just to distract from their own beliefs and practices. One of the problems with political power is that once it changes hands the payback never seems to end.

EDUCATION RADICALIZED

American culture shapes the way people live and the choices they make, and often helps to clarify personal beliefs. There is a synergism between people and culture. Changing culture changes people and changing people changes culture. Some of the more prominent shapers of American culture are found at the college level. Institutions of higher learning directly impact America's K–12 classrooms in many ways. Therefore, it is not an understatement to argue that the progressive left has had great effects upon American education and national culture, as well.[20]

These effects upon American education are real, tangible, and even measurable. This is clear from the data. Surveys indicate the magnitude to which teachers and teachers' unions support progressive and leftist causes.[21] There is very little political balance within this progressive large-scale ideological entity.[22]

There are some conservative and moderate teachers (and students) mixed within the system of public education, but these minimized human voices are not allowed to have an equal share at the table of conversations. Voices other than those of the progressives are not allowed to dissent, and, therefore, freedom of speech is stunted within classrooms. The established narratives of the left have predetermined that conservatives are the radicals. This only enhances the political divide and exacerbates any possible congeniality, or even any meeting of the minds.

The issue for many American parents dealing with radicalism at their schools has reached critical levels. Parental concerns over radical teachers in their children's schools are not unfounded. "Many embedded assumptions lurk below the surface of innocuous-sounding terminology. Stealthy deception is one of the main methods by which unpopular ideas are being smuggled into our children's classrooms."[23]

Ideological Creep

Remember when just one or two teenagers wanted to use school bathrooms of their choice, because they thought they were of the opposite sex and gender? In less than a decade, American students have seen a definite shift in the ways that gender-confused classmates are now treated. What began with school bathroom choice has migrated to locker rooms, made its way into board rooms, and now protects biological males in competition against biological females in athletics.

Medical communities are participating in the transitioning of children to something to which they were not born. These so-called professionals are making every attempt to change biological nature under the guise of affirming care. Physicians are stealthily practicing gender-affirming care by prescribing medicine to block human growth and are performing surgeries that remove and construct human body parts.[24] By all measures, American culture has been radically bombarded by sex and gender ideology.

The US military has a growing number of transgender recruits, and it will not be long before even professional athletics sees its share, given the propensity to move a radical practice along within mainstream wokeness. As a primary reflection of culture, schools and teachers are subject to ideologies in education and have no recourse but to go along. If they refuse, they may lose everything for which they worked.

The pressure on America's corporate and business board rooms has intensified, and billions of dollars have been shelled out to racial and gender lobbies to keep the peace and avoid lawsuits. The changes are terribly noticeable. All one has to do is to watch any cable television program or tune in to a progressive news station. It is made to appear that everyone is a person of color, or married to one, or that the LGBTQ+ population is massive and mainstream. The strategy is clear that bombarding viewers with ideologies will eventually sink into the psyches of these same viewers. Thus, culture can be changed by indoctrination led by the media and its workings.

The race and LGBTQ+ ideologies have deeply radicalized America. From Obama to Biden, the specter of *community organizing* is considered by critics as stealth talk for the strategies and tactics of Saul Alinsky. Then there is Trump the disrupter. He sauntered into Washington, DC, with an alternate ideology that claimed to place *America First*. His critics claim this phrase was a dog whistle to white nationalists.

Each of these elected officials developed ideologies that appealed to swaths of the American voting populace. In Trump's case, it was the appeal to populism, which emphasized the people of the nation over the elites of the nation. Each official has seen his or her share of radical activism both for and against him or her. Sadly, riots, violence, and destruction took place on their watches. There is no surprise that radicals acted out on their behalf, given the highly politically divided nation.

Simona Trip, Carmen Hortensia Bora, Mihai Marian, et al., see radicalism as "a process of developing extremist beliefs, emotions, and behaviors. The extremist beliefs are profound convictions opposed to the fundamental values of society, the laws of democracy and the universal human rights, advocating the supremacy of a certain group (racial, religious, political, economic, social, etc.)."[25]

The extremists who openly share "emotions and behaviors may be expressed both in non-violent pressure and coercion and in actions that deviate from the norm and show contempt for life, freedom, and human rights."[26] The reader should take note in the statement above, the possibility of violence has been left on the table of radical actions and serves as an imprimatur for groups willing to take up the call.

THE DANGERS OF RADICALIZATION

Radical ideological worldviews can be dangerous for many reasons. One of these reasons is because they are often embedded in revolutionary discourse and serve as motives toward taking extreme action. Even before the time of Christ, known empires feared being overthrown by oppositional forces. These fears continued throughout the ages and have not disappeared in the present.

Emerging worldviews spin sets of beliefs that, in turn, develop into ideologies. But there really is nothing new that is established. Take socialism, for example. A new wave of political socialism has struck the halls of Congress. Some radicalized elected officials are bereft of the history of socialism and the evil outcomes that resulted from its enforcement upon people around the world during the twentieth century. Some elected officials would take the United States down a socialist pathway that has been tried by other countries with disastrous outcomes.[27] Nevertheless, when indoctrination into an ideology produces a radical, it is at this point that consequential thinking becomes blurred.

Today a person can be radicalized by one of many ideologies, including:

- radical sexual ideology
- radical gender ideology
- radical racial ideology
- radical political ideology
- radical religious ideology
- radical nationalistic ideology
- radical progressive education ideology
- radical social justice ideology

Expectations Associated with Radicalization

Activism is not a separate ideology, in itself. One of the reasons some ideologies are more dangerous than others, however, does come down to activism. Activism means action and this action is often an expected byproduct of being radicalized.

The last sixty years of American history have seen their share of activists. When recalling an ideology in history, there are likely characters whose names are synonymous with radical activism. Whenever the term activism is used, it is usually associated with a near-opposite ideology of the status quo. In the past, activism was seen "as a crusade, youthful dalliance, or career opportunity."[28] Today, activism is as much as about destruction as it is deconstruction.[29]

Diversity. When activists use terms such as diversity, they are often misapplied and result in either distractions or miscommunications. "Most consider diversity as simply welcoming people of all ethnic backgrounds to the table."[30] However, for example, diversity "on the lips of a critical social justice activist means something else. While an activist might occasionally claim to be tolerant of different ideas and political viewpoints and nod towards philosophical differences, he focuses almost entirely on physical and cultural differences, which he evaluates according to the critical social justice conceptions of privilege and marginalization. He therefore aims to privilege the marginalized and marginalize the privileged in order to redress the imbalances it sees in society."[31]

Equity. Diversity and race activists "believe invisible systems of power and privilege hold some people back in invisible ways because of their race, gender, sexuality, or other marginalized identity factors. Therefore, equity requires giving some identity groups privileges in order to redress the perceived imbalance."[32] This practice has become something of an expectation placed on America.

However, these privileges are one-sided. A good example is on college campuses where students are protesting speakers scheduled to visit campus. If students do not want these speakers, small groups of radicals can get them canceled. Diversity and inclusion of those outside the progressive camp are found to be intolerable, per se.

WORLDVIEWS LEAD TO RADICALIZATION

World views are not vacuous. Worldviews are shaped by inputs of individuals and groups. Some or all of these inputs may also be responsible for pushing Americans to extreme measures, while others may appear harmless for the moment. The consideration of worldviews means careful examination of the inputs that help to craft them. These include indoctrination, one-sided education, direct support from radical mentors, online groups that encourage certain behaviors, issue affinities, and close friends and families.

Generally, worldviews are belief systems that people attempt to apply to most areas of their lives. They are often referred to as lenses through which to view life. Belief systems affect (1) perspectives on money and finances, (2) views on politics, (3) understanding of social and moral issues, (4) appreciation of art and music, (5) what one believes about sex and gender issues, and (6) how one approaches religion and faith.

David Noebel, author of *Understanding the Times*, contributes the following: "A worldview is a framework from which we view reality and make sense of life and the world. It's any ideology, theology, movement or religion that provides an overarching approach to understanding God, the world, and man's relations to God and the world."[33]

Philosophers and theologians such as the late Francis Schaeffer and the late R. C. Sproul brought Christianity and culture together in ways that demonstrated contrasted incompatibility, as well as compared insightful overlap. Noebel, in reference to Schaeffer's perspective, writes: "Through books, like *How Should We Then Live*, videos, and his L'Abri Study Center, Schaeffer made worldview thinking accessible and applicable to non-academics, demonstrated the broad relevance of Christianity to culture, paved the way for para-church organizations committed to Christian worldview thinking, and influenced the worldview writings of individuals such as Charles Colson and Nancy Pearcey."[34]

Anyone with a toddler understands the rudimentary aspects of a worldview. Most toddlers' words and actions imply they are content to be the focus of the world. Self is supreme. When we understand the differences between worldviews, we can begin to understand why people believe abortion is a choice, gender is fluid, love is love, and design in the universe happened by chance.

Influencers

Those who wish to promote widespread acceptance of an ideology are typically called influencers. Influencers are often found celebrating their worldviews on social media, seeking to persuade others to follow their ideas. Two realities come into play when finding oneself persuaded to a worldview, especially by serious engagement of emotions. These realities inform us that, (1) many evangelists of causes exist in the world and most of them believe in their own *good news*, and (2) people come to believe in an ideology because of the influence of something or someone rather than critically discovering a belief by personal thought and reflection. In terms of determining worldviews, three questions should come to mind.

Three Questions Pertaining to Worldviews

The following three questions are important to consider because their answers provide insight into how someone views the world.

Question 1: Where did we come from and why are we here?

There are two fundamental worldviews to consider here. One worldview involves some type of *purpose and design*, while the other involves a naturalistic, *random* evolutionary and humanistic worldview. How a person views the world will definitely have an impact on the answer to this question and impact whether or not there is purpose to life and living.

Question 2: Is anything right or wrong with the world?

The answers to this question vary depending on who is in power and whether or not people or events—or a combination of both—are the cause of what is both right and wrong with the world. Adding a religious element then brings in a different aspect, such as responsibility for the world in the form of stewardship, as well as whether mankind's nature is fallen and sinful. A Christian will answer this question differently than an atheist. These worldviews are drastically different.

Question 3: If there are right or wrong things with the world, then how can the world be improved upon, or fixed?

Worldviews will affect the answer to this question significantly. If a worldview is based in religion or morality, then returning God into secular culture may be an answer to how the world can be fixed. If a secular view is applied, then mankind bears the responsibility for the things that are both right and wrong with the world, or mankind is basically victimized randomly. As with questions one and two, there is an undergirding issue regarding the value of truth and whether truth is objective or purely situational and subjective.

The three questions have great importance for parents to consider in terms of who their children's teachers are and their own personal and familial worldviews. The reason it is important for parents is because, "There is an exploding realization among many parents that the now dominant progressive ideology of the public schools is incompatible with their bedrock beliefs."[35] Parents should also be concerned because "Polling data on the beliefs of young Millennials . . . underscore the impact of the ideologized and politicized instruction they received in the public schools."[36] Gen Z is now showing similar signs, as these young adults are demonstrating some extremely radical behaviors.[37] These behaviors have been motivated by Gen Z's view of the world.

WHAT DOES IT MEAN TO BE RADICALIZED?

The bottom line is that in order to have a radical there must be radicalization. In order to have radicalization, there must be exposure to radical ideas that are accepted and supported. In order for many radical ideas to be accepted and supported, they must be believed as just and true, and this usually occurs through the process of indoctrination.

The process of radicalization occurs from at least two points of functionality. In terms of this *function*, to be radicalized is the process of preparing for "intergroup conflict and subsequent engagement."[38] Therefore, the process of radicalization is defined as preparation for intergroup conflict and subsequent engagement.[39] Pertaining to *descriptive aspects*, being radicalized "refers to a change in belief, feelings, and behaviors that justify intergroup violence, in defense of their own group."[40] When the two are present, the process of radicalization can be said to be satisfied. However, there are other issues to consider beyond function and description in coming to understand radicalization.

Reasons Radicalization Occurs

A recent study conducted by the RAND Corporation concluded that the factors of social marginalization and sacred values were key components in radicalization and subsequent action. Scott Atran writes, "The research used ethnographic surveys and psychological analysis to identify 535 young Muslim men in and around Barcelona—where ISIS-supporting Jihadis killed thirteen people and wounded one hundred more in the city center in August 2017."[41]

Along with financial support from the Minerva Research Institute, the National Science Foundation, as well as the US Department of Defense, "the first neuroimaging study of a radicalizing population was published."[42] The findings of the study suggest some interesting ideas worthy of consideration.

First, "sacralization of values interacts with willingness to engage in extreme behavior in populations vulnerable to radicalization."[43] For example, if a population is considered, by itself or others, as vulnerable to radicalization, the addition of a sacred belief can bring group differences to a head more rapidly. Likewise, "social exclusion appears to be a relevant factor motivating violent extremism and consolidation of sacred values."[44] Atran suggests that if this is the case then "counteracting social exclusion and sacralization of values should figure into policies to prevent radicalization."[45] The question is: Whose responsibility is it to counteract these? A more localized application question is: To what extent did sacralization of ideologies occur through the social exclusion that resulted from two years of COVID-19 lockdown?

Second, in the United States, the antiracist, oppressor-oppressed based, and neo-Marxist ideology assumes that whites are vulnerable by birth to be racists. Thus, when children and young adults are told these things, there may be a tendency toward developing extreme reactions toward political organizations or fringe groups that badger those unwilling to accept social extremism.

In some ways, the RAND study relates to American radical extremism. One of these ways is that "sacred values tend to be associated with unconditional cooperation for those who hold to such values, as well as intractable conflict with those who don't."[46] Americans who are on the fence politically are finding that when their values are attacked, or the group within which they associate is castigated, there is a shift in mind sets and behaviors[47] as a result.

Additional details from the RAND study reported that the men studied in Barcelona showed "the neurological impact of being excluded,"[48] which led to their sense of being excluded for reasons that were greater than mere involvement in an activity. Thus, "issues that they had previously considered non-sacred became far more important and were now deemed similar to those considered sacred and worth fighting and dying for."[49]

Next, the study showed that a willingness "to fight and die . . . is greatest for those who believe they are fighting for sacred values, and who also perceive spiritual strength . . . as more important than material strength."[50] One of the most important findings of the study should catch the attention of policymakers. The study found that "people are willing to sacrifice everything, including their lives—the totality of their self-interests—[and] will not be lured away just by material incentives or disincentives such as pay, promotion or punishment."[51]

Regardless the nation, the conclusions of the study bear witness that "enticements or threats to compromise or abandon values that have become

sacralized, usually backfire when competing sacred values are involved, leading to enduring conflict, as we find in the case of Palestine and Israel . . . the
abortion standoff, gun rights and now the recently sacralized issue of immigration that has accompanied intense political polarization."[52]

The dynamics of radicalization, some would argue, seem to mimic what
tends to occur in religious indoctrination. However, there is a far cry between
Hare Krishna asking for money on the streets, the threats and violence committed in the name of Scientology, the contemporary evangelical practice of
sharing the Gospel of Christ with the lost, and offering alternate care for those
considering abortion.

Where choice is restricted and participation is mandatory to demonstrate
allegiance, there is generally a tendency toward radicalization. Are not
restricted choice and mandatory allegiance by radicals a prominent characteristic of what besets American public school classrooms?

CHARACTERISTICS OF BEING RADICALIZED

The radicalization of students is not just an American concern. In the United
Kingdom, the Devon Children and Families Partnership (DCFP) works with
the Devon-Cornwall Police to protect children from being radicalized. The
DCFP defines radicalization as "when someone starts to believe or support
extreme views, and in some cases, then participates in terrorist groups or
acts."[53] They posit that "people may be radicalized in many different ways,
and very different time frames from as little as a few days or hours, or it may
take several years."[54]

The DCFP found that "anyone can be radicalized, but factors such as
being easily influenced and impressionable make children and young people
particularly vulnerable."[55] In fact vulnerable children[56] may sense or have
experienced one or more of the following:

- low self-esteem;
- victimization by bullying
- a desire to belong and fit in
- a hyper-awareness of others' feelings toward them
- judged by their sexual identity or cultural claims, or their religious beliefs
- inner-anger about people
- indoctrination and pressure to fight for causes of the so-called oppressed

The data from the DCFP show that "teenagers can be at greater risk
because they are more independent, exploring new things and pushing
boundaries as they grow and discover more about their identity, faith, and

sense of belonging."[57] When young people are targeted for indoctrination and extremism, they are often radicalized by the internet and social media. Unless a nation blocks internet access for its people, social media can make it appear that "everyone" is on board with a cause and that radical extremism is a norm.[58] The old axiom that "everyone is doing something" is assurance that not everyone is doing it.

When people are radicalized both by online and in-person relationships, they may become victims of:

- being groomed online or in person
- exploitation, including sexual exploitation
- psychological manipulation
- exposure to violent materials
- risk of physical harm through extremist acts

Some of the signs that a child or young adult is being radicalized[59] or has already succumbed to radicalism, include:

- uncharacteristic changes in behavior
- dropping friends to associate with a new group of friends
- withdrawing and isolating from family and acquaintance with different views
- talking in bumper-sticker narratives and with a repetitive script
- suddenly disrespecting and name-calling others
- an increase in anger and a shorter fuse
- an increase of secrecy with smartphone and internet use
- accessing extremism material online
- deciding that they are a different gender
- referring to all people as either oppressed or oppressors
- using terms that marginalize groups and individuals, or is found inciting violence
- creating artwork, online videos, banners, protest signs, and so on, that promote an extreme ideology
- attending Antifa or Black Lives Matter rallies regularly

THE METHODS AND PROCESS OF RADICALIZATION

When a person is radicalized, there is a process he or she is exposed to and developed by, and to which he or she eventually succumbs. The process can be identified within a particular culture, or as a result of cross-culture exposure. Thus, extremism in literature refers both to "political ideologies and to methods through which political actors try to achieve their aims."[60]

The methods that are associated with extreme radicalization demonstrate a blatant "disregard for others' life, liberty, and human rights."[61] Trip et al., provide clarification:

> Radicalization is a process of developing extremist beliefs, emotions, and behaviors. The extremist beliefs are profound convictions that oppose the fundamental values of society, the laws of democracy and universal human rights by advocating the supremacy of a particular group (racial, religious, political, economic, social, etc.). The extremist emotions and behaviors may be expressed both in non-violent pressure and coercion and in actions that deviate from the norm and show contempt for life, freedom, and human rights. There is a clear distinction between [the] terms counter-radicalization, de-radicalization, and disengagement. Counter-radicalization involves social, political, legal, and educational prevention programs designed to discourage disgruntled and perhaps already radicalized people. . . . De-radicalization implies a cognitive trajectory, thus programs focus on changing the cognitive framework of radicalized individuals with the aim of discouraging their involvement in violence.[62]

Danielle Serio, who also goes by the online name of "Flint," posted on TikTok that she had amassed a sizeable queer library and that this library "was available to students and has been active for five years."[63] When challenged, Serio resorted to hiding behind a fallacy called the Motte and Bailey Doctrine. Serio stated that her library was meant to liberate and be available to all. When asked "whether she thought it's important to have a queer library on campus," she retreated to a safe place and then changed the framing of the question, by replying "In my educational experience, books are always a good thing and books that support our students, I'm for."[64]

The issue is that Serio was solely in charge of determining that a queer library benefited her students. In fact, her ideology is so pervasively a part of her identity that she "questioned why parents have a hard time trusting educators."[65] The easy answer to getting parents to trust teachers with their children is not to indoctrinate or groom them, by allowing one's personal ideology or lifestyle to become so important that being queer means more than academics.

Trust by parents is earned, and it is obvious that Serio is ignorant of this, or just does not care, when she states, "It's been so long since they were in school . . . I'm wondering if they have extreme or outdated views about what's happening in the classroom."[66] The problem for Serio, and others like her, is that parents are discovering this type of radicalism and voicing their distaste for what they are seeing.

RADICALIZATION BY THE LEFT AND THE RIGHT

There are three basic educational questions that run from general to specific, and capture the essence of concern about radical ideologies. The answers to these questions will vary. However, the answers should generate parental awareness regarding the depth of the radicalism they may confront. Parents should consider asking the following questions of school board members, school principals, and their children's teachers:

1. How has the mission of education changed in this age of wokeness and indoctrination?
2. How is indoctrination affecting students mentally, physically, emotionally, spiritually, and sexually?
3. What would convince a child to alter, change, or remove body parts to conform to an ideology that states a person can choose their own sense of identity?

To review, radicals adopt worldviews as a result of being indoctrinated into a belief system. Radical ideologies can lead to radical actions, since radicals are not content with mere belief systems. Actions taken by radicals are often marked by extreme behaviors. Radicals in America are especially politically active. As such, radicals in the United States can easily present a façade, in order to appear (1) concerned about moral and ethical issues, (2) patriotic, (3) focused on government, freedom, and rights, and (4) focused on religion.

Radical ideologies that impact schools and students lean left today. The same applies to American universities and colleges. Likewise, teachers and professors, offices of the media elites, entertainers, and Hollywood share in similar political leanings.

Much of the leadership of corporate America, military brass, and even presidential administrations have been left-leaning for some time. Nevertheless, radicalism does not always lean left, as stated earlier in the chapter. Whether a person is a political conservative or liberal, moderate or progressive, everyone should be concerned about extremism, radicalism, and indoctrination. Unfortunately, in terms of political ideology, darker forces that either occupy the underbelly of the political beast in the nation, or are part of emerging conspiracy theories, are not content to leave well enough alone.[67]

So much of what takes places today is filled with rage and heat. Voices from all sides appear radicalized and even poised for physical battle. This is not a good place to be as a nation. The thirst for power and control over the masses results in oppressing voices of opposition. Those not in power are content to ride their opponents' power until it is stripped away. Once that happens, then another form of indoctrination may occur, as a replacement to the previous status quo. This may be followed by the emergence of another group of indoctrinated radicals. As the cycle repeats, radical extremists may take their radicalism to the streets to express power. Table 2.1 illustrates ideologies on the left and on the right.

THE MAINSTREAMING OF RADICALIZATION

There is no secret that Christians around the world represent the largest persecuted religious group.[68] This persecution has come to the United States. William Wolfe writes in *The Christian Post*: "Even though the United States is, arguably, the freest nation on the planet, and offers First Amendment protection, Christians still face already-and-increasing persecution between our shining seas."[69] Threats to Christian ministries, and others, are occurring almost daily over disagreement with same-sex marriage, the LGBTQ+ agenda in schools, and positions against mutilating children for the sake of the transgender movement. A more high-profile case involves J. K. Rowling, author of the *Harry Potter* literature series. She is facing threats of all sorts, including being killed, by transgender activists of the LGBTQ+ movement.[70]

Although Christians have not yet had to die massive martyrs' deaths in America, like they have at the hands of Muslim radicals in Nigeria and elsewhere,[71] everything short of that has already come about.[72] The persecution slope manifests itself first by way of a change in worldview, then by ideologies from colleges and bureaucrats, marginalization by beliefs, and then legal restrictions. Americans have endured backlash against Muslims (after September 11, 2001), persistent anti-Semitism, and now Christo-phobia.

Since America was founded on Christian principles and our legal system and laws are evidence of our reliance on biblical principles, it is becoming increasingly clear that Christians who speak their mind about the direction of American culture are labeled as haters of progress and despisers of democracy.

Table 2.1. Examples of Radical Ideologies on the Left and the Right

RADICAL IDEOLOGIES ON THE LEFT	RADICAL IDEOLOGIES ON THE RIGHT
Anarchism	Alt-Right
Antifa (Fascism)	Christian Nationalism
Antiracism	Conservatism
Communism	Fascism
Critical Gender Theory	Neo-Nazi
Critical Race Theory	Q-ANON
Progressivism	Racism
Socialism	White Nationalism

Something is terribly wrong in American culture when the foundations of the nation's morality and legal system are accused of being racist. Likewise, something is equally as wrong with American culture when the foundational truths of the nation are supplanted. Revisionists have taken aim at theology and have redefined away absolutes and queered Christian theology.

Christian theology has been affected deeply by the LGBTQ+ apologists who are hoping to derail millennia of scriptural teachings. This is not a small issue. Rather than seek mainstream acceptance, Martin Duberman, veteran activist, argues the LGBTQ+ should heed the call "to return to its radical activist roots."[73]

Claims of revelatory superiority are nothing new and are often responsible for new religious cultic ideologies. From the woke, that emphasize race and gender—as well as other progressive efforts to erase America's history—to the outright blasphemy by radical sex and gender groups, America is moving closer each decade to the brink of moral implosion, and this is not hyperbole. Parents from all walks of life, including from all political perspectives, are fearful of the direction that is being pushed by radicals in American schools.[74] This may be one reason that more than half of Americans surveyed desire to bring God back into American culture, while declaring the United States as a Christian nation.[75]

Woke as a Radical Religious Worldview

The term *wokeness* was added to the *Merriam-Webster Dictionary* in 2017. It is defined as, "aware and actively attentive to important facts and issues—especially issues of racial and social justice." *The Oxford Dictionary* adopted the term in its publication the same year defining it as "alert to racial or social discrimination and injustice."

Culture of wokeness means staying consciously aware, and actively pointing to racism and white supremacy where it is assumed to exist. Wokeness is a mindset that is evidenced by a consciousness that things in American society are fundamentally unjust. It also implies that activism is necessary to fix things and this is considered as *radical antiracism*.

The completely woke activist is referred to as an antiracist—one who actually seeks out perceptions and assumptions of racism to cancel them. An active antiracist is a follower of teachings such as those of Ibram X. Kendi, a person who claims to be certain of the motivations of whites and their actions. This pertains to all white people around the world, and not just those living in the United States. As an example of the thinking of antiracists, Kendi assumes that the only reasons white people adopt black children, or children of color, is because they are natural colonizers. According to Kendi, whites simply want to "virtue signal" how wonderful they are by glorifying their personal virtuous actions. Meanwhile, the adopted black children are denigrated and devalued in comparison to what their adoption does for the white adoptive parents.

One of the problems with antiracism is the assumption that racism exists in all systems; it assumes the worst about human nature and actions. It is pessimism colored by melanin. Antiracism is pure inescapable determinism. So, anytime people of color excel, the worldview according to the ideology of antiracist wokeness designates that the excellence achieved by blacks is actually only permitted to exist because it is of overall benefit to whites. The phrases *checking one's whiteness* and *checking one's privilege* are the requirement that one sees their actions through the lens offered by antiracists. Although affecting many people of color, this ideology is actually a slight upon those whose skills and abilities enabled them to be accomplished in America.

If one holds to a woke worldview, it is because the lens of American history is clouded with assumed injustices and that the *system is* rigged against people of color. Either a person or group is oppressed by historical oppression, or is presumed guilty of implicit bias and is guilty of said oppression.

The woke worldview colors everything with shades of melanin and racism. The following exists unshakably in the minds of those claiming to be woke. Commentator Van Jones writes, "even the most liberal, well-intentioned white person has a virus in his or her brain that can be activated at an instant."[76] Students around the nation are indoctrinated about race by means of racist ideology. This ongoing indoctrination continues to divide the nation by skin color.

Analysis of a Woke Worldview

What are some characteristics of a woke ideological worldview? Woke ideology is based on a binary worldview that includes a belief system, with divisions primarily focused on social justice, race, and gender. Woke ideology claims racism has been a part of America from the beginning and still infiltrates every system and institution herein. This is where the radical modern critical race theory (CRT) comes into play.

An increasing number of scholars in all disciplines, and of all skin colors, are making the claim that the ideology behind wokeness resembles a cult-like false religion, and that CRT lays out some of the doctrines of this religion. The ideology springs from the worldview that negates grace. The general philosophy of CRT negates grace while doubling down its own virtues instead—which are (1) based on inversion of the Golden Rule, and (2) accentuate long-term grudge-bearing and un-forgiveness, over the past. As such, the ideology plays on negative emotions.

Theological and secular views of human nature extend into the classrooms across America. That being said, one tenet of woke ideology means that *original sin*, or racism, is endemic and thereby renders historical figures as irredeemable. In other words, racism has been and always will be a stain on the United States.

Drilling down on the core of this quasi-religion reveals that any person born as white is automatically classified as a member of the oppressor class.[77] For insight into the mind of an antiracist, one needs to look no further than Kendi. In the words of Kendi, "The only remedy to racist discrimination is antiracist discrimination. The only remedy to past discrimination is present discrimination. The only remedy to present discrimination is future discrimination."[78] As a radical ideological maxim, it is obvious that antiracism is the arbiter of vengeance and payback for the past. It is a religion of racial animosity and vitriol—one where there is a void of forgiveness.

Wokeness breaks down people into groups and marginalizes them, just as Marxism does the same. It is no mere coincidence that Marxism, critical race theory, and antiracist ideology have much in common. All are truly dystopian ideas touted as answers to imagined problems. The marginalization that occurs includes the breaking down of people who believe humans are made in God's image. This breaking down process is called *deconstruction*. After deconstruction, the ideology calls for reconstruction, promising to right the past wrongs of racism in America by installing sweeping, systemic changes. However, radicals rarely offer post-destruction rebuilding plans.

There is a type of Marxist utopian ideology that remains popular in higher education and has spread to teacher training institutions. For example, it calls for breaking down the system of public education on behalf of the *oppressed* for the purpose of social justice and educational equity. The ideology calls for provisions of guaranteed outcomes, equating accomplishments and achievements realized by others by means of merit, and those with whom the government selects as winners. It should not surprise many to discover that nearly one-half of American young adults favor socialism as much as they do capitalism.[79] Marxism is a societal disincentive on many levels.

In my recent book, *From Character to Color*, I state: "There has never been a utopian society. Furthermore, even the notion of one built by imperfect humans is a ridiculous idea, given any view of human nature. Even those who claim to be woke politically and spiritually reborn, with a renewed sense of secular-spiritual identity, are as human as everyone else. . . . *It is by grace we are saved, and not by race.* Believers in grace comprehend it is the color of shed blood that unites all believers in grace and not the color of skin. They are also aware that the color of blood runs red on any shade of melanin."[80]

Proponents of wokeness expect political activism as evidence of true belief in their ideology. According to woke antiracists, activism is the natural expression of being woke and clear evidence that they believe in the ideology. Americans should also be cautious when "a theory explodes in popularity and grips the nation's attention as CRT has . . . people should take a step back to consider its tenets, and what it asks of them."[81]

John McWhorter summarizes woke culture masterfully in the foreword to Bonnie Kerrigan Snyder's book titled *Undoctrinate*:

> The antiracist commitment strangling America's educational system, which includes colleges and universities as well, is couched in elaborate verbiage. Too, in involving whites actually voluntarily giving up their power, it is an unprecedented development in human social history. This is part of why its participants are so narcotically devoted to the paradigm.
>
> They feel anointed, like people blazing a path towards, well, redemption. They are parishioners amidst a religion. Unfortunately, it is a religion committed to logic, dehumanization, and destruction, sacrificing all civic sense, as well as genuine concern with black and brown people's fate, to focus on virtue signaling. Dedication to being nonracist leads them to construct a movement, modus operandi and policing system that thrives by leaving people cowering to be called racist, forced into accepting actions, opinions, and programs they never would under other circumstances, such as excusing brown students from having to do real work or behave themselves. This is a collapse of post-Enlightenment thought, forced by people many of whom will quite openly condemn the Enlightenment as—what else?—too white. . . . The white professional antiracists have challenged themselves to give up their power as whites. The rest of us—who at this point are a cowering majority—must stand up and challenge ourselves. The modern antiracists hold us in their grip solely via their ever-looming threat to call us racists in the public square.[82]

CHRISTIANITY: QUEERED AND RADICALIZED

The LGBTQ+ movement has garnered much attention in the United States. It has moved from a sociocultural movement into the realm of theology and religion, seeking to supplant traditional Christianity with a new religion.[83] Religion is a main target for the LGBTQ+ activists. To be sure, their activism is a variation of wokeness that has serious spiritual implications for its advocates. What follows is the belief system of the radical queer ideology that is impacting not only people of faith but has also migrated to America's public schools.

Woke LGBTQ+ churches have adopted innovative but politically correct biblical narratives like the following:

Although the story of Sodom and Gomorrah has been interpreted as evidence of God's punishment of LGBT people, queer biblical scholars have argued that the story is actually a condemnation of the sin of "inhospitality" toward strangers, which had life or death consequences in the harsh desert environment of the biblical world. . . . Nancy Wilson and Kathy Rudy have "queered" the Sodom narrative by placing hospitality at the center of queer theological reflection. For example, Wilson has constructed a "queer theology of sexuality" by focusing on the gift of "promiscuous" or "bodily hospitality" that many LGBT people have. Rudy, an open lesbian ethicist at Duke University, has suggested that non-monogamous sex acts—including anonymous and communal sex—can be viewed in terms of a progressive ethic of hospitality.[84]

Wilson argues that LGBT people can be found in a number of biblical narratives—including David and Jonathan, Ruth and Naomi, the Roman Centurion, the Ethiopian Eunuch, and Mary, Martha, and Lazarus—which she refers to as "our gay and lesbian tribal texts."[85]

Patrick Cheng adds, "From the perspective of queer theology . . . the doctrine of revelation is more than just a matter of scripture or reason. It is also a matter of experience. Specifically, the doctrine of revelation can be understood as *God's coming out as radical love*. In other words, the doctrine of revelation parallels the self-disclosure that occurs when an LGBT person comes out to someone she or he loves about her or his sexuality and/or gender identity. God reveals Godself to us because God loves us and wants to share Godself with us. . . . Ultimately, God's coming out is an act of radical love because, like the coming out experience for LGBT people, it results in the dissolving of existing boundaries."[86]

Olive Hinnant agrees with Cheng: "In the same way that Jesus is the embodied revelation of the ineffable God, coming out allows the LGBT minister to become an embodied revelation of the abstract notion of homo-sexuality, or queerness. In this way, the boundaries between LGBT people and the church are dissolved."[87] Readers should take note of the repeated idea of *dissolving of boundaries*, which is a term used by radicals to deconstruct and remove obstacles to their radical ideas. Cheng's theological radicalism borders on blasphemy, with, "As Christians, we are the body of Christ, and, as such, we are all brought into the Trinity itself and become part of the divine dance of radical love."[88] LGBT members who claim radical queer theology are clearly delusional in thinking they can become as God.

Radical LGBTQ+ sex and gender ideologies are making the rounds in American schools. It is also showing up in Christian schools and colleges. The ability to change one's identity by choice essentially brings a person a new reality within their emotional being. The claim to be able to do so has an aura of self-divinity attached to it. The ideologies that involve radical queering have brought American culture from secular to sensual and then to sexual. All of these impact children in schools in the United States. We also need to add churches into the equation. The same students and their families may be radicalized at schools and also at their churches.

Why Christianity Is Considered Radical

Gavril Andreicut writes the following piece in a 2018 *Baptist News* publication titled, "In the US, Are Christians Really Different from Secular Culture?" He writes, "There is a line that separates Christianity from the secular world, because there is an absolute antithesis between Christianity's values and those of the secular world. According to the Bible, the objectives and standards of the world are not God's objectives and standards, and if the Bible is a Christian's main source and authority, we should take its words seriously. . . . Christianity must change the secular culture according to its principles."[89]

Andreicut provides exactly why Christianity is considered radical. Cultural shifting from the values upon which the United States was founded have caused a steady erosion of what it means to be American. This is obvious in the anti-American protests on American college campuses. From this nature grows radicals who are antiracist, anti-White, anti-science, anti-marriage, anti-life, anti-family, anti-Christian, and so on. Christianity, and the biblical principles that are found in it, as Andreicut argues, must change the secular culture. This statement alone is considered radical to the current culture that celebrates secularism, sensuality, sexuality, and gender expression. Andreicut is clearly on the right. He continues, "People changed by God cannot be changed by the secular culture; indeed, they must change it. If they do not, they certainly are not animated by God's will and Spirit. . . . 'Do not be conformed to this world, but be transformed by the renewing of your minds, so that you may discern what is the will of God—what is good and acceptable and perfect' (Romans 12:2)."[90] Hence the battle for the soul of a nation for the right and the left continues with no clear ending point in sight.

Del Tackett, creator of series *The Truth Project*, shares the importance of worldviews: "It is hard to imagine anything more important for the Christian, especially in the times in which we live, than to stand firmly upon a solid biblical worldview foundation . . . one that provides a comprehensive and systematic understanding of every area of life and reality. Whether conscious or subconscious, every person has some type of worldview. A personal worldview is a combination of all you believe to be true, and what you believe becomes the driving force behind every emotion, decision and action. Therefore it affects your response to every area of life . . . everything."[91]

The contrast of worldviews could not be clearer. The secular, humanistic worldview is all about serving self and one's personal goals and improvement.

The biblical-Christian worldview is about serving God and loving and serving others. In contrast, both are considered as radical worldviews and ideologically and theologically very different. People find it difficult to fully love themselves and fully love others at the same time. The question remains, what actions prove themselves to be more radical. Certainly, it would be a mistake to place all people who disagree on the margins, as radicals, in the strictest sense. Holding to radical ideologies demonstrates differences.

FIGHTING RADICALIZATION WITH RADICAL TRUTH

Radical ideologies continue to challenge America's heritage and history. The way to fight radicalism is by truth—truth that is recognized by all races and social conditions. Wisdom is found in the book that is the all-time best seller, and contains the principles of truth upon which America was built. This biblical truth is meant for the Christian but is worth applying, in contrast to the ideologies that are based in something other than truth.

First, Americans should be warned about not being taken captive by ideologies and views that are counter to truth. Each idea should be tested. For the Christian, truth resides in the person claiming to be the truth (John 14:6). Colossians 2:8 states, "See to it that there is no one who takes you captive through philosophy and empty deception in accordance with human tradition, in accordance with the elementary principles of the world, rather than in accordance with Christ" (New American Standard Bible, NASB).

Second, people are warned about deception by those claiming to be the answers to all of our problems. Whom it is we follow has implications on beliefs and behaviors. Jesus Christ warned, in Matthew 24:3–5, "Watch out that no one deceives you. For many will come in My name, saying, 'I am the Messiah,' and they will deceive many" (NASB). For the Christian, voices that repeat the idea that societies can build their own utopias, and that Americans should follow their cultural prophecies on race, sex, and gender, are preaching errant views.

Students who come from Christian families and attend public schools are taught they are the center of the education universe and they can be anything they want to be. This now includes branding an identity of a new gender. Such ideas are not only radical but they are also deceptive and lead to all sorts of confusion. God is not the author of confusion (1 Corinthians 14:33).

Woke teachers who advocate for interpreting the world and its problems according to woke ideology settle on sociology over science. Influencing children to do the same is to place opinions and emotions above facts. Once again, such an approach is not education; it is indoctrination. A similar warning is issued to woke churches. There should be worry about woke pastors and woke Bible teachers. They interpret Scripture through a non-biblical lens. When one wades into culture to search for truth, the doctrinal waters become murky at best.

Third, people are warned not be drunk on what may be described as new ideas, revolutionary truths, and the like. Sobriety, in the main, means avoiding fads and not buying into deceptive teachings and dangerous practices. 1 Peter 5:8 puts it this way for the Christian: "Be of sober *spirit*, be on the alert. Your adversary, the devil, prowls around like a roaring lion, seeking someone to devour" (NASB; emphasis mine). As Saul Alinsky warned his readers in *Rules for Radicals*, Lucifer was the biggest radical of all.[92]

Fourth, we are warned to guard our hearts and minds. Thoughts and ideas need to be taken captive and compared to truth. (2 Corinthians 10:4–5, Proverbs 4:23). In America's schools, less students are allowed to think on their own or to think critically. Students are primarily taught what to think and not necessarily how to think. Critical thinking is vital for the mind to be on guard. It is the same with the heart, or the center of emotions and feelings.

There is an old saying that a person can claim to be of the utmost in sincerity about a belief or idea. However, in this claim of sincerity, this person can also be sincerely wrong. If a person is not allowed to criticize and dissect other peoples' ideas, how then will he or she be able to determine error from truth? Without being wrong, how can there be correction applied? Truth and open discussions must be allowed to flourish in public schools.

Last, a Christian is warned "not to be conformed to this world, but be transformed by the renewing of your mind, so that you may prove what the will of God is, that which is good and acceptable and perfect" (Romans 12:1–5; NASB). The purpose of secular education may not entail the biblical renewing of a person's mind. In public education, it is indoctrination that seeks to capture minds and hearts. Nevertheless, renewing one's mind comes through a process and focusing on *truth*, which happens to be an inconveniently messy word when considering indoctrination and radicalism.

In closing, expediency wins in public education and with it comes politics and radical ideologies. Is there any wonder why American students' international assessment test scores are poor? Maybe it is time to drive out woke radicalism from schools and radicalize our approach to learning, assessments, and building of character in students. Not all radicalism is bad. Not all indoctrination is bad. But parents and concerned educators must be on guard and speak up when appropriate. A *radical shift* in education policy at the state and federal levels can begin when people vote in officials that understand the concerns and the principles addressed in this chapter.

NOTES

1. Bonnie Kerrigan Snyder. *Undoctrinate: How politicized classrooms harm kids and ruin our schools—and what we can do about it.* 2021. Nashville, TN: Post Hill Press, p. 216.

2. Saul Alinsky. *Rules for radicals.* 1971. New York: Random House, pp. 126–127.

3. Staff. "Recent cases on violence against reproductive health care providers." United States Department of Justice. 2022. Retrieved October 31, 2022, from https://www.justice.gov/crt/recent-cases-violence-against-reproductive-health-care -providers.

4. Staff. "23 pro-life organizations vandalized, firebombed by pro-abortion activists in recent weeks." Right to Life of Greater Cincinnati. 2020. Retrieved October 31, 2022, from https://cincinnatirighttolife.org/media/23-pro-life-organizations -vandalized-firebombed-pro-abortion-activists-recent-weeks.

5. Carolyn Downey. "Pro-abortion group publicizes conservative supreme court justices' home addresses ahead of planned protests." *National Review.* May 5, 2022. Retrieved October 31, 2022, from https://www.nationalreview.com/news/ pro-abortion-group-publicizes-conservative-supreme-court-justices-home-addresses -ahead-of-planned-protests/. Cf. Bart Jansen. "Republicans hit democrats over Roe protests at justices' homes, calling them mob rule." *USA Today.* May 12, 2022. Retrieved October 31, 2022, from https://www.usatoday.com/story/news/politics /2022/05/11/protests-supreme-court-justices-homes/9714925002/?gnt-cfr=1.

6. Eric McQueen. "Examining extremism: The oath keepers." Center for Strategic & International Studies (blog). June 17, 2021. Retrieved October 2, 2022, from https: //www.csis.org/blogs/examining-extremism/examining-extremism-oath-keepers.

7. Brian Michael Jenkins. "The origins of America's jihadists." RAND Corporation. December 5, 2017. Retrieved June 3, 2022, from https://www.rand.org/pubs/ perspectives/PE251.html.

8. Cornelius Van Til. *Essays on Christian education.* 1974. Nutley, NJ: Presbyterian and Reformed Publishing Co., p. 26.

9. Rousas John Rushdoony. "Appendix E: The impossibility of neutrality," in Colin Gunn and Joaquin Fernandez (eds.). *Indoctrination: Public schools and the decline of Christianity.* 2012. Green Forest, AR: Master Books, p. 366.

10. Ibid.

11. Samuel Blumenfeld and Alex Newman. *Crimes of the educators: How utopians are using government schools to destroy America's children.* 2021. Nashville, TN: Post Hill Press, p. 230.

12. Ibid., p. 227.

13. Ibid., p. 208.

14. Ibid., p. 366.

15. Snyder. *Undoctrinate,* p. 147.

16. Ibid., p. 85.

17. "Radical." *Merriam-Webster's Unabridged Dictionary.* 2022. Retrieved September 24, 2022, from https://www.merriam-webster.com/dictionary/radical.

18. Elga Sikkens, Marion van San, Stijn Sieckelinck, et al. "Parents' perspectives on radicalization: A qualitative study." *Journal of Child and Family Studies* 27: pp. 2276–2284. 2018.

19. Edward Graham. "Who is behind the attacks on educators and public schools?" *NEA Today*. December 14, 2021. Retrieved October 5, 2022, from https://www.nea.org/advocating-for-change/new-from-nea/who-behind-attacks-educators-and-public-schools.

20. Will Flanders and Dylan Palmer. "From the top: The impact of college-level indoctrination on K–12 education." Wisconsin Institute for Law and Liberty. July 2022. Retrieved July 30, 2022, from https://will-law.org/wp-content/uploads/2022/07/FromTheTop2.pdf.

21. Staff. "Following the money in politics: Summary." *Open Secrets*. 2021–2022. Retrieved October 6, 2022, from https://www.opensecrets.org/industries/indus.php?ind=I1300.

22. Charli Brown. "For teachers' unions, back to school means a return to leftist indoctrination." Freedom Foundation. August 15, 2022. Retrieved August 20, 2022, from https://www.freedomfoundation.com/education/for-teachers-unions-back-to-school-means-a-return-to-leftist-indoctrination/.

23. Snyder. *Undoctrinate*, p. 107.

24. Staff. "Gender surgeons in the United States." TranHealthCare. 2022. Retrieved October 15, 2022, from https://www.transhealthcare.org/usa/.

25. Simona Trip, Carmen Hortensia Bora, Mihai Marian, Angelica Halmajan, and Marius Ioan Drugas. "Psychological mechanisms involved in radicalization and extremism: A rational emotion behavioral conceptualization." *Frontiers in Psychology* 10(437): pp. 1–8. March 6, 2019. Retrieved September 15, 2022, from https://www.frontiersin.org/articles/10.3389/fpsyg.2019.00437/full.

26. Ibid.

27. Rainer Zitelman. "Socialism: The failed idea that never dies." *Forbes*. March 16, 2020. Retrieved October 27, 2022, from https://www.forbes.com/sites/rainerzitelmann/2020/03/16/socialism-the-failed-idea-that-never-dies/?sh=1022039523cc.

28. John Patrick Leary. "Activism isn't a coherent ideology." *New Republic*. November 26, 2021. Retrieved June 3, 2022, from https://newrepublic.com/article/164412/activism-isnt-coherent-ideology.

29. Mike Gonzalez. "To destroy America." The Heritage Foundation. September 3, 2020. Retrieved November 27, 2022, from https://www.heritage.org/civil-society/commentary/destroy-america.

30. Snyder. *Undoctrinate*, pp. 106–107.

31. Ibid.

32. Ibid., p. 107.

33. David A. Noebel. *Understanding the times: The religious worldviews of our day and the search for truth*. 1994. Eugene, OR: Harvest House Publishers. Cf. Francis Schaeffer, *How should we then live? The rise and decline of Western thought and culture*. 1983. Wheaton, IL: Crossway Books.

34. Noebel, *Understanding the times*.

35. Lance Izumi, Cassidy Syftestad, and Christie Syftestad. *The corrupt classroom: Bias, indoctrination, violence, and social engineering show why America needs school choice.* 2017. San Francisco, CA: Pacific Research Institute, p. 106.

36. Ibid.

37. Giorgio Grande. "Gen Z is radical, you should be too." *Ethical Magazine.* January 27, 2021. Retrieved October 12, 2022, from https://ethicalmag.com/brand/radical-gen-z-is/.

38. Clark McCauley and Sophia Moskalenko. "Mechanisms of political radicalization: Pathways toward terrorism." *Terror and Political Violence* 20(3): pp. 415–433. 2008. Retrieved September 12, 2022, from https://www.tandfonline.com/doi/full/10.1080/09546550802073367.

39. Ibid.

40. Ibid.

41. Scott Atran. "How people become radicalized." *Scientific American.* January 28, 2019. Retrieved September 8, 2022, from https://blogs.scientificamerican.com/observations/how-people-become-radicalized/.

42. Ibid.

43. Ibid.

44. Ibid.

45. Ibid.

46. Ibid.

47. Anne Muxel. "Political radicalism among the younger generations." *Youth and Globalization.* 2(2): pp. 123–136. December 31, 2020. Retrieved October 9, 2022, from https://doi.org/10.1163/25895745-02020001.

48. Atran. "How people become radicalized."

49. Ibid.

50. Ibid.

51. Ibid.

52. Ibid.

53. Staff. "Child abuse: Radicalism and extremism." Devon Children and Families Partnership. 2022. Retrieved September 4, 2022, from https://www.dcfp.org.uk/.

54. Ibid.

55. Ibid.

56. Ibid.

57. Ibid.

58. Ibid.

59. Ibid.

60. Trip, Bora, Marian et al. "Psychological mechanisms involved in radicalization and extremism."

61. P. Neuman. "Prisons and terrorism radicalization in 15 countries." A policy report published by the International Center for the study of radicalization and political violence (ISCR). 2010. Retrieved September 13, 2022, from https://www.clingendael.org/sites/default/files/pdfs/Prisons-and-terrorism-15-countries.pdf.

62. Trip, Bora, Marian et al. "Psychological mechanisms involved in radicalization and extremism."

63. Hannah Grossman. "A California high school teacher boasts queer library included a book which said kink/BDSM was sexual liberation." Fox News. September 8, 2022. Retrieved September 9, 2022, from https://www.foxnews.com/media/california-high-school-teacher-boasts-queer-library-with-material-on-orgies-bdsm-kink.

64. Ibid.

65. Ibid.

66. Ibid.

67. Nathan Bomey and Jessica Guynn. "How QAnon and other dark forces are radicalizing Americans as the COVID-19 pandemic rages and election looms." *USA Today*. August 31, 2020. Retrieved October 5, 2022, from https://www.usatoday.com/in-depth/tech/2020/08/31/qanon-conspiracy-theories-trump-election-covid-19-pandemic-extremist-groups/5662374002/.

68. Doug Bandow. "Christianity is the world's most persecuted religion, confirms new report." CATO Institute. March 7, 2022. Retrieved October 7, 2022, from https://www.cato.org/commentary/christianity-worlds-most-persecuted-religion-confirms-new-report.

69. William Wolfe. "Yes, Christians are being persecuted in America. Here's how we can respond." *The Christian Post*. July 18, 2022. Retrieved October 12, 2022, from https://www.christianpost.com/voices/yes-christians-are-being-persecuted-in-america.html. CF. Lindsey Grewe. "Focus on the Family headquarters sign vandalized in wake of Club Q shooting." KKTV. November 25, 2022. Retrieved November 26, 2022, from https://www.kktv.com/2022/11/25/focus-family-headquarters-sign-vandalized-wake-club-q-shooting/.

70. David Artavia. "J. K. Rowling says she faces threats of hundreds of trans activists amid controversy." *Yahoo Entertainment News*. July 20, 2021. Retrieved November 26, 2022, from https://www.yahoo.com/entertainment/jk-rowling-says-threats-trans-activists-203717514.html.

71. Staff. "President Joe Biden has turned a blind eye to the killing of Christians in Nigeria." Stop Killing Christians. Revelation Media. 2022. Retrieved October 23, 2022, from https://stopkillingchristians.com/?utm_source=BABSKC1.

72. David Curry. "Are American Christians on the path to severe persecution for their faith?" Religion News Service. September 19, 2022. Retrieved September 24, 2022, from https://religionnews.com/2022/09/19/are-american-christians-on-the-path-to-severe-persecution-for-their-faith/.

73. Samantha Allen. "Martin Duberman: Why LGBT activism needs to return to its radical roots." *The Daily Beast*. June 30, 2018. Retrieved November 26, 2022, from https://www.thedailybeast.com/martin-duberman-why-lgbt-activism-needs-to-return-to-its-radical-roots?ref=scroll.

74. Yael Halon. "Face the nation focus groups of GOP, Democrat parents sound off on woke culture overtaking US education." Fox News. October 23, 2022. Retrieved October 24, 2022, from https://www.foxnews.com/media/face-the-nation-focus-groups-parents-sound-off-woke-culture-overtaking-us-education.

75. Stella Rouse and Shibley Telhami. "Most Republicans support declaring the United States a Christian nation." *Politico*. September 21, 2022. Retrieved

September 25, 2022, from https://www.politico.com/news/magazine/2022/09/21/most-republicans-support-declaring-the-united-states-a-christian-nation-00057736.

76. Larry Emmons. "Watch: CNN analyst says all white people have virus of racism." *PM*. May 30, 2020. Retrieved September 5, 2022, from https://thepostmillennial.com/watch-cnn-analyst-says-all-white-people-have-virus-of-racism. Cf. Joe Concha. "Van Jones: A white, liberal, Hillary Clinton supporter cam pose a greater threat to Black Americans than the KKK." *The Hill*. May 29, 2020. Retrieved September 7, 2022, from https://thehill.com/homenews/media/500158-van-jones-a-white-liberal-hillary-clinton-supporter-can-pose-a-greater-threat/.

77. Peter W. Wood. *1620: A critical response to the 1619 project*. 2020. New York: Encounter Books.

78. Ibram X. Kendi. *How to be an antiracist*. New York: One World Books, p. 19.

79. Lydia Saad. "Socialism as popular as capitalism among young adults." *Gallup*. November 25, 2019. Retrieved October 10, 2022, from https://news.gallup.com/poll/268766/socialism-popular-capitalism-among-young-adults.aspx.

80. Ernest J. Zarra, III. *From character to color: The impact of critical race theory on American education*. 2022. Lanham, MD: Rowman & Littlefield Publishers, p. 61.

81. Ibid., p. 62.

82. John McWhorter. Foreword in Bonnie Kerrigan Snyder. *Undoctrinate: How politicized classrooms harm kids and ruin our schools—and what we can do about it*. 2021. Nashville, TN: Post Hill Press, pp. xiii–xiv.

83. Ernest J. Zarra, III. "Straight talk about radical love." *National Association of Scholars*. October 7, 2022. Retrieved October 8, 2022, from https://www.mindingthecampus.org/2022/10/07/straight-talk-about-radical-love/.

84. Patrick S. Cheng. *Radical love: An introduction to queer theology*. 2011. New York: Seabury Books, pp. 12–13.

85. Nancy Wilson. *Our tribe: Queer folks, God, Jesus, and the Bible*. 1995. San Francisco, CA: Harper San Francisco, pp. 231–280.

86. Cheng. *Radical love*, p. 45.

87. Olive Elaine Hinnant. *God comes out: A queer homiletic*. 2007. Cleveland, OH: Pilgrim Press, p. 168. Cf. Cheng. *Radical love*, p. 47.

88. Cheng. *Radical love*, p. 61.

89. Gavril Andreicut. *Baptist News* publication titled, "In the US, are Christians really different from secular culture?" *Baptist News*. 2018.

90. Ibid.

91. Focus on the Family. The Truth Project—Teaser trailer TruthProject. Posted on January 21, 2007. YouTube video. Retrieved October 19, 2022, from https://youtu.be/-nUXTLy_M-w.

92. Alinsky. *Rules for radicals*.

Chapter 3

Radicals and Their Radicalism

Tendentious, activist teaching isn't merely a political or pedagogical problem. It is also developmentally damaging. . . . Many students today . . . experience rejection in the classroom and are therefore learning to be guarded and inauthentic in their classroom interactions.

— Bonnie Kerrigan Snyder, *Undoctrinate*[1]

Radicalism begins as a seed in the indoctrination foreplay of the mind. It comes to life in minds when the seeds of curiosity and interest are embedded in the senses. The short journey from the eyes and ears to the heart enjoins the emotions and the process of indoctrination takes hold. The potential for all sorts of radical actions is now conceived. What is key is that no person has ever acted as a radical without first being radicalized.

It is not uncommon for the outspoken to monopolize the conversational environment in school classrooms. Teachers must never assume that quieter students have less to say. Boisterous classroom environments that encourage messages align only with an instructor's bias, or a few strong-willed students' ideas—while shutting downs opposing ideas—are actually indoctrination-friendly centers. The reality is that radicals nudge others from conversations by making the environment for dissent an unfriendly one. By so doing, this detracts from classroom unity and assures that opposing viewpoints are not welcome in the echo chamber of permitted ideologies. This is controlled by the teacher.

There is an aphorism that states *a radical is a radical to another radical.* Semantically, an anti-radical can be presumed to be a radical in his or her own right. However, radicals generally stand in contrast to the status quo, and seek to weaken or even abolish the system which is called into question. More often than not, leftists call for the eradication of some form of democratic government or capitalist rule. Generally, the greater the call to dismantle and destroy what exists, the greater the radicalism.

Leftist radicals claim to be better educated, elitists, more in touch with progressive politics and believe themselves to be in better positions to lead the rest of Americans.[2] The radicalization of students is prominent at colleges and universities and now includes K–12 schools in America. Radical leftists are especially characterized by their efforts at silencing dissent.[3]

R. C. Murray alludes to the leftist notion of intellectual superiority by stating, "Because stupid people are easily led (or misled), it's important for those who would rule over us to deconstruct the language and math skills of as many people as possible. Education involves academic as well as moral and spiritual training."[4] Radicalism in American society is nothing new. It still remains dangerous.

HISTORICAL SNAPSHOT OF
RADICALISM IN AMERICA

The term *radical*

is popularly used to designate individuals, parties, and movements that wish to alter drastically any existing practice, institution, or social system. In politics, radicals are often seen as individuals and/or parties reflecting "leftist" views. Etymologically, this meaning originated during the French Revolution (1787–1789), where those most opposed to the king sat in the National Assembly at the far left, and those most committed to the king at the far right. It is therefore common to designate points on the political spectrum, reading from left to right, as radical, liberal, conservative, and reactionary.[5]

Political radicalism became prominent in the nineteenth century in America, as Republicans were given that moniker, after they emerged as a new political party to challenge to political order at the time.[6] In fact, after Republicans won the presidency in 1860 and 1864, the radicals among the party were at the forefront in the impeachment trial of Andrew Johnson, who was vice president to Abraham Lincoln at the time of Lincoln's assassination—and who also was targeted for assassination, which failed to materialize when the conspirator George Atzerodt lost his nerve.[7]

Moving forward in history, there is an interesting yet peculiar theory that has a clear foundation rooted in classical Marxism. Its origin dates back to early twentieth-century Germany.[8] This theory has evolved over time in the United States, impacting academe over the past few decades. The theory changed its look as it added cultural issues to the original theoretical tenets.

Since the 1960s and 1970s, the United States has seen a steady rise in cultural and racial neo-Marxism. The most recent appearance in the United

States is largely at the higher education levels and is referred to simply as critical theory. As critical theory adopted race into its fold, critical race theory was born. This later triggered the statement from the American Bar Association, claiming, "CRT is not a diversity and inclusion 'training' but a practice of interrogating the role of race and racism in society that emerged in the legal academy and spread to other fields of scholarship."[9]

The man credited by some for the rise of cultural Marxism, and responsible for some of its clash with capitalism, is the "Italian communist, Antonio Gramsci. . . . Gramsci proposed that capitalism could be overthrown gradually, by infiltrating and transforming society's major institutions—e.g., education establishments, media, law, religion, and the family."[10] Cultural Marxism, and the public's exposure to critical race theory (CRT), has grown exponentially in the United States within the last few decades. CRT is now a front-and-center theory that needs to be taken seriously, analyzed, and open to dismissal—as with all radical ideologies.

Contrasting History with the Present

At the end of the twentieth century, the mention of any one of several events, or persons, would have brought about many negative reactions and personal recollections. These events were the causes of many active protests on the streets and in the halls of Congress. Some of these historical events included: (1) women's suffrage, (2) Prohibition, (3) the Bolshevik Revolution, (4) World War I, (5) the Great Depression, (6) the rise of socialism, communism, and fascism, (7) oil robber barons, (8) Prohibition, (9) monopolies and anti-trusts, (10) tycoons, (11) World War II, (12) Nazis, Stalinists, and Maoists, (13) McCarthyism, (14) the Korean War, (15) the Vietnam War, (16) affirmative action, and (17) abortion.

There have always been radicals who protested politically under the protection of the First Amendment. Education has had its radicals also, along with politics and religion. Sometimes an ideology encompasses all three. However, given the events of the recent past, it seems that violence, destruction, and even killing have become a pastime for modern radicals. Radicalism has become more flagrant[11] and seemingly more violent. Such tactics are not protected under the First Amendment. But this matters little when a government tends to overlook the actions taken by the radicals it favors. A culture that accepts the practice of these tactics is not a healthy culture, and there is great concern over radicalization in America, especially given the entrance of the blend of politics and religion into the picture.

Politics and religion provide significant impacts on what children see and learn about American values and the nation's history. Children see that radical changes can be made by radical actions. The reality is that what many learn and are encouraged to practice (praxis), some will follow through in fulfilment of radical activist expectations. This is one of the outcomes to guard against when concerned about student indoctrination. Teenagers were found to be part of the 2020–2021 riots of Portland, Oregon, involving Antifa.[12] In terms of religion, another outcome may result in the proclamation of war in the name of God. Fundamentalist Islamic jihadists still make this claim against the United States with the chant, "Death to America."

So many of the atrocities committed by radicals and revolutionaries of the past go either unnoticed in the annals of history, or suffer from the fate of historical revisionism. Radicals on the left create a narrative to preserve the message that radicalism and acts of violence in the name of a higher cause are not bad things. This is the case even if the expression of the radicalism is murderous, such as was experienced by the terrorist attacks on September 11, 2001. Another example pertains to young Chinese, in their understanding of just how ruthless Mao was when he tortured and killed millions of Chinese, as starvation and execution became methods to exact compliance to the Cultural Revolution in China.

Conflicts as those that arose during the Cold War, Vietnam, and the War on Terror are often covered without the requisite details, in terms of ideologies and methods used to radicalize masses of people.[13] How can people learn from history if history is not learned? America is now on the edge of radicalization that will affect its identity as a nation internally for years to come.

CRITICAL THEORY RADICALISM

There have been many attempts to define and refine what is meant by the term critical theory. The intention is to lean into two basic meanings that have arisen within the ideology of critical theory. The *first* is a narrow meaning of the term, which pertains to the "generations of German philosophers and social theorists in the Western Marxist tradition known as the Frankfurt School."[14] According to this group of theorists, "a theory is critical to the extent it seeks human 'emancipation from slavery,' acts as a liberating influence, and works to create a world which satisfies the needs and powers of human beings."

The *second* basic meaning of critical theory is the broad view. The theorists that hold to the broad view of critical theory connect their ideas to social movements "that identify varied dimensions of the domination of human beings in modern societies."[15] As one would expect, both meanings bring implications concerning radicalism, as both address liberation and domination and may result in subsequent antiracist actions.

Identity Radicalism

The following are brief samples of the current radicalization occurring among Americans. This radicalization will eventually result in severe consequences.

- "A record 7.1 percent of US adults self-identify as lesbian, gay, bisexual, transgender or something other than heterosexual, and members of Generation Z are driving the growth."[16]
- "86.3% say they are straight or heterosexual, and 6.6% do not offer an opinion. The results are based on aggregated 2021 data, encompassing interviews with more than 12,000 US adults."[17]
- Bisexual is the most common LGBT status among Gen Z, millennials, and Gen X, while older Americans are about as likely to say they are gay or lesbian as to say they are bisexual.
- Overall, 15 percent of Gen Z adults say they are bisexual, as do 6 percent of millennials and slightly less than 2 percent of Gen X.
- "Women (6.0%) are much more likely than men (2.0%) to say they are bisexual. Men are more likely to identify as gay (2.5%) than as bisexual, while women are much more likely to identify as bisexual than as lesbian (1.9%)."[18]
- People leave churches because the church teaches something that goes against their new-found emotional identity.
- Students today are not certain about their worth and value as humans. The fact that some are willing to re-create their identities is a demonstration of discontentment. They are suffering from a loss of the historical understanding of the theological principle of *imago dei*.
- Suicide ideation and suicidal attempts are growing because of several factors. Part of the blame is on schools that celebrate students who are confused about their own identities. There is an overwhelming feeling of purposeless and a lack of acceptance, among youth. When one's purpose is tied to what one feels about oneself and then this feeling shifts, for whatever reason, the results can be devastating.
- What sex and gender groupings do not share publicly is that de-transitioning and re-transitioning of people back to their scientific-based biology is growing each year. There is an emotional mind-warping that occurs when a person comes out and declares a lifestyle change. Some psychologists attribute this to dysphoria.[19]

The radical shift of people confused about their identities did not originate in a vacuum. There had to be others who were influencing people along the way to question themselves and to celebrate an identity they felt that they could control within themselves. There is more than coincidence about young people spending hours-per-day online during the COVID-19 lockdowns and the rise of identity issues. Along with sex and gender, people today are radically questioning their identities in a number of ways. Some additional ways include radicalization by way of racial groups and partisan politics.

Race Radicalism

Prejudice, discrimination, or antagonism directed against a person or people on the basis of their membership in a particular racial or ethnic group is called *racism*. Racism is the belief that different races possess distinct characteristics, abilities, or qualities, especially so as to distinguish them as inferior or superior to one another. The existence of systematic policies or laws and practices that provide differential access to goods, services, and opportunities of society by race is defined as *institutional racism*. Some other terms to consider include *systemic racism, microaggressions, white privilege, white supremacy, white fragility*, and *intersectionality*.

Systemic racism is the belief that "systems and structures . . . have procedures or processes that disadvantage African Americans." Glenn Harris, president of Race Forward and publisher of the digital media platform *Colorlines*, defined it as "the complex interaction of culture, policy and institutions that holds in place the outcomes we see in our lives."[20] *Racial Microaggressions are* "verbal and nonverbal assaults directed toward People of Color, often carried out in subtle, automatic or unconscious forms."[21] These aggressions can be real and direct, unintentional, and in some cases imaginable and assumed.

White privilege refers to the myriad of social advantages, benefits, and courtesies that come with being a member of the dominant race,[22] which then leads to the term white supremacy. *White supremacy* is a set of beliefs and ideas purporting natural superiority of the lighter-skinned, or "white," human races over other racial groups.

When white persons become defensive, and persons of color sense an obligation to comfort the white persons, this is referred to as *white fragility*. This is also the result of living within a white-dominated environment.[23] Also, white fragility refers to feelings of discomfort that white persons experience when they witness discussions around racial inequality and injustice.[24]

The last term is the theoretical notion of *intersectionality*, which asserts that "overlapping sources of oppression compound one another, rendering racial and ethnic minorities, gays and lesbians, and economically disadvantaged groups even more marginalized and victimized by society in proportion to their accumulating victim identities."[25]

Establishment and Beliefs of Race Radicalism

Some would argue that the creation of American race radicalism was born in Europe, and there is good evidence to draw this conclusion. Several dozen legal scholars

> met at a convent outside of Madison, Wisconsin, on July 8, 1989, as Public Enemy's *Fight the Power* topped the Billboard charts. They came together to forge an antiracist intellectual approach known as *critical race theory*. Thirty-year-old UCLA legal scholar Kimberlê Williams Crenshaw organized the summer retreat the same year she penned *Demarginalizing the Intersection of Race and Sex*. The essay called for *intersectional theory*, the critical awareness of gender racism (and thereby other intersections, such as queer racism, ethnic racism, and class racism). . . . One of the greatest offshoots of the theory was critical Whiteness studies, investigating the anatomy of Whiteness, racist ideas, White privileges, and the transition of European immigrants into Whiteness. Critical race theorists, as they came to be called, joined antiracist Black Studies scholars in the forefront of revealing the progression of racism in the 1990s.[26]

All ideologies have tenets that are sometimes woven together into a larger manifesto. Often, however, radical ideologies are a bundle of disparate ideas that accumulate as an ideology grows. What follows are tenets accepted by race-based radicals. These statements can be found in classroom materials and adjusted to grade levels, at a teacher's discretion.

- Critical race radicals (CRITS) oppose Martin Luther King Jr's idea of "color-blindness."
- CRITS do not believe that universal values are possible as long as whites hold a grip on society.
- CRITS do not wish to improve upon American society but, rather, to deconstruct and transform it.
- The majority of America's values are based on whiteness and the oppression of people of color. Reiterating the words of Kendi, "The only remedy to racist discrimination is antiracist discrimination. The only remedy to past discrimination is present discrimination. The only remedy to present discrimination is future discrimination."[27]
- Racial integration was a ruse. CRITS oppose racial integration, since such a concept meant people of color were to assimilate into white culture. White values are not the values of people of color. Whites and blacks coming together through a common culture is not possible.
- CRITS push back against assimilation and call for black liberation. They actively promote the liberation from a melting pot idea and encourage the "oppressed" to assert their power toward freedom. So, marginalized

groups might fight back in order to avoid having their culture and beliefs stripped from them by assimilating.
- CRITS teach "race-consciousness," not race-blindness.
- There is no such thing as objective truth. This is a white supremacy value. Truth is subjective and changes according to culture. This is why fluidity in cultural areas of sex and gender is viewed as a new normal. It is also where a Christian must see that any deviation from the norms of God's truth, both in creation and lifestyle, is dangerous.
- CRITS assume the Western Christian understanding of God is as a white man's God.

As the reader might have already gathered, the tenets of CRT set the stage for antiracist actions that race radicals can take to ameliorate what they consider racist in American history and modern American society. The following section provides examples of race radicalism in America.

Examples of Race Radicalism in America

While critical race ideology has been around for a few decades, it really has gained prominence and social traction since the rise of the Black Lives Matter (BLM) movement. The ideology serves as radical and with intellectual underpinnings in order to grant the movement an appearance of legitimacy—as a civil rights movement—rather than merely a violent reaction to a man's killing.

The 1619 Project attempts to bring radical ideas together with historical forces to reimagine and revise the historical narrative of America. The central premise is that America was not founded in 1776, or in the early colonies, or when the Declaration of Independence was written, or when the United States Constitution was ratified. According to this new interpretation, the functional founding of America began when the first enslaved Africans arrived on the North American continent. Furthermore, supporters of the 1619 narrative claim the colonists fought the Revolutionary War primarily to protect the slave trade.[28] This radical interpretation of history, supported as a project by the *New York Times*, had mixed and dubious acceptance by history and economics scholars. That being said, the narrative about the 1619 America is being taught in many American public schools as fact, even as it runs afoul of a growing number of Blacks who think such attempts by racial identitarians are "exacerbating an identity crisis" for Blacks.[29]

In the mostly white Peninsula School District of Gig Harbor, Washington, the published 2022 *Statement on Human Dignity* on race and identity was published as follows: "Recognizing and valuing that we are a diverse community, part of our mission is to provide a positive, harmonious environment where diversity is respected and encouraged. We are engaged in work around equity, race, and identity to better foster and support an environment in which our students, families and staff grow and thrive."[30] Schools, regardless their population and demographics, felt pressure to apply woke race radicalism to their school policies.

There is a radicalization taking place in the United States military. In terms of the United States Air Force, Lynne Chandler Garcia, a professor of political science at the United States Air Force Academy, stated,

I teach critical race theories to our nation's future military leaders because it is vital that cadets understand the history of the racism that has shaped both foreign and domestic policy. Critical race theory provides an academic framework to understand these nuances and contradictions. It helps students identify the structural racism and inequality that has been endemic in American society. And it provides methods for deconstructing oppressive beliefs, policies and practices to find solutions that will lead to justice.[31]

Thomas Spoehr, director of the Center for National Defense at the Heritage Foundation, elaborates on the woke culture found within today's military. Spoehr writes: "Much of the emphasis of wokeness today is on promoting the idea that America is fatally flawed by systemic racism and white privilege. Our fighting men and women are required to sit through indoctrination programs, often with roots in the Marxist tenets of critical race theory by Pentagon diktat or through carelessness by senior leaders who delegate their command responsibilities to private diversity, equity, and inclusion instructors. These indoctrination programs differentiate service members along racial and gender lines, which runs completely counter to the military imperative to build cohesiveness based on common loyalties, training, and standards."[32]

The race radicalization movement in America has not left medicine and university hospitals out of its focus. The University of Washington School of Medicine's leadership stated that they would establish more effective and required antiracism training for members of their community and improve their support for the professional development of a diverse leadership team. UW Medicine's *Healthcare Equity Blueprint* recommends that the school "provide training to the workforce regarding implicit bias, diversity, cultural humility and respectful conversations."[33]

The plan also recommends that the school "Assess existing training options for implicit bias, diversity, inclusion, cultural humility and respective conversations available to UW Medicine workforce members. Create an action plan to provide training to existing UW Medicine workforce and to insert training into new hire onboarding."[34] The University of Washington is not alone.

Many university and private hospitals have taken the same radical route. How can they not, when funding streams are tied to politics through woke-focused legislation?

POLITICAL RADICALISM

When a person becomes a community organizer, or an organizer of like-minded individuals, "you're supposed to love everybody (at least everybody on your side). That's part of what makes the fighting of tyranny of the annoying so hard. It means dealing with disruptive people so that the rest of the folks who are ready to get to work can spend their time on productive and often fun organizing tasks."[35]

Grassroots "mass movements can move mountains if you give each person a shovel. If you give your base some effective tactics that they can rinse and repeat to make progress on a strategic plan, then your movement will be very effective. But to make a revolution, you also need to discover a rinse-and repeatable way to grow."[36]

Radicals are told to keep in mind that "there's no such thing as a single-issue revolution. The revolution is about everything. The people live in communities affected by all the issues, and all of our struggles are connected. What's more, it's going to take all of us, each motivated by the issues that directly affect us, working together to build the revolution."[37] Likewise, when it comes to engaging in politics to enhance a movement, those in charge must strive to remember, "Each movement that brings in all these new people is a chance to build to transformational change—to take a real revolution all the way."[38]

Anne Applebaum reveals the nature of modern political radicalism in her piece in *The Atlantic*. Referring to the election of 2020, and the reelection bid of Donald Trump as president, she writes:

> But anyone who is truly worried by these tendencies should fear the consequences of a second Trump administration even more. Anyone who actually cares about academic freedom, or the future of objective reporting, or the ideas behind the statues built to honor American democrats in the country's public squares, must hope that Trump loses. If he wins a second term, extremism on the left will not be stopped. It will not grow quieter. Instead, extremism will spread, mutate into new forms, and gradually become entrenched in more areas of American life. Radicalism of all kinds will spread, on the right as well as the left, because America will find itself deeply enmeshed in the same kind of death spiral that the country experienced in the 1850s.[39]

Applebaum has a point. There were rises in political opposition that were based on race. In fact, the Proud Boys, led by the Latino Enrique Tarrio, had the reputation for being a white supremacist group.[40] One of the more recent and infamous incidents occurred on January 6, 2021, when a group of rioters broke into the United States Capitol building after a rally held by then President Trump.

Some of the rioters were members of the Oath Keepers group, an ultra-right politically radical group. Members of the group were indoctrinated to believe that the presidential election of 2020 was stolen. One transgender member of the group was arrested and describes her ordeal on the day of the riot. Jessica Watkins expressed "remorse for her participation in the events of that. . . . At the time, I felt like it was this heroic American moment where *We the People* were going into our House and were going to be heard . . . I basically lost all objectivity . . . I was just another idiot running around the Capitol."[41]

Watkins attributed her actions to a "steady diet of the right-wing show InfoWars and its host, Alex Jones . . . though she described herself as gullible to the conspiracy theories spread by Jones and other right-wing media."[42] Fortunately, Watkins was able to shake free of her radical indoctrination. But some the far left Antifa members also shake their indoctrination, over time.

In entertainment, musician Winston Marshall, formerly of Mumford and Sons, was on the extreme side in support of leftist causes, but began to question what he believed. He bucked the far left and became highly criticized over his support of an anti-Antifa book written by gay journalist Andy Ngo. As Marshall explains, "My hill I ended up dying on, which I didn't think it would be, was far left extremism in the United States."[43] Radical political extremism occurs within the minds and actions of those on the right and those on the left.

For years, in teacher education institutions, prospective teachers were instructed to make certain that students were kept in the dark about teachers' politics and personal beliefs. After all, it was said that student learning was of the greatest importance, and teachers' personal lives were just that—personal!

Until recently, indoctrination was not part of teacher training. The focus was on teaching methods of content, content mastery, and classroom management. Indoctrination and radicalization of students as activists was the farthest things from the mission and mindsets of teachers. Unfortunately, winning students to an ideology today is front and center, and teacher education programs are not shy about their mission. In fact, in terms of race, as an example, one is either an antiracist or a racist. There is no in-between,

The real win for radical teachers today is the activism of students. What is lost when teachers and students have activism like-mindedness? For those in the "education profession . . . if your students know your political ideology, you're doing a bad job as their teacher. . . . Effective instruction requires fair implementation of competing views without deletions or distortions."[44] Effective instruction takes a serious hit and learning comes by way of the indoctrinator.

Effects of Political Radicalism

Institutions of higher learning are replete with examples of greater leftist tilts in academe. Reports on faculty beliefs and political party affiliation reveal much. Cornell University is not an outlier when it comes to the demographics of humanities departments. Of the ninety-nine humanities professors, across the breadth of the humanities disciplines, ninety-eight were Democrats. No one is surprised by the political affiliations of professors at American universities—especially in the undergraduate humanities departments.

The leftist tilt, politically and socially, has been occurring for some time. What is most important is that students are still exposed to only one side of many issues, which amounts to certain indoctrination. Not all universities are this extreme, but the tilt left is obvious and problematic.[45] How are students expected to develop the requisite balance necessary to enhance their critical thinking abilities?

An issue that is missed by people on both extremes is that the "excessive leftward tilt in academia likely harms liberal-leaning students as much as, if not more than, conservative-leaning ones; this makes perfect sense when you consider that only the conservative students are being exposed to disconfirmation tests and have to seek out more information in order to back up their views. Studies have, in fact, shown that conservatives understand liberals better then liberals understand conservatives."[46]

Certain events accelerate political and social advocacy. This was the case in both 2016 and 2020 election cycles. "While rising for some time, the 2016 presidential campaign seemed to supercharge bias in the classroom."[47] Randi Weingarten, head of the American Federation of Teachers, alluded to what she described as a "Trump Effect," and without clear data, Weingarten claimed Trump's rhetoric emboldened students, and the result was the creation of "a climate of bullying at schools."[48] In fact, Trump's opposition claimed Trump's rhetoric encouraged "violence and racism—not only on the campaign trail, but also in the classroom."[49] They labeled this as the "Trump Effect."

The Trump Effect

Lance Izumi writes, "The Trump Effect campaign talking points filtered down to state and local officials who then turned the talking points into biased classroom instruction. In San Francisco, the teachers union, the United Educators of San Francisco, issued an anti-Trump lesson plan that could be used by its 6,000 members."[50] This lesson plan labeled Trump as a racist and sexist man, bolstered and elected by his supportive base comprised of the same. At this same time, teachers around the nation began instructing from the materials based in biased, anti-Trump premises.[51] The Trump Effect produced a host of hateful *anti-Trump rhetoric and actions*, which smacked of Alinsky's tactics.

Political Radicalism and Political Enemies

The reality is that bullying is actually nothing new on college campuses. The radical leftists have seized control of the campus narrative. In so doing, the colleges and universities that produce teachers unleash classroom educators who are radicalized and bring their radicalism into K–12 classrooms. The bias is stark against those who support conservative values.

Conservatives are connected to Trump by progressives in an attempt to smear and exenterate by association nearly 75 million Trump voters with the label of neo-fascists. Anyone supportive of Trump is stamped a racist, bigot, and is indicted by political affiliation or ideological association. This is directly out of the playbook of Saul Alinsky, in *Rules for Radicals*.

Saul Alinsky got his start in the shadow of the mass industrial labor movement of the 1930s. While working on his PhD in sociology in the low-income Back of the Yards neighborhood of Chicago, he participated in the birth of a community organization led by priests and other neighborhood leaders. With support from the Catholic Church and major, corporate-funded foundations, Alinsky hired organizers to launch community organizations in other cities, and eventually he formed a training school for community organizers and wrote books on his philosophy of organizing, including the now classic *Rules for Radicals*.[52]

At the heart of Alinsky's methods is "one-on-one personal relationship between the organizer and the subject who was to be organized."[53] Furthermore, Alinsky exhorts, "when we organize, we strive to create the conditions that allow people to work together to win the change they want to see in the world."[54]

Rules for Radicals, which was published in 1971, encapsulates this organizing philosophy. Some of these rules are tactical and helpful to any activist, such as: "A good tactic is one your people enjoy," and "The threat is usually more terrifying than the thing itself," and "Pick the target, freeze it, personalize it, and polarize it. . . . Alinsky believed that the purpose of building power was not to put the people in power, but to compel negotiation."[55] Observe the following example.

PRESIDENT BIDEN CO-OPTS ALINSKY'S RADICALISM

Saul Alinsky's Rule 4 states, "Fighting racism must be at the core of the message to everyone. If it is not led by people of color and immigrants, if it . . . doesn't have fighting racism and xenophobia at its core, and if it is not mobilizing white people to lead other whites to choose multiracial solidarity over fear and hate—then it's not a revolution."[56]

President Joseph Biden, in a 2022 speech in Philadelphia, given at Constitution Hall,[57] used an Alinsky set of tactics to embolden Americans against conservatives and "Make America Great Again" (MAGA) supporters. The bias was clearly presented and fed progressives' angst about the possibility of anyone supportive of the MAGA movement. As America discovered with Trump, presidents have sway over the creation of narrative through the means of the bully pulpit and national audiences.

It turns out that the gist of President Biden's speech was reminiscent of Barack Obama's community organizer stratagem, which also hailed from Saul Alinsky's *Rules for Radicals*. The exception to the Obama comparison was the context from within which Biden framed his speech. Biden made radicals out of his fellow Americans of a different political party and those that hold to a different political philosophy. The opposition, as Biden saw them, were categorized as violent, semi-fascist, anti-democratic, and anti-Constitution. Specific statements where Biden utilized Alinsky's tactics are addressed in the following section.

Saul Alinsky: The Radicals' Mentor

Saul Alinsky is listed as one of the top fifty most influential progressive radicals of the twentieth century.[58] The following excerpts and interpretations explain President Biden's co-opting of Alinsky's approach in *Rules for Radicals*.

- **Alinsky Rule 1**. "Ridicule is man's most potent weapon. It is almost impossible to counterattack ridicule. Also it infuriates the opposition, who then react to your advantage."[59]
- Biden's Rhetoric: Biden ridiculed Trump supporters and dismissed the MAGA group as semi-fascists.
- **Alinsky Rule 2**. "The threat is usually more terrifying than the thing itself."[60]
- Biden's Rhetoric: Biden constructed a threat and accused the MAGA group as being harmful to democracy and said that their presence is an existential threat to changing America back to before he took office

- **Alinsky Rule 3**. "If you push a negative hard enough and deep enough it will break through to the counter-side."[61]
- Biden's Rhetoric: Emphatic statements repeated with the imperative "Look!" are intended to press the American psyche that the problem being addressed, namely revolution and disrespect for the US Constitution, are real threats to democracy.
- **Alinsky Rule 4.** "Pick the target, freeze it, personalize it, and polarize it."[62]
- Biden's Rhetoric: Biden went after the MAGA group and froze it, isolating it from the rest of democracy-loving Americans. Freezing creates isolation and brings fear of the group. Biden then marginalized the MAGA group from any other Republicans that do not support the MAGA agenda, or Trump. Biden also warned that the ultra-Maga "fringe" is akin to terrorists and capable of violence at any time. He used rhetoric from the January 6, 2021, riot at the United States Capitol to make his point.

Alinsky warns that when a radical takes the approach similar to Biden's approach, and "as you zero in and freeze your target and carry out your attack, all of the *others* come out of the woodwork very soon. They become visible by their support of the target."[63]

Political Bias

Once the MAGA supporters come out of the woodwork, in dissent or protest, the government will begin rounding them up for prosecution and a fascist label will be affixed. Social media will assist in cancelling the voices of many of the opposition's supporters. What will be the reason for the cancellation? The government will have decided who is fascist and who poses a threat to democracy.

Politics provides clear and obvious biases, due to the nature of binary partisanship. However, in K–12 American education, the political has usurped the need for true learning, conversation, dialogue, debate, and critique. Disagreement is no longer allowed on many college campuses. Biden's speech may potentially cause greater rifts between teachers, professors, and students. What is certain is that Biden's rhetoric was supported by the majority of leftists in the media and in academe.[64]

In addition to whites being called racists, these same people, if supportive of conservative values, the MAGA philosophy, or even supportive of Trump, have to deal with labels like neo-fascist, anti-democratic, and even pro-insurrectionist. Alinsky lives on in the minds, hearts, and actions of true radicals. His instruction in radicalism is quite basic. Politicians who can marginalize their opposition taint the opposition in the minds of the public. Thus, propaganda and indoctrination are keys to a politician's toolbox. These are especially relevant just prior to an election year.

The battle over who controls the classrooms and K–12 education positions in America will not end anytime soon. Conservative teachers are being pushed out, censored, or taking early retirement due to the direction of education in America. The reality is that "demographic trends indicate that this disparity will tilt much more heavily to the Left in coming years."[65] This process of "accelerating the tilt"[66] is nearing its completion, with the rash of Baby Boomer retirements.

GENDER RADICALISM

Perhaps, in today's culture, there are few topics that set off fierce firestorms of debate than those pertaining to gender. American students have been bombarded into believing that people can choose to belong to any race, have any sexual orientation, and choose to express any one of nearly seventy genders. Students have been taught, through the neglect of facts, that science means very little and sociology is of great importance. Some radicalized students would have great difficulty distinguishing between the two disciplines today. Students do not hear much to negate their radical views, unfortunately, and follow leftist professors as they would online influencers whose tasks are similar in their indoctrination.

There is no doubt that traditional and historical American identity continues to be deconstructed as gender identities expand and as more children reject their own biology. Changing a nation can be accomplished by changing its people. Schools and school districts have welcomed the radicalization of students by sex, gender, and the newly-arrived group of *queer identitarians.*

One example hails from a California school district, where it is claimed that there are "over 10 sexual orientations, and eight genders."[67] This open-ended, non-scientific set of opinions is what is being rolled out as factual, across the United States in K–12 schools and in humanities departments in higher education. The fact is that state and federal dollars are being spent to both accommodate sex and gender ideologies, as well accentuate minor students' and young adults' choices to transition from one gender to another. In some cases, these transitions begin without parents' knowledge of the choices. Parents should rise up and question why schools are promoting these practices and why tax dollars are funding them.

In Portland, Oregon, a war has been launched "against the gender binary and adopted a radical new curriculum teaching students to subvert their sexuality of white colonizers and begin exploring the infinite gender spectrum."[68]

This is one ideology that is being used to radicalize children to disregard their religious teachings, and their family's values and upbringing. Apparently, along with race, Americans have been accused of hating those who have sex with the same sex and suffer from gender confusion.

Lessons from the Portland Public Schools reveal that the school system is content with turning what is known as academic queer theory "into an identity-formation program for elementary school students."[69] Written explanations in the academic program include the challenge for students to come to terms with the fact that "gender is colonized, and that western societies have used language to erase alternative sexualities."[70]

As a result of Eurocentric gender and sexuality, that appear problematic to the leftists in Portland Public Schools, their thinking is that "Gender is something adults came up with to sort people into groups."[71] The solution, according to school officials and teachers is "to obliterate the white colonizer conception of sexuality, with its rigid male-female binary, and encourage students to inhabit the infinite gender spectrum . . . and promoting queer and trans-identities."[72]

In order to accomplish this "teachers are told to eliminate the terms *girls* and *boys*, *ladies* and *gentleman*, *mom* and *dad*, *Mrs.*, *Mr.*, *Miss*, and *boyfriend*, *girlfriend*, in favor of terms such as *people*, *folx*, *guardians*, *Mx*, and *themfriend*."[73] Sex and gender radicalization has revealed far beyond the personal choices of a group of people with differences. There are now mandates for teachers to accept and recognize all pronouns and genders of any students.

Students in the Portland Public Schools are being radicalized on behalf of the LGBTQ+ push for normalcy and credibility. If an entire generation makes a commitment to change, then the chances of changing American culture become greatly assured. Indoctrination of the masses of young minds means that, at adulthood, there are radicalized adults seeking comprehensive change in the entire American system.

Some of the commitments that are packed into the Portland gender and sex curriculum are summarized[74] in the following:

- Commitment to learning more about LGBTQ history and how the movement has changed throughout the years.
- Commitment to learning about the history of black trans women.
- Commitment to practicing pronoun correctness.
- Commitment to attending queer group meetings and LGBTQ meetings at school.
- Commitment to becoming an outspoken leader of LGBTQ issues at school.

- Commitment to becoming a political activist for queer academic theory, the practices of LGBTQ, and play a role in the sexual and gender revolution to expel colonized gender ideas from culture.

TRANSGENDER RADICALISM

Students making the claim that they are transgender suddenly began to appear in the news in the early 2000s. The point of entry was use of restroom of their choice and use of locker room they claimed best fit their chosen identities. Some referred to this as advancement and progress. Others referred to this as social engineering and a problem of gender identity confusion.

As with all leftist claims, once a door is opened, it is propped open by radicals. Claims then become marching orders toward ensuring access and the granting of special rights to marginalized groups. In less than twenty years, America has gone from mixed gender restroom use to transgendered military and non-binary political appointees of the highest levels of government. The nation has slipped into practices that celebrate a form of medical mutilation of young children's bodies by chemical and physical castrations.[75] Children are given hormone blockers to stem the onset of puberty and schools are now indoctrinating children to the ideology that *who they are* and *what they are* is subject to their own choices, and that doctors and parents can make mistakes about gendering them at birth.[76] Make no mistake about it. These are radical actions that have their genesis in radical ideology.

Colleges give priority status to the LGBTQ+. For example, biological males transgendered as women, have been allowed to compete against biological women in NCAA athletics. Athletic organizations have become radicalized and obviously recognize males as females, over actual females, in terms of athletic competitions.[77] Science is overlooked by anti-science ideology.

The book *Who are you?* specifically informs the reader, the minor child, that doctors and other adults (parents) merely guess at gender when a baby is born and that there are times when the doctors guess wrongly. The reason for this, as gender radicals state, is because genitalia exemplify sex and do not define gender.[78]

For purposes of clarity, the radical sex and gender ideologies can be understood in the following analogy. Genitalia is to the body, as gender is to the soul. The latter is why expression is so important to gender radicals. The expression may not be in alignment with the genitalia and this presents a problem of dualism that must be explained by the advocates of gender theory.[79] Some argue this is why the concept of fluidity was rolled out. Others struggle and decide to have any reminder of their sexuality removed. The idea is that without designated genitalia, a person can overcome biology with identity. The truth is that they cannot.

TEACHER AND PROFESSOR RADICALISM

Do radicals make good public school teachers? "A good teacher is a guide, not an interpreter. Their assigned role is to faithfully instruct students in the curriculum as established by the school, which is overseen by a school board, and state boards of education in a public school. Private schools have more flexibility in how they operate, but they still have a clear responsibility to communicate ethically and honestly with their customers (parents and students) in describing the mission, methods, and modes of instruction to be undertaken in the school, along with the curricular aims to be pursued."[80]

Radical Educators

Lance Izumi, of the Pacific Research Institute, "points out that the teaching profession is more liberal than the acting profession."[81] Izumi writes, "Among English teachers, there are 97 Democrats for every three Republicans, with the proportion being even more one-sided among health teachers, with 99 Democrats for every one Republican. While there are slightly more Republicans among math and science teachers, among high school teachers overall, there are 87 Democrats for every 13 Republicans."[82]

Humanities and social science professors "skew much further to the Left than the physical sciences. Over 80 percent of English professors, for example, identify on the political Left. Subjects such as history, political science, sociology, and fine arts typically approach or exceed 70 percent. In short, the humanities and social sciences have become ideological monoliths."[83]

Schools of teacher education wield tremendous influence. Not only do they train in instructional methodologies and assessments, they also spend time winning over the trainees into the political and social beliefs that permeate public education. "Imagine you want to become a teacher, but you're conservative or a libertarian. You will have to sit through hours of Far Left indoctrination that most Democrats would shun, and do it in a classroom of people hostile to your beliefs."[84] The facts are that the more liberal a teacher, in K–12, the more likely they are to be actively hostile to conservative colleagues.[85]

Izumi writes, "Perhaps no other issue will cause a parent who wants to take their child out of a school than when the child's safety is in question."[86] The issue of safety now comes with a much broader definition. Safety of soul is as important as safety of mind and body. When addressing safety in schools the element of physical safety is still in the mix. However, the emotional, psychological, spiritual, and sexual safety are now in real jeopardy in many schools across America. Whether "deliberate or accidental, these teachers do their young, impressionable charges a great disservice by treating them as mere means to be exploited in furtherance of a cause. Their unique access to minor children places them in a position to potentially harm them."[87] This is not just a K–12 public school concern.

Private schools do "have greater latitude to attempt to impose belief systems (and some of these are religious schools) but should surely only do so with good faith, full disclosure, and transparency of their belief systems and ideological aims, so that potential parents and students are not misled or deceived into making a choice to enroll there. Anything else would risk falling into false advertising or breach of implied contract territory."[88] But in some public schools, Snyder claims, "this lack of transparency is deliberate, with the intent to conceal motivations, when an activism-oriented teacher senses that not everyone in the community shares the educators' allegiances."[89]

Samuel J. Abrams, in his article titled "On Leaving Professional Organizations," expounds on what is happening to a colleague. As an example of the radicalization of higher education, Jonathan Haidt, professor at NYU's Stern School of Business, recently submitted a letter of resignation to the Society for Personality and Social Psychology (SPSP), his "primary professional society."[90] The reason for Haidt leaving the organization when his dues are up, is because "all social psychologists are now required to submit a statement explaining whether and how . . . [research] submission advances the equity, inclusion, and anti-racism goals of SPSP."[91] Radicalism has become professionalized and even tenure cannot escape its grasp.

The radicalization of college departments, according to Abrams, continues unabated. "The American Association of University Professors found that almost a quarter of universities require DEIO statements for tenure evaluations, and that nearly 40 percent of institutions are reported they are considering the idea."[92] Abrams concludes, "Those who care about the future of education and inquiry must push back when and where they can and demonstrate the peril of injecting politics into research and inquiry."[93] That's precisely why education—and higher education specifically—are now radicalized and held hostage by DEIO (diversity, equity, inclusion, and opportunity) offices for their indoctrination and output requirements.

Michael Metarko writes, "Our education system is such a part of us and of society that we no longer even think to question it. We accept it, work within its boundaries, polish it to look better, and rename it to sound better."[94] These words are a panacea to radicals and those wishing access to unobstructed points of entry to indoctrinate students.

Erwin Lutzer asserts: "Unfortunately, our schools are all too often indoctrination chambers where children come to be scrubbed of their trust in parents, their church, and their sexual identity, and are force-fed a diet of secularism and immorality. . . . Indeed, there are some public schools that are still committed to education and not to indoctrination—but it is indicative of a trend in our schools that cannot be ignored."[95] R. C. Sproul Jr. enjoins with the statement, "There are at least three major battlefields in this one great war, three theaters in which the fighting goes on. We fight over who is called to do the teaching. Is the education of children a function of the state, the church, or the family? We fight over what should be taught, the content of our curriculum."[96] These are worthy battle in which to fight.

Snyder addresses how bad teaching weakens schools and does a great disservice to parents and students. She concludes that "tendentious, agenda-driven, biased teaching yields compliancy, complacency, obedience, and listlessness. It weakens mental capacity, and its one-sidedness renders it incomplete and insufficient."[97] Bruce Shortt perceives the handwriting on the wall as he states, "there are now many in government school administration that are actively seeking to drive out teachers who haven't bought into the latest school of iteration of indoctrination."[98] If schools want good teachers, they first need to know what good teachers look like in practice. Then, once hired by the schools, the institutions need to stop driving them away by force-feeding radical ideology.

Moreover, "In addition to the loss of veteran teachers, many aspiring teachers who would be great educators never make it to the starting line today because they are repulsed by the rank pedagogical and political stupidities served up in the curricula of schools of education."[99] Those that remain in public school classrooms run the risk of having their goodness swallowed up by acceptable radical ideologies of colleagues. Shortt addresses this concern: "The bottom line is that capable, conscientious teachers and administrators are going to be increasingly isolated. . . . For the diminishing remnant . . . government schools will become lonelier places by the year."[100]

Radical Curriculum

For several years, public school districts have made the claim their teachers are not teaching critical race theory to their students. At the same time, parents and savvy teachers and stealthy students have proven them wrong. Jason Rantz illustrates that, "left-wing educators often frame material through a CRT lens, precisely the complaint from parents, politicians, and commentators. This framing allows educators to indoctrinate students by reinforcing a claim that this country was founded on white supremacy and installed systems of oppression that students must dismantle."[101]

An example of CRT in the Washington State's K–12 curriculum is in the course description of the classes in which it is taught. "The classes are intended to give students the tools to discuss left-wing views on race and use [a] progressive world view to be leaders in the community."[102] Moreover, in this curriculum are components for student activism, which happens to be one of the major outcomes expected from students while taking classes that emphasize CRT. Phrases like "transforming society," and taking "leadership roles in the community," are buzz phrases tied to the courses encouraging activism.[103]

In an essay posted by the National Education Association, one known progressive activist teacher at Bellevue High School, Lukas Michener, writes, "We try to make black students fit into a white system. More than 80 percent of teachers today are white, and that doesn't reflect the young people in our classrooms."[104] Aside from admitting that assimilating into culture is not the focus, Michener attempts to persuade the very readers that there is a problem with racial balance in America's schools.

As Rantz aptly point out, "Michener has not given up his teaching position for a person of color to replace him at Bellevue High School. Bellevue High School has an estimated 3.5% black student demographic."[105] His concern for students of color must not run beyond self-validating virtuous rhetoric. This happens to be a trait of many white woke elitists.

Parents, with whom there has been correspondence, have been quick to note their frustration that an activist teacher prioritizes antiracist activism and indoctrination. Teaching erroneous history means more than adequately preparing students for the rest of their lives as citizens. As a substitute for good teaching, Michener is about marginalizing whiteness and churning out white radicals on behalf of his sordid ideology. The facts are that "most Americans of all colors don't view the country as institutionally or systemically racist. They certainly don't want a teacher training students to be activists."[106] Yet, this is what transpires daily in many American public school classrooms.

BREEDING ACTIVISM

In order for students to become activists, several components are necessary. *First*, there must be a teacher who is himself or herself already radicalized and committed to the same in the training of students. Radicals are not educated; radicals are trained—and often in some of the best colleges and universities in the nation.

Training is the *second* element involved in radicalizing students. There must be an ideology that marginalizes groups, or specifically alienates one group from the rest. *Third*, there must be supportive curriculum adopted that serves as the foundation and basis for radicalism. *Next*, schools and activist teachers must get creative in changing terms from those laden with baggage in the community, to terms softer and more acceptable. *Last*, students must be given opportunities to demonstrate their activism, through participating in new civics programs such as the "Generation Citizen Action Civics" in middle schools in Massachusetts.[107]

At the college level, some professors offer extra credit to their students if they attend protests. This was the case in Michigan, where Jeanne Lorentzen, professor of sociology at the Northern Michigan University, offered extra credit to attend a local "Occupy the Upper Peninsula"[108] protest. Students who objected at the time were given a paper to write as a substitute that was to be twenty pages amounting to "a critical sociological analysis of a particular movement,"[109] including "substantive concepts"[110] from the class textbook.

Criticism came from Sarah Morrison, the president of the NMU Chapter of College Republicans at the time, which stated, "Overall, I feel that Dr. Lorentzen's extra credit opportunity was politically biased . . . there was no equal opportunity presented for students who hold opposing view-points."[111] Schools in Michigan, California, and Washington State are not the only ones dealing with radicalized teachers and activist-grooming curriculum. Objections like Morrison's are few and often dismissed by college administrations.

The West Bonner School District in Idaho is another example. It was here that the local school board "revoked its approval of the district's English language arts curriculum . . . after accusations that its social emotional learning (SEL) component would lead to liberal indoctrination, sexual grooming and critical race theory."[112] Bonner's indoctrination concerns largely stemmed from SEL components in the K–5 curriculum, *Wonders*, and the 6–12 curriculum, *StudySync*. Parents do have a say and need to exercise their voices of protest, when necessary.

Traditional publishers with storied histories of producing quality literature are now heavily invested in the woke radicalism that plagues our schools. Even previously reliable kids' programs such as *Sesame Street* have become radicalized. A social-emotional component "was added to *Wonders* in 2020 after McGraw Hill collaborated with the Sesame Workshop, the nonprofit organization that produces the children's television show Sesame Street. Over the past few years, Sesame Street's wokeness has pushed parents away by incorporating same sex marriage, LGBTQ+"[113] and "BLM materials into their programming,"[114] in their attempt to normalize what parents want to remain on the moral fringes of culture in the United States.

Radicalism and Teacher Shortages

States are realizing extreme shortages of teachers. The problems are at such critical levels in some states that state officials are waving the state level requirements for certification. In lieu of these requirements, states are relinquishing the responsibility of teacher training and teacher certification requirements to colleges and universities. One such state is New Jersey, which just recently allowed teachers in the state's teacher pipeline for certification to waive mandatory assessment tests for earning a state teaching license. The state did reveal that teachers would have to pass another test, eventually. But for now, there is a shift in "the burden of certifying teachers from the state's shoulders to the colleges that train them."[115] The more radical the teacher training program, the more radical one can expect its graduates to be upon finishing the college's teacher education program.

In addition to not being able to find enough teachers to fill classrooms, Washington State illustrates there are other serious issues that are becoming worrisome for America's public schools. One of the serious concerns for Washington relates to parents removing their children from the state's public schools. Washington State public schools are reeling from a shortage of teachers, and now the state's schools are hemorrhaging students. There are at least three good reasons why this is the case. These are identified by Liv Finne, the director for the Center for Education.[116]

First, on the fifth of May, 2021, Washington State Governor Jay Inslee signed into law the requirement that schools must teach critical race theory. Not all teachers have bought into the radical ideology, which dictates that there are white oppressors of people of color, and that being an oppressor group is a hallmark of being white. This is part of the ideological tenets of CRT. Most parents are understandably upset when they hear their children share this ideology at home.

Second, Finne mentions how parents are often kept in the dark about some of the material children are learning at their schools: "The state legislature mandated a radical sex education curriculum to children as young as five and six years old, without consultation with parents. The classroom curriculum includes graphic materials and requires discussion of physical, gender, and sexual issues at inappropriate ages."[117]

Finne includes a *third*, but two-part reason parents remove their children from the state's public education system. *Primarily*, "some school officials require teachers to give students passing grades for work that does not meet state learning standards to prevent students and parents from knowing about educational failures."[118]

Secondarily, the Washington State superintendent of public instruction laid out a policy that would eliminate grades, which would prohibit education stakeholders and parents "from receiving an accurate assessment of a child's failure or progress."[119] This is a dumbing down of education and does not appeal to most parents. Especially after the COVID-19 pandemic, parents sense an urgency to get their children caught up on two lost years, academically.

Nationally, in some educational institutions, "ideological buy-in is so complete that educators and administrators are sincerely unaware that other positions on social issues even exist, and hence they see no need to disclose, discuss, or justify their actions, since there is no alternative reasonable position to hold, in their limited view."[120] This is the result of indoctrination and radicalizing and the expectation is to make certain the jaded, one-sided ideologies are shared with students to create monolithic and systemically radicalized by-products. Unfortunately, there is the appearance of success to these ends.

Some teachers take matters into their own hands and teach to what angers them in the news. For example, a Michigan middle school teacher was so triggered by the Brett Kavanaugh SCOTUS hearings that he wanted to use a tactic he had learned in his teaching training—"Creative insubordination"[121]—but was fearful his principal would find out he was injecting personal bias into a lesson to lead his students to his conclusions. Some teacher training institutions are making certain to provide practical radical strategies for the teachers they radicalize.

MEDICINE AND RADICALISM

Psychology and sociology college disciplines have diluted science with theories about psychological fluidity, and have revised facts and truth by substituting emotion and social constructs in their places. The nexus of these replacements has reached its zenith in Gen Z. Today's teachers stress that knowledge is not as important as what is felt about the knowledge. Knowledge and facts are often cancelled by those whose voices are largely elevated by media influencers from various platforms. If an influencer comments on something outrageous, followers may *feel* the comments are *true*.

Social media and large technology companies are replete with Gen Z voices, which adds another level of concern when discussing indoctrination and activism. As stated earlier, Gen Z is more susceptible to emotional pleas, even if science refutes their feelings. Science is overlooked and claims that rely on science are ridiculed as hateful, among other accusations. Truth is no longer a thing to be grasped and has become as emotionally fluid as one's claimed identity.

There is little wonder why growing percentages of Gen Z and Millennials claim to struggle with their identities, or hold the view they are not who adults claim they were at birth.[122] Remarkably, science only seems to be science when it either justifies a non-scientific question, or when it fits a niche of radical ideologies. One can hardly view a video on YouTube, scroll through Instagram or TikTok posts, or suffer through Twitter rants without seeing college-age students sharing their personal ideologies about life.

Medicine itself has been radicalized. Medical schools are increasingly requiring their physicians-in-training to recognize the emotional identities of their patients. In other words, men can now be viewed as women and women as men. Psychology, sociology, women's and gender studies are now in competition with biology, physiology, and anatomy when it comes to medical training. There is obvious brainwashing that is occurring when physicians claim that men can be women after studying human anatomy and biology. It is one thing to say that people make these claims. It is another thing for a physician to state a biological error as fact for ideological purposes, or to generate revenue for research hospitals.

At the University of Minnesota Medical School's white coat ceremony, students took an oath that bore no resemblance to the traditional Hippocratic Oath: "Do no harm."[123] Although not legal or binding, the new oath has medical students committing to "uprooting the legacy and perpetuation of structural violence deeply embedded within the health care system."[124] This oath, which exudes antiracism ideology, was written by some students, in consultation with a few faculty advisors.

In addition to pledging to be antiracists in 2021, students added to their oath that they "recognize inequities built by past and present traumas rooted in white supremacy, colonialism, the gender binary, ableism, and all forms of oppression."[125] Furthermore, as these medical students "enter this profession with opportunity for growth,"[126] they commit themselves to "promoting a culture of antiracism, listening, and amplifying voices for positive change . . . pledge to honor all Indigenous ways of healing that have been historically marginalized by Western medicine. Knowing that health is intimately connected to our environment, we commit to healing our planet and communities."[127]

The University of Minnesota Medical School has become fully woke as "evidenced by its participation in an Antiracist Transformation in Medical Education program."[128] (ATME) In terms of the ATME, and "despite sounding admirable, anti-racism is a term popularized by Ibram X. Kendi, who explicitly calls for discrimination in his writings."[129] Kendi's ideas of antiracism and the impact of the new oath taken by medical students have played directly into the recent "Minneapolis teachers' union contract, which requires laying off white teachers first,"[130] as the university moves in the direction of recovery from its own "whiteness."[131] Welcome to equity, where quality of person is sacrificed for quotas based on melanin.

Many pediatricians and other medical professionals fear that if scientists and physicians can be discounted as experts in their fields, which includes human anatomy expertise, and are relegated to that of "guessers" over what they see at birth—or in the genetics, gametes, or any other scientific determination—then the authority for identity is as fluid as are claims of gender. Oddly, this is precisely what some authors are writing within the pages of children's literature. This, again, is indoctrination.

Psychology, sociology, and humanities departments are churning out ideologies as fast as sympathetic journals can publish them. There are now dozens of gender claims, thanks to psychology. American parents do not need to look any further than America's schools and social media influencers for some accountability. Many of these influencers exist to support and groom children *from clarity and security to confusion and insecurity*. This radicalization strips away norms and reality and does result in confusion in the lives of children. However, there is a down side for today's radicals.

Gen Z are suffering from a lack of understanding of who and what they are. They are bringing this confusion into the workplace and, when they are emotionally agitated, or casually dissatisfied, they mobilize and take to the streets as groupie sycophants, via the clarion call of social media networks and influencers paid to motivate the sympathetic troops. The reality is that from their caloric moodiness, Gen Z are more likely to display gender dysphoria and emotional dysfunction. This is the onset of the beginning of a trend that may result in great numbers of students needing serious mental health therapies, deprogramming interventions, and other health treatments in the near future.

CLARITY OVER CONFUSION

Where does this all shake out? Gen Z lives at a time when the phrase *follow the science* had become a mainstay, especially during the COVID-19 pandemic. Most Americans believed that scientists had allowed themselves to acquiesce to controlled mandates by their state and local governments. Amidst that acquiescence, students were also told that a basic understanding of biological science does *not* apply. Rather, sociologists and psychologists, actually, were allowed to circumvent facts of science. Like many other things, once something is radicalized, the indoctrinated rally to defend even the most erroneous of ideologies. In this case, science has been radicalized and is to be followed when it seems to fit the politics, and not the other way around.

Every generation—albeit every normally developed human—has emotional reactions on some level. The phrase "go with your gut-level feelings," is an example of that. However, what we have today in the United States is a panoply of pressures upon students, right where they spend most of the hours of their days. These hours are spent at schools, playing sports, participating in community activities, attending churches, and online.

Gen Z is very different than previous generations. Gen Z and, for that matter, some younger millennials are seeking deeper spiritual experiences and have found a radical culture willing to provide these experiences. The ticket for admission to this radicalism is becoming a convert and indoctrinated into woke ideologies concerning race, sex, and gender identity. As a substitute for truth, the cultural ideologies that are ensnaring millions of children and young adults offer no answers to the confusion created by them in the hearts and minds of radicalized Americans.

NOTES

1. Bonnie Kerrigan Snyder. *Undoctrinate: How politicized classrooms harm kids and ruin our schools—and what we can do about it*. 2021. Nashville, TN: Post Hill Press, p. 166.

2. Staff. "A wider ideological gap between more and less educated adults." Pew Research Center. April 26, 2016. Retrieved November 1, 2022, from https://www.pewresearch.org/politics/2016/04/26/a-wider-ideological-gap-between-more-and-less-educated-adults/. Cf. Tristram Hooley. "What is radical education?" *Adventures in Career Development*. May 29, 2014. Retrieved November 1, 2022, from https://adventuresincareerdevelopment.wordpress.com/2014/05/29/what-is-radical-education/.

3. Angie Speaks. "The left is weaponizing misinformation to silence dissent: Opinion." *Newsweek*. February 3, 2022. Retrieved November 1, 2022, from https://www.newsweek.com/left-weaponizing-misinformation-silence-dissent-opinion-1675949.

4. R. C. Murray. "Dumbing them down," in Colin Gunn and Joaquin Fernandez (eds.). *Indoctrination: Public schools and the decline of Christianity*. 2012. Green Forest, AR: Master Books, pp. 78–79.

5. "Radicals and radicalism." *Encyclopedia.com*. 2022. Retrieved October 20, 2022, from https://www.encyclopedia.com/history/dictionaries-thesauruses-pictures-and-press-releases/radicals-and-radicalism.

6. Ibid.

7. Ibid.

8. Stephen Sawchuk. "What is critical race theory, and why is it under attack." *EdWeek*. May 18, 2021. Retrieved May 20, 2021, from https://www.edweek.org/leadership/what-is-critical-race-theory-and-why-is-it-under-attack/2021/05.

9. Janel George. "A lesson on critical race theory." *Human Rights*. American Bar Associatio. 46(2): n.p. January 11, 2021. Retrieved October 19, 2021, from https://www.americanbar.org/groups/crsj/publications/human_rights_magazine_home/civil-rights-reimagining-policing/a-lesson-on-critical-race-theory/.

10. Carol M. Swain and Christopher J. Schorr. *Black Eye for America: How critical race theory is burning down the house*. 2021. Rockville, MD: Be the People Books, p. 21.

11. Lindsey Grewe. "Focus on the Family headquarters sign vandalized in wake of Club Q shooting." KKTV. November 25, 2022. Retrieved November 26, 2022, from https://www.kktv.com/2022/11/25/focus-family-headquarters-sign-vandalized-wake-club-q-shooting/.

12. Christopher F. Rufo. "The child soldiers of Portland." *City Journal*. Spring 2021, Retrieved November 17, 2022, from https://www.city-journal.org/critical-race-theory-portland-public-schools.

13. Lance Izumi, Cassidy Syftestad, and Christie Syftestad. *The corrupt classroom: Bias, indoctrination, violence, and social engineering show why America needs school choice*. 2017. San Francisco, CA: Pacific Research Institute, pp. 26–32.

14. James Bohman. "Critical theory." *Stanford Encyclopedia of Philosophy*. 2005. Palo Alto, CA: Stanford University Press, p. 1.

15. Ibid.

16. Julianne McShane. "A record number of US adults identify as LGBTQ. Gen Z is driving the increase." *The Washington Post*. February 17, 2022. Retrieved July 7, 2022, from https://www.washingtonpost.com/lifestyle/2022/02/17/adults-identifying-lgbt-gen-z/.

17. Jeffrey M. Jones. "LGBT identification is US ticks up to 7.1%." *Gallup*. February 17, 2022. Retrieved July 7, 2022, from https://news.gallup.com/poll/389792/lgbt-identification-ticks-up.aspx?utm_source=twitterbutton&utm_medium=twitter&utm_campaign=sharing.

18. Ibid.

19. Michael S. Irwig. "Detransition among transgender and gender-diverse people—and increasing and increasingly complex phenomenon." *The Journal of Endocrinology and Metabolism*. June 9, 2022. 107(10):e426-e262. Retrieved August 7, 2022, from https://academic.oup.com/jcem/article/107/10/e4261/6604653.

20. N'Dea Yancey Bragg. "What is systemic racism? Here's what it means and how you can help dismantle it." *USA Today*. June 15, 2020. Retrieved July 2, 2022, from https://www.usatoday.com/story/news/nation/2020/06/15/systemic-racism-what-does-mean/5343549002/.

21. Lindsay Perez Huber and Daniel G. Solorzano. "Racial microaggressions as a tool for critical race research." *Race, Ethnicity, and Education*. 2015. 18(3): pp. 297–320. 2015.

22. Richard Delgado and Jean Stefancic. *Critical race theory: An introduction*. 2012. New York: New York University Press, p. 87.

23. Timothy J. Legg and Jessica Caporuscio. "Everything you need to know about white fragility." *Medical News Today*. June 12, 2020. Retrieved September 23, 2022, from https://www.medicalnewstoday.com/articles/white-fragility-definition.

24. Julica Hermann de la Fuente. "White fragility." *Unitarian Universalist College of Social Justice*. 2022. Retrieved September 23, 2022 from, https://uucsj.org/study-guide/who-are-you/white-fragility/.

25. Swain and Schorr. *Black Eye for America,* p. 3. Cf. Kimberlê Crenshaw, "Mapping the margins of intersectionality, identity politics, and violence against women of color." *Stanford Law Review.* 1991. 43(6): 1241–1299.

26. Ibram X. Kendi. *Stamped from the Beginning: The Definitive History of Racist Ideas in America.* New York: Bold Type Books, pp. 443–444. Cf. Crenshaw. "Mapping the margins of intersectionality, identity politics, and violence against women of color," p. 1242.

27. Ibram X. Kendi. *How to be an antiracist.* 2019. New York: One World Publishers, p. 19.

28. Stephen Sawchuk. "What is critical race theory and why is it under attack?" Staff. "Explore the data." *Critical Race Training in Education.* 2022. Retrieved September 21, 2022, from https://criticalrace.org/.

29. Derryck Green. "Black nationalism." *First Things.* August 2022. Retrieved November 25, 2022, from https://www.firstthings.com/article/2022/08/black -nationalism.

30. Staff. "Diversity, Equity, and Inclusion." *Peninsula School District.* 2022. Retrieved October 20, 2022, from https://www.psd401.net/about-us/equity#:~:text =Peninsula%20School%20District%20Statement%20on%20Human%20Dignity &text=We%20expect%20this%20value%20to,and%20staff%20grow%20and %20thrive.

31. Lynne Chandler Garcia. "I'm a professor at a US military academy. Here's why I teach critical race theory." *The Washington Post.* July 6, 2021. Retrieved July 5, 2022, from https://www.washingtonpost.com/opinions/2021/07/06/military -academies-should-teach-critical-race-theory/.

32. Thomas Spoehr. "The rise of wokeness in the military." *Imprimis.* June/July 2022. 51(6–7): 3.

33. Staff. *Healthcare equity blueprint.* University of Washington Medicine. April 21, 2017, p. 2. Retrieved November 1, 2022, from https://depts.washington.edu/ uwmedptn/wp-content/uploads/UW-Medicine-Healthcare-Equity-Blueprint-2017.05 .01.pdf.

34. Ibid.

35. Becky Bond and Zack Exley. *Rules for revolutionaries: How big organizing can change everything.* 2016. White River Junction, Vermont: Chelsea Green Publishing, p. 85.

36. Ibid., p. 153.

37. Ibid., p. 159.

38. Ibid., p. 177.

39. Anne Applebaum. "The answer to extremism isn't more extremism." *The Atlantic.* October 30, 2020. Retrieved June 2, 2022, from https://www.theatlantic.com /ideas/archive/2020/10/left-and-right-are-radicalizing-each-other/616914/.

40. Julio Ricardo Varela. "Former Proud Boys' leader Enrique Tarrio serves as a brown face of white supremacy." MSNBC. March 15, 2022. Retrieved October 5, 2022, from https://www.msnbc.com/opinion/msnbc-opinion/former-proud-boys -leader-enrique-tarrio-serves-brown-face-white-n1291949.

41. Holmes Lybrand and Hannah Rabinowitz. "In surprise testimony, Oath Keeper apologizes for going into the Capitol on January 6." CNN. November 16, 2022. Retrieved November 17, 2002, from https://www.cnn.com/2022/11/16/politics/jessica-watkins-oath-keepers-testifies.

42. Ibid.

43. Cortney O'Brien. "Winston Marshall has no regrets leaving Mumford & Sons after getting canceled: I'm liberated." Fox News. November 17, 2022. Retrieved November 18, 2022, from https://www.foxnews.com/media/winston-marshall-no-regrets-leaving-mumford-sons-getting-canceled-im-liberated.

44. Snyder. *Undoctrinate*, p. 122.

45. Gigi De La Torre. "Democrats outnumber Republicans 98 to 1 in Cornell humanities departments." *The College Fix*. October 14, 2022. Retrieved October 15, 2022, from https://www.thecollegefix.com/democrats-outnumber-republicans-98-to-1-in-cornell-humanities-departments/.

46. Snyder. *Undoctrinate*, p. 123. Cf. Jonathan Haidt. *The righteous mind: Why good people are divided by politics and religion*. 2013. London, UK: Penguin Books, p. 334.

47. Izumi, Syftestad, and Syftestad. *The corrupt classroom*, p. 17.

48. Tim Devaney. "Teachers union: Trump's comments encourage school bullies." *The Hill*. May 5, 2016. Retrieved August 30, 2022, from https://thehill.com/regulation/278911-teachers-union-trumps-comments-encourage-school-bullies/.

49. Ibid.

50. Izumi, Syftestad, and Syftestad. *The corrupt classroom*, p. 18.

51. Ibid., p. 17.

52. Bond and Exley. *Rules for revolutionaries*, p. 7.

53. Ibid.

54. Ibid., p. 84.

55. Ibid., p. 8.

56. Ibid., p. 36.

57. Joe Biden. "Biden delivers speech on battle for the soul of the nation in Philadelphia." CBS News. Posted September 1, 2022. YouTube video. Retrieved October 1, 2022, from https://www.youtube.com/watch?v=NA3Outfs7K8.

58. Peter Dreier. "The fifty most influential progressives of the twentieth century." *The Nation*. October 4, 2010. Retrieved October 20, 2022, from https://www.thenation.com/article/archive/fifty-most-influential-progressives-twentieth-century/.

59. Saul Alinsky. *Rules for radicals*. 1971. New York: Random House, p. 128.

60. Ibid., p. 129.

61. Ibid., p. 129.

62. Ibid., p. 130.

63. Ibid., p. 133.

64. Ben Jacobs. "Biden defended democracy—and pounced on a political opportunity." *Vox*. September 2, 2022. Retrieved September 4, 2022, from https://www.vox.com/policy-and-politics/2022/9/2/23334115/biden-maga-republicans-pennsylvania-speech. Cf. Ryan Mills. "Democrats praise Biden's soul of the nation speech as inspiring, urgent war-time address." *National Review*. September 2, 2022. Retrieved

September 4, 2022, from https://www.nationalreview.com/news/democrats-praise
-bidens-soul-of-the-nation-speech-as-inspiring-urgent-war-time-address/.

65. Snyder. *Undoctrinate*, p. 33.

66. Jacobs, "Biden defended democracy."

67. Hannah Grossman. "California district curriculum claims there's 10 sexual orientations, including skoliosexual and gynesexual." Fox News. August 31, 2022. Retrieved September 2, 2022, from https://www.foxnews.com/media/california -district-curriculum-claims-10-sexual-orientations-skoliosexual-gynesexual.

68. Christopher F. Rufo. "In Portland, the sexual revolution starts in kindergarten." *City Journal*. July 27, 2022. Retrieved July 29, 2022, from https://www.city-journal .org/in-portland-the-sexual-revolution-starts-in-kindergarten.

69. Ibid.

70. Ibid.

71. Ibid.

72.Ibid.

73. Ibid.

74. Ibid.

75. Abigail Schrier. *Irreversible damage: The transgender craze seducing our daughters*. 2021. Washington, DC: Regnery Publishing.

76. Brook Pessin-Whedbee. *Who are you?* 2017. London, UK: Jessica Kingley Publishers, pp. 6, 15.

77. Staff. "Participation of transgender athletes in women's sports." Women's Sports Foundation. Downloadable PDF. 2022. Retrieved September 25, 2022, from https://www.womenssportsfoundation.org/wp-content/uploads/2016/08/participation -of-transgender-athletes-in-womens-sports-the-foundation-position.pdf.

78. Brooke Pessin-Whedbee. *Who are you: The kids guide to gender identity*.

79. Pessin-Whedbee. *Who are you?* pp. 6, 15.

80. Snyder. *Undoctrinate*, p. 85.

81. Ibid., p. 34.

82. Lance Izumi. "Why are teachers mostly liberal?" Pacific Research Institute. April 3, 2019. Retrieved September 7, 2022, from https://www.pacificresearch.org/ why-are-teachers-mostly-liberal/.

83. Snyder. *Undoctrinate*, p. 34. Cf. Philip W. Magness. "Here is proof that the leftist tilt on campus has gotten dramatically worse." American Institute for Economic Research. May 1, 2019. Retrieved September 6, 2022, from https://www.aier.org /article/here-is-proof-that-the-leftist-tilt-on-campus-has-gotten-dramatically-worse/.

84. Snyder. *Undoctrinate*, p. 35.

85. Ibid, p. 33.

86. Izumi, Syftestad, and Syftestad. *The corrupt classroom*, p. 35.

87. Snyder. *Undoctrinate*, p. 31.

88. Ibid., p. 188.

89. Ibid., p. 27.

90. Samuel J. Adams. "On leaving professional organizations." *National Association of Scholars*. September 29, 2022. Retrieved October 4, 2022, from https://www .mindingthecampus.org/2022/09/29/on-leaving-professional-organizations/.

91. Ibid.

92. Ibid.

93. Ibid.

94. Michael Metarko. "America's Trojan horse: Public education," in Colin Gunn and Joaquin Fernandez (eds.). *Indoctrination: Public schools and the decline of Christianity*. 2012. Green Forest, AR: Master Books, p. 27.

95. Erwin Lutzer. "When a nation forgets God: Authoritarianism and government schools," in Colin Gunn and Joaquin Fernandez (eds.). *Indoctrination: Public schools and the decline of Christianity*. 2012. Green Forest, AR: Master Books, p. 230.

96. R. C. Sproul. "The goal of education," in Colin Gunn and Joaquin Fernandez (eds.). *Indoctrination: Public schools and the decline of Christianity*. 2012. Green Forest, Arkansas: Master Books, p. 230.

97. Snyder. *Undoctrinate*, p. 31.

98. Bruce Shortt. "Appendix A: Postscript to teachers and administrators," in Colin Gunn and Joaquin Fernandez (eds.). *Indoctrination: Public schools and the decline of Christianity*. 2012. Green Forest, AR: Master Books, p. 349.

99. Ibid.

100. Ibid., p. 350.

101. Jason Rantz. "Rantz: Bellevue High School teaches critical race theory with intent to create activists." *My Northwest*. April 6, 2022. Retrieved August 27, 2022, from https://mynorthwest.com/3420690/rantz-bellevue-high-school-teaches-critical -race-theory-crt/.

102. Ibid.

103. Ibid.

104. Staff. "Lukas Michener: Uniting for social justice with NEA." National Education Association. June 16, 2020. Retrieved September 2, 2022, from https://www .nea.org/professional-excellence/leadership-development/member-spotlight/lukas -michener-uniting-social.

105. Rantz. "Rantz: Bellevue High School."

106. Ibid.

107. Kelly Field. "Teaching action civic engages kids—and ignites controversy." *The Hechinger Report*. August 1, 2001. Retrieved September 1, 2022, from https: //hechingerreport.org/teaching-action-civics-engages-kids-and-ignites-controversy/.

108. Shaina James. "Extra credit brings up questions." *The North Wind*. November 3, 2011. Retrieved September 4, 2022, from https://thenorthwindonline.com/3862745 /news/extra-credit-brings-up-questions/.

109. Ibid.

110. Ibid.

111. Ibid.

112. Sadie Dittenber. "Indoctrination concerns prompts West Bonner trustees to yank curriculum." *Idaho Ed News*. August 31, 2022. Retrieved September 7, 2022, from https://www.idahoednews.org/news/indoctrination-concerns-prompt-west -bonner-trustees-to-yank-curriculum/.

113. Paulina Firozi. "Family with two dads debuts on Sesame Street during pride week." *The Washington Post*. June 21, 2001. Retrieved July 5, 2022, from https://

www.washingtonpost.com/arts-entertainment/2021/06/21/sesame-street-pride-month
-episode/.

114. Staff. "Coming together: Celebrating every child's race, ethnicity, and culture!" Sesame Workshop. African Australian. Posted 2022. Retrieved September
13, 2022, from https://www.sesameworkshop.org/what-we-do/race-ethnicity-and
-culture. Cf. *"Sesame Street* explains Black Lives Matter." Posted June 6, 2020. You-
Tube video. Retrieved September 12, 2022, from https://www.youtube.com/watch?v
=xBUFcv0y0yk.

115. Mary Ann Koruth. "Victory for all future educators: NJ does away with
teacher certification test—sort of." *NorthJersey.com.* September 27, 2022. Retrieved
September 28, 2022, from https://www.northjersey.com/story/news/education/2022
/09/27/teacher-shortage-nj-mandated-assessment-test-to-be-replaced/69520248007/.

116. Liv Finne. "Reasons parents are leaving Washington State public schools."
Washington Policy Center. March 2022. Retrieved August 12, 2022, from https://www
.washingtonpolicy.org/library/doclib/Finne-Reasons-parents-are-leaving-Washington
-state-public-schools.pdf.

117. Ibid.

118. Ibid.

119. Ibid.

120. Snyder. *Undoctrinate*, p. 30.

121. Ibid., p. 29.

122. Erin Doherty. "The number of LGBTQ-identifying adults is soaring."
Axios. February 19, 2022.   Retrieved March 4, 2022, from https://www.axios.
com/2022/02/17/lgbtq-generation-z-gallup.

123. Anthony Gockowski. "Med students take antiracism oath at University of
Minnesota." Alpha News. September 2, 2022. Retrieved September 3, 2022, from
https://alphanews.org/med-students-take-anti-racism-oath-at-university-of-minnesota
/.

124. Ibid.

125. Ibid.

126. Ibid.

127. Ibid.

128. Ibid.

129. Ibid.

130. Ibid.

131. Ibid.

Chapter 4

Generation Z as the New Radicals

I hope that these pages will contribute to the education of the radicals of today, and to the conversion of hot, emotional, impulsive passions that are important and frustrating to actions that will be calculated, purposeful, and effective.

—Saul Alinsky, *Rules for Radicals*[1]

A few years back, my publisher, Rowman & Littlefield, released the following two books: (1) *The Entitled Generation: Helping Teachers Teach and Reach the Minds and Hearts of Generation Z*, and (2) *Helping Parents to Understand the Minds and Hearts of Generation Z*. At the risk of hubris, those two books were somewhat prescient, as they laid out the susceptibility of Generation Z to fall prey to whatever seasonal social and emotional winds blew in their direction. The present reality is that this vulnerability remains and, fueled by very strategic social media influences, places Gen Z in a continued high-risk category, susceptible to indoctrination and radicalization.

The phrase "perfect storm" may be overused by writers, but it fits here and can be applied to explain an uncanny, yet perceptible alignment of trends, laws, voices in the media, education, and changes in American culture. In the eye of this perfect storm, there is a conscious but quiet sense of pending cataclysm. This is a sense some veteran teachers experienced when beginning to work with a growing number of Gen Z graduates from college, just a few years ago.

Why have history and Gen Z fallen into alignment for a time such as this? How has a generation so quickly turned its back on certain realities of settled science, while at the same time elevating the pretense of feelings as a gauge for truth? Moreover, why is the dismantling of the nuclear family and the disrespect for birth identity so welcome? The question remains: Why are these so important to current-day radicals?

More recent optimism about Gen Z centers on a hopeful, maturing genera-tion of purpose-seeking young adults. One wonders if they will ultimately reject the ideology that puts them at odds with parents and some colleagues. Educators at the forefront of working with students tell a different story, as they see concerning signs. Those of us in the classrooms at the time saw firsthand the sociocultural interests and group tendencies of Gen Z, some of which raised eyebrows at the time, because they began to mirror the activism of millennials[2] and outdo them in their push leftward.

What transpired is that individuals started to become less important. Groupthink and tribalism became acceptable and expected. The group real-ity had become so intransigent that to go against one person's beliefs or disagree with behaviors and practices meant an attack on a neighborhood of individuals. This is especially true today with the all-purpose pejoratives used to categorize critics, as well as the cancel culture practiced by the fragile left-ists—especially at universities.

GENERATIONAL DIFFERENCES OBSERVED

Veteran educators have observed the escalation of differences between them and Gen Z and began to understand what were once concerns had actually become generational problems. Those who wish to predict what comes next for a generation can find the answers in working to prepare teachers who will take over the schoolrooms of America, for the generation-in-question.

The next generation of teachers is a good gauge as to what students and young people will come to believe or reject. To this end, some of the gradu-ates of teacher education programs, which include Gen Z, are leading the charge toward things that are both radical[3] and practical.[4] For all intents, it remains clear that Gen Z are the newest of radicals on both fronts.

Indifferent teachers see these changes, but are unwilling to talk about them for fear of losing everything for which they have worked.[5] Others think there is hardly anything for which to be concerned. Why is this? Gen Z is quick to vent their angst over the simplest of issues that arise. Not getting along with a person or a group qualifies as justification for some form of cancelation. They have been taught to emote, which is more than a reaction. For this genera-tion, emotion is reality and truth. To put it differently, and with apologies to Descartes: *I feel, therefore I am.*

Along with the changes that present themselves with Gen Z, there has come a heightened sensitivity toward being criticized. They have been labeled as "the most sensitive generation"[6] and often any criticism leveled at one of them results in a claim of microaggression, and on to the social media attack they go.

Technically, psychologists see Gen Z from several different vantage points. In addition to these perspectives, the reality is hyper-emotionality and the ease by which people are manipulated by social media influences;[7] Gen Z raises concerns unlike those with which previous generations have had to contend. The major reason for this is twofold: (1) schools indoctrinate without fear and (2) social media–support mobs are just an icon swipe away. Technology has exacerbated radicalization of students by providing access to radical ideas, social fads, and emotional support.[8]

Educational researchers have made careers out of documenting ideological shifts in schools. They continue to study how actions based on beliefs coincide in concert with variations of social and cultural norms. It is no secret that as ideologies change, so also do the actions that result from these ideologies.

Older generations anticipate that major changes in culture tend to alter the mores of the status quo, hence their generation. Thus, previous generations are wary of the changes with which they are confronted. The older the generation, the greater the longevity, the greater awareness of the radical nature of any generational paradigm shift.[9] Teacher training across generations has changed drastically.

Substantively, Gen Z teachers in training are required to take classes on psychology, student trauma, social justice, diversity, brain development, and social-emotional learning. Several of these have underlying racial components to their content. Teachers today focus on emotional intelligence (EI), or EQ, over IQ. Students, therefore, are now being taught to learn by feelings and emotions and given subsequent tasks to accomplish, based on the same. Gen Z has been trained to express and to emote, rather than reflect and consider. When they are hired in public schools they bring their training into the classrooms.

One of the characteristics shared by Gen Z and other more recent generations is that the more youthful a demographic, the more inclined the demographic is to impulsiveness. Many of Gen Z have picked up the mantle of millennial radicals before them and have exceeded their impulses. However, one generation's radicals are different from another generation's radicals, because people are as different as the causes they undertake.[10] So why is Gen Z so radicalized?

REASONS FOR GEN Z RADICALIZATION

Nicole Neily, president of Parents Defending Education, puts it like this: "Young children and adolescents are highly vulnerable. It's a developmental period that's naturally full of insecurity and confusion. Since when did it become OK for non-family adults to influence children on such intimate

topics behind parents' backs? School officials have decided they're in charge
of those intimate topics. They get to decide what's right and what it means to
be male and female. And parents get no say. How dare these radicals decide
that they know our children better than we do! How dare they use their
agenda to dictate our children's emotional, social, and physical lives?"[11]

One reason that helps us understand why Gen Z is open to being radicalized is as Neily points out. It is their emotional vulnerability. Another reason
is that there is a definite shift in worldviews among the Gen Z population
in America. Gen Z's views on religion, church, and God are vastly different
from the views of older generations.[12] A third reason for the radicalization
of Gen Z is that the colleges they attend are intentional about producing
agents of change and activists on behalf of social justice, race, and gender/
sex causes.

Politics is an inescapable feature of today's Gen Z radicals, for those both
on the left and the right. Politics is inescapable at the college level and, as
an influence, especially favors those that claim progressive positions and the
Democratic Party.[13]

This reality became more apparent when a recent Mt. Holyoke graduate,
Annabella Rockwell, declared herself deprogrammed after being "totally
indoctrinated into viewing the world as a toxic patriarchy and . . . had a duty
to fight on behalf of other victims: women, people of color and LBGTQ
folks."[14] Rockwell stated "the professors encouraged alienation [from par-
ents] and even offered their homes to stay in. They'd say, like, don't go see
them, come stay with us for the holiday. Most of my classmates believed all
this stuff, too. If you didn't you were ostracized."[15]

Rockwell's mother hired a deprogrammer to rescue her daughter from
the indoctrination she experienced at the all-girls' college. These types of
experiences are not uncommon and equate to those that far too many college
students are subjected to. Why are these younger adults becoming so radically
divergent from the previous generation and their elders?

Rarely does radicalism of people occur at the grassroots level and work
its way upward. Today's radicalism is no exception. It comes from the top
levels in society and then works its way down from there.[16] (See chapter 5.)
Political leaders and university professors are ground zero for most radical
ideas that affect Gen Z.

Gen Z Searching for Identity

Gen Z is more susceptible to radicalization because as a group they are
searching for identities that exist merely within their emotions. Some are trying to find their way in politics, as the first group of Gen Z candidates has run
for office in 2022. Others are up to their necks in the LGBTQ+ movement,

trying to determine which gender they belong to and which sexuality to express. There is a lot of confusion among developing factions in Gen Z, and this confusion has made them especially vulnerable to new ideas that come along.[17]

One of the more serious concerns among Gen Z is their abdication of faith.[18] The faith that gave them a sense of purpose, and an understanding that each of them were unique in the world, has been left behind. In fact, "suicide is the sixth leading cause of death for five-to-fourteen-year-olds. The idea of child suicide was unheard of before the schools became atheistic. It is true that family dysfunctions can depress a child, especially if that child has no recourse to God, because the school told him that there is no God, just as there is no Santa Claus. . . . Simply put, godless education leads to depression, suicide, and antisocial behavior."[19]

Gen Z as a Target

The majority of college professors, social media influencers, racial groups, and others do not hide the fact that they target children and young adults. They do so within the context of schooling. Culture changes quickly, and when media is behind the push for change, culture changes radically. Young people are often swept up by catalysts for change, and Gen Z fits the bill.

There is no doubt that the lurch leftward by progressives is a planned strategy to change culture. But who is harmed by all of this? The children are harmed, and most often they are those of the economic disadvantaged middle and lower classes. For those that doubt the ultimate goals of progressive radical activists, the following statement by Saul Alinsky should set that straight.

Alinsky claims,

> Activists and radicals, on and off our college campuses—people who are committed to change—must make a complete turnabout. With rare exceptions, our activists and radicals are products of and rebels against our middle-class society. All rebels must attack the power states in their society. Our rebels have contemptuously rejected the values and way of life of the middle class. They have stigmatized it as materialistic, decadent, bourgeois, degenerate, imperialistic, war-mongering, brutalized, and corrupt. They are right; but we must begin from where we are if we are to build power for change, and the power and the people are in the big middle-class majority.[20]

Gen Z Is Not Traditional

Generation Z is not a traditional generation. As a group, the data demonstrate that they are shunning their parents' values and leaning toward much more radically secularized values. The work ethic of the generation is more unstable, in that today's younger workers have no problem with walking away from work if they decide it lacks interest, or if their employment counters the purposes of their personal beliefs. They want to be treated as individuals, but they count on their importance in belongs to a larger group. Gen Z takes pride in belonging to groups that have cultural power.[21]

The erratic temperament of some radicals in Gen Z was manifested when they first spoke about tolerance as a virtue and then began demonstrating their own intolerance. As Gen Z entered the workplace, there was a distinct veering toward leftist values and intolerance of those opposite them in values. Calls for intolerance of those with whom they disagreed quickly supplanted previous generic calls for acceptance. Snitching and canceling became virtuous.

Researchers are finding that some in the Gen Z teacher work force come across as more boisterous about the radical views than any previous generation of educators, dating back to the 1960s. As a result, they are more than primed to instruct and indoctrinate students to radical ends.[22] Media accounts attest to this growing radicalization.

Gen Z and COVID-19

A consequence associated with the recent COVID-19 pandemic revealed how some schools and teachers were leading students directly into ideological conflicts with students' home lives. Zoom teaching and learning revealed some very stark messages about public educators. Some parents became irate when they heard their children's teachers on Zoom, while eavesdropping in on their children's classes. What some parents heard were comments made by adults promoting racial and sexual content, considered by parents as out-of-bounds for their children—and rightly so!

As a result of some teachers being required to be in their actual classrooms while on Zoom, parents saw flags and posters celebrating radical gender and radical race ideologies. As a result of these actions, growing groups of parents and community members became concerned, mobilized, and began to speak up. The main concern was that their children were not being educated. They were, instead, being indoctrinated. Matters have accelerated since COVID-19.[23]

Teachers and parents agree on one unfortunate thing. Schools have become places where students are encouraged to question their personal lives and values, and their families' values. They are also encouraged to become activists for causes they choose. In some cases, these causes are the result of exposure to radical teachers and other influences seeking similar outcomes. If there was a silver-lining to the COVID-19 pandemic, it is that parents became more involved in their children's education.

THE RAND STUDY ON EXTREMISM

What follows are some of the questions and findings of a study conducted by the RAND Corporation. The RAND Corporation conducted a study in 2021, seeking to determine the mindsets and actions of former radicals and extremists in America. Some of the questions asked in the study include: (1) "Who is at risk of joining violent extremist organizations?" and (2) "Can families and friends recognize whether someone is becoming radicalized?[24]

Some of the characteristics of those radicalized include:

- the amount of student consumption of propaganda, both online and in written materials;
- the sense of being part of a group by which the radicals identified, and
- the direct and indirect recruitment of those already radicalized.[25]

The following tactics pose great concerns for many parents with younger children:

- race and sex and gender propaganda,
- LGBTQ+ group pressure for inclusiveness and recruitment at schools,
- and the fact that children are being taught by teachers with an agenda to propagandize toward activism.

Throughout all of the interviews performed in the RAND study, "Many interviewees noted the importance of childhood as a critical time to be exposed to diverse ideas, develop critical thinking skills, participate in social activities designed to promote positive behaviors and inclusiveness, and be exposed to members of different racial or cultural groups."[26] The concerns are real and, despite what activists in classrooms and culture say to the contrary, their efforts to capture the minds and hearts of the young in schools are having negative effects on their lives and their choices, and sometimes terribly so.

What child in his or her right mind would demand to be surgically or medically altered for life, absent input from an adult proponent? How does this even occur, without the persistent drumbeat of propaganda by adults breaking down the barriers of conscience? Grooming tactics provide a sense of uniqueness for a child, including the promotion of another sense of belonging to a group of uniquely-altered individuals.

The fact remains, however, that children have been exposed to radical ideas online and practices by influencers during their formative years. The same exposure also applies to parents of these children. These parents favor medical or surgical castration and disfiguring their children long before their children's brains and bodies have had a chance to manifest whether they truly like one flavor of ice cream over another.

TWELVE ASSERTIONS ABOUT GEN Z RADICALISM

The following assertions about radicalism are derived from research and help to provide the reader with a conceptual framework about radicalism and how it affects students and education.

1. There are cultural issues in postmodern American society that are leading to radicalization of students beginning as early as kindergarten. These issues are accentuated, as well as exacerbated, by social media platforms, television and cable programming, and even extending to entertainment (Disney) and athletics. The COVID pandemic also left its mark on students. Each cultural institution in the United States can be found promoting and forcing values that stand in conflict[27] with millions of mainstream American families.[28]
2. Schools and colleges are promoting primarily radical ideas found most often on the far left of the political, social, and moral spectra. American high schools are breeding grounds for radical activists (Freshmen Beliefs and Behaviors Survey).[29] Colleges are hotbeds of leftist radicalism, which surveys of students and professors (AAUP) confirm. Gen Z is both in college and somewhat newly-minted as employees in the work place. "An essential aspect of this process is that no one, expert or amateur, gets to claim special authority simply because of who he happens to be."[30] Gen Z may have to wrestle with identity in the workplace.

When it comes to how things have changed at college, a stark realization is that "blatant advocacy was not traditionally a stance associated with academia, but with the inclusion of identity studies departments (women's studies, gender studies, ethnic studies—which have been jokingly, collectively, called studies studies), activism is now widely practiced within certain segments of the academy. This means students and professors in these fields typically seek to advance a set of ideology and policy positions, and political uniformity in those fields is nearly total. Agreement with often unstated aims is assumed at the outset."[31]

The fact is that "it's pretty well accepted that political correctness dominates the scene in American higher education, but when this same problem appears at the K–12 level, it is potentially far more damaging because it targets children."[32] This is precisely why radicals seek to impact children and why parents strive to protect children from being indoctrinated.

3. There is a recent phenomenon affecting younger students. Students as young as six are claiming a gender other than what theirs was at birth. They are told that doctors and parents guess at their gender and sometimes they guess wrongly.

Older K–6 students are opting to physically alter their bodies. Even at this young age, children are swept up into a response to an insidious, radical gender ideology. Pressures placed on them by family members do not alleviate any of their confusion over who and what they are told they can choose to become.

A dangerous level of indoctrination has to occur to convince, and later affirm, that a child is not who they were born to be. The radical physical changes that a child eventually goes through, by medical castration or the literal removal of body parts, in many cases, are permanent and unrecoverable.

On the flip side, numbers indicate that as children grow, so too do conversion regrets. Consequently, reversion and re-transitioning are gaining traction.[33] However, for far too many, mutilating and dismembering their bodies is a painful and sometimes botched reminder of the immaturity of choices they made as pubescents and prepubescents. The sad part is that these choices are often made with the blessings of adults in their lives. Where young children are supported and affirmed in extremes,[34] there are often radicalized persons influencing the younger persons toward a particular ideology.[35]

1. America is divided into extremes. Tribalism by race, politics, and LGBTQ+ factions have usurped the unity of the masses as well as marginalized the population into combative anti-American factions.[36] Some of these marginalized groups are the result of radicalization, while others are the result of natural interests and curiosities. Each contributes their share to the growing discontent in American society.

2. Influencers have taken over social media and are affecting millions of Gen Z students and teachers. Activism does not happen in a vacuum. Students are easily influenced by the time spent following those whom they respect as online influencers. This also leads to periodic protests over beliefs, which may result in corresponding behaviors, such as a rise in teenage terrorism.[37]

3. American parents are aligned with their choice of left-wing or right-wing ideologies, and conflicts are becoming all too common at schools, at sporting events, and so forth. There are clear lines drawn across political differences and radicalism can occur from both extremes. Unfortunately, this type of partisan alignment often results when children are the targeted focal points of radicals.

4. There is a very obvious red-state/blue-state divide in America. The political divide has caused severe mistrust in the system of elections and representative governance. Politics today is being used for vengeance toward political enemies and as imprimatur for radicals to change the social and moral landscapes of traditional America. A win-at-any-cost ethic is now a virtue to radicals—especially those that are involved with politics.

5. Support for the nuclear family is viewed as a radical attempt to close off nontraditional families, and the forming of such a unit is even considered to have been erroneous.[38] The definition of family has changed radically and has deviated from the traditional norm. What used to be the norm is now considered as white supremacy.

6. Absolutes are quickly fading from culture in favor of subjective political, sociological, and psychological truths. The truth of science is now questioned as if it is a sociological dilemma to be solved from within an undergraduate women's studies class. It is not uncommon to hear that men can be women, and women can be men, and that both can have babies.[39] This radical ideology countermands science but is the new illogic that is being used to justify transgenderism as a new social norm. As logic would have it, if trans women and trans men are truly women and men, then there can be no actual trans anyone.

7. The radicalization of Gen Z and their activism on behalf of any number of social issues may well be a permanent fixture in American culture. This radicalization has affected students in education in American schools negatively, and the fruit of this radicalization will only lead to a more unstable and divided America.

8. There is an increase of violent acts that are committed as radicalization takes hold ideologically and deepens in the psyches of the actors. This violence occurs along religious, racial, sexual/gender, and political lines. The increase of lawless behaviors is caused by multiple factors, each intertwined. Government officials are attempting to solve problems created by their own politically binary positions and subsequent actions.

9. In terms of religion, "promoting belief of faith systems in secular schools violates the legal principle of the separation of church and state. You are entitled to your own belief system, and to behave accordingly to the dictates of your own conscience, but not to impose it on others. This is foundational to the social compact we pledge to one another in our pluralistic society."[40] While this is true, generally, any Christian not wishing to violate his or her conscience with regard to services that promote a radical sex or gender ideology is held in contempt as hateful.

RADICALISM, GROOMING, AND SEX EDUCATION

Who are the radicals among us and how did they arrive at the point of being radicalized? The boisterous, quick-to-cancel Gen Z radicals are sometimes as vicious as they are vocal. Many of the Antifa radicals were proven to be younger adults.[41] College campuses are replete with over 90 percent leftist professors in many of the nation's humanities departments. Name-calling is now a basic hallmark of radicalism and a justification for eradication of those who become marginalized—and it begins early in the lives of some children.

The Little Book of Little Activists is an example of the indoctrination of the minds of children. Children ranging from five months to age fourteen are photographed at a women's march, from 2017, as they wear signs promoting any and all issues that adults determined were pertinent to women. Children holding signs when they have absolutely no idea what is written, or the meanings of the words, slogans, and phrases. Such actions are a co-opting of innocent children on behalf of adults. Such actions are also examples of adults radicalizing children by placing them in an environment of protest.

The purpose of the book in question is to expose children to protests and groom them, as the title of the book makes clear, to be "little activists." For example, there is photo of an eighteen-month-old girl named Birdie holding up a sign with the phrase, "I dissent." There is another photo of twins named Sophie and Emma, both around age five, holding a sign from their joint stroller that reads, "Where there is oppression there is resistance." A third and final example from the many included in the book is of five-month-old Leha. Her sign reads "I marched before I walked."[42]

Radicals do not need to be extroverts and to be calling attention to their actions through violence and defacement. Those are only the boisterous ones, but the majority of the indoctrinated are usually followers. The radicalization often occurs gradually and the indoctrination occurs as it creeps slowly around inside the mind of the supporter. Hence, the term *grooming* is most applicable.

Once convinced that fighting for a cause by any means is the right thing to do, then tribalistic groups, also called *the warriors*, attend to the natural, active part of expressing radical discontent. There are radical professors inciting students to action, public school teachers radicalizing students toward action civics that fit a leftist agenda, and there are ways younger children are being groomed by radicals beyond even the areas of sexuality, gender, and race.

The Pressures of Radicalism and Activism

Examinations of current sex education standards and curriculum in some states reveal that CRT includes LGBTQ+ as part of the education. BLM has made no secret of its desire to be included in school curricula. The reason BLM exists is based on the notion that America is systemically racist, and this racism is endemic in law enforcement. For this ideology to take hold, Americans have to experience the reality of it for themselves. This is how the George Floyd killing was used to radicalize Americans into factions. BLM has migrated from the George Floyd killing to the defund-all-police, sever the traditional nuclear family from society, and deconstruct whiteness and hetero-sexuality movements, and the list goes on. A recent book, *When the Secular becomes Sacred* (2021), addresses these and many other attacks carried out by radical activists, including those in BLM.[43]

Here is one example. Critical race theory does little to elevate the impor-tance of learning civics. Rather, certain tenets of the theory pose as a primer for social activism. As Stephen Sawchuk admits, laws that are written to forbid racial demagoguery in classrooms "could also become a tool to attack other pieces of the curriculum, including ethnic studies and 'action civics'—an approach to civics education that asks students to research local civic problems and propose solutions."[44] Some of the local problems still appear on nightly cable broadcasts.

Often radicals exude an enviable zeal about their ideology and extol extreme actions that may stem from its adherents. Some radicals do not understand why others cannot be as excited about their ideology as they are. As a result, disappointment may set in. An up-side to youthfulness and radicalism is that both seem a natural fit, in terms of maturity of mind and expressions of emotion. These are necessary to continue the drive toward their pursuit of idealism to which followers ascribe.

But radicals be warned. Advocates of CRT must come to admit, as Snyder puts it, that it is "a popular academic theory, and some K–12 teachers want to teach it, having studied it themselves in college. Here's the thing: while it is *a* theory, it is not *the* theory, and it is definitely not the *only* theory. Whether or not it is included in the existing curriculum is a reasonable discussion, but it is unreasonable to assert that it should replace all the oxygen in the classroom. It shouldn't preempt, conclude, or disallow all other discussions. It definitely shouldn't prevent and preclude the possibility of disagreement. . . . Though it may be taught informationally, so that students understand it, it can't be promoted as a system of belief in a public school, any more than religious precept can."[45]

Civic activism, along with antiracist training, does very little to unify the nation and its students. Values such as love, joy, peace, and patience are sacrificed for identity, tribal unity, disruption and destruction, and intolerance. Planting seeds of discontent and focusing on race are attempts to guilt people into understanding and compliance. Students should never be used in promoting a racial or sexual agenda. Yet, that is exactly what is being done, as activists take the messages they hear and promote them forward to recruit new radicals.

At one of the so-called elite academic institutions in America, Harvard University, there exists a typical example of radicalization that has overtaken institutions of higher education. Paralleling the fact that equity policy fuels the admissions process at most universities today, it would not be a surprise to discover that radicals only want other radicals of similar mindsets, or those who may be open to so-called change, to occupy their campuses.

Upon examination of Harvard's student admissions, there are very few conservatives on campus (6.4 percent). The majority of graduating students in 2022 wanted Immigration and Customs Enforcement (ICE) abolished (54.1 percent) and the percentage of very progressive students increased dramatically after four years.[46] This should not come as surprise to anyone.

Sawchuk rightly describes the current state of education in America, as it relates to impacts of dangerous ideologies, such as Marxism, in schools. He insists, "As the school-aged population became more diverse, these debates have been inflected through the lens of race and ethnic representation, including disagreements over multiculturalism and ethnic studies, the ongoing 'canon wars' over which texts should make up the English curriculum, and the so-called 'Ebonics' debates over the status of Black vernacular English in schools."[47]

Sawchuk also includes a recent example that demonstrates the intensity of the Gen Z advocacy and debate over CRT in America's schools. The example he cites is the furor surrounding the *New York Times*'s 1619 Project, "which sought to put the history and effects of enslavement—as well as Black Americans' contributions to demographic reforms—at the center of American history."[48] This material is accepted and used in many public schools across America.

According to Snyder, critical race theory was once relegated to the theoretical and discussed in the academy, primarily in law schools. It migrated into the humanities and, according to Andrew Sullivan, "Now it has become the core, underlying philosophy of the majority of American cultural institutions. . . . CRT advocates have brilliantly managed to construct a crude moral binary to pressure liberals into submissions. Where liberalism allows neutrality or doubt or indifference, CRT demands an absolute and immediate choice between racism and anti-racism . . . and no one wants to be a racist, do they?"[49] This is exactly what has trickled down into elementary and middle schools. Yet, there are still people purposely claiming that CRT is not taught in America's public schools.

Grooming and Sex Education

Grooming is generally defined as when someone builds a relationship, trust, and emotional connection with a child or young person so they can manipulate, exploit, and eventually abuse them. What was once taboo is now being pushed daily into the psyches of Americans. Therefore, parents should be alert and vigilant.[50]

What were once deemed as aberrational and abnormal personality disorders are now viewed, with greater frequency, as psychologically normal. Who would ever have considered a time when children would be brought to bars and transvestite shows? What person would have considered drag queen shows and story time with transvestites in classrooms as acceptable for seven-year-olds? What schools would celebrate lifestyles that were once deemed as radical and carnal cultural aberrations? The LGBTQ+ activists now react viciously at even the notion of questioning their lifestyle choices.[51]

As an example of how quickly culture has changed, pedophilia is quickly gaining acceptance and will soon be removed from the label of perverse psychological dysfunction in favor of a valid and accepted sexual orientation. The same winds that blew in the direction for acceptance of LGBTQ+ normalization will soon make room to include acceptance and validation of pedophilia as a valid sexual orientation. The same winds that blow for an imagined utopia, blow just as strongly in the pursuit of sex and gender as ultimate identity. Such pursuits are, in reality, dystopian and, at their core, dissatisfying.[52] This is why the moral envelope is continuing to be pressured leftward.

Not all parents will accept this normalization, especially when it comes to exposing children to its more radical side, usually through the avenue of graphic sex education programs. This is a major reason why some schools keep the parents away from knowing about people that are invited to their children's campuses.

Students across the nation are being exposed to a radical sex and gender revolution and it is happening right in the schools they attend. It is happening directly in some of the classrooms. Some radical LGBTQ+ teachers are lobbying for pedophiles to be referred to as minor attracted persons (MAPS),[53] even as some of the more conservative members of the sex and gender acronym fight against what they view as unfair association with pedophiles.[54] Samuel Blumenfeld explains a bit more in detail:

Before the widespread implementation of "sex ed" in government schools, people somehow managed to fall in love, get married, and have families. Countless Americans lived happily ever after; some did not. So how did humanity manage to deal with sex before it became a subject to be taught to children at school? Simple: religious and cultural institutions, as well as parents, generally dealt with such matters—all of which have been shoved aside as the state increasingly seeks to usurp their roles. It is true that there has always been some titillating secrecy on the subject. However, adherents to biblical religion understood that premarital sex, also known as fornication, is a sin. Obviously, it was not a perfect world, but neither is the current sex-saturated environment in which high school students openly complain that their schools are not doing enough to protect them from the consequences of their own immoral and depraved behavior.[55]

The bottom line then, is that "sex education as presently taught in the schools contributes to the delinquency of minors. Thus, it's a crime."[56]

The last stronghold for childhood innocence is the family. Radicals are chipping away at family authority. Even corporations like Disney,[57] and others, were discovered promoting non-traditional norms and producing anti-family offerings. But families are fighting back against what they perceive as grooming of their children.[58]

What were once marginalized groups are now normalized radical voices chirping away at the moral framework that helped to define America at her beginning and was a focal point of national pride. Pride in a nation has shifted to pride in radical sexual and gender expressions, as well as in race radicalism. Consider the normalized actions below that are tell-tale descriptors of radicalization of American culture:

- ivory tower professors in non-science academics dictating science
- leftward lurching toward DEI, sensitivity training, whiteness deconstruction
- selection of one's own gender and pronouns
- grooming of students as sexual objects
- exposing young children to urban sexual language and imagery of adult sexual practices

A good two-part test to apply to any questionable voices online, or in person, is to *first* determine whether radicalism has taken hold of a group and if there is evidence that the group is in sync with the thoughts and feelings about a topic or issue. *Second*, when in touch with any member, or members of a group, ask whether the individuals and the group are open to having their ideology and practices questioned and openly critiqued by dissenters. This test, when applied to most professors' classes in college, or other radicals with

power, demonstrates the extent of radicalization and the depth of indoctrination. It also calls out the façade of any tolerance mantra.

COMBATTING STUDENT RADICALIZATION

The facts are quite clear that each generation is different and the nation is
more divided today along social and moral lines. Students are right in the
middle of this generational and culture divide. The gateway of Gen Z's moral
filters and behavioral guardrails are stuck in open mode.

As mentioned earlier in the chapter, students today come across as easier to
seduce psychologically and emotionally. They are emotionally vulnerable to
being led astray and to feeling things they deem as right are because of emotional sensations and validations from influencers, both online and in person.
Sometimes these influencers take things too far. As an example, a growing
number of students seem to be having sex with teachers who are just a few
years older than them.

On that note, the sexual abuse problem at colleges became so bad a few
years back, that institutions began implementing policies forbidding professors from having sexual relations, or even emotional relationships, with their
students. Ironically, some states dropped their restrictions on teachers having
sexual relationships with students, if the students were eighteen or older.[59]
The slippage began by advocates of relationships between teachers/professors
and their students.

When it comes to teenagers in high schools and young adults in colleges,
there are some things that are recommended by the National Education
Association (NEA) to help with preventing student radicalization.[60] However,
what the NEA omits is that leftist ideology itself is indoctrination, as its
worldview is dispensed from the front of classrooms every day by teachers
sold out to the gender, sex, and race ideologies that are prominent within
the radically progressive worldview. As long as the NEA is in bed with the
leftists and beholden to one political party, their objectivity will continue to
be skewed.

Can Radicalism Be Resisted?

As mentioned above, the NEA has recommended several strategies to guard
against student radicalization. However, their overall concern is about those
who may have interest in right-wing extremism.[61] There are three strategies
offered by the NEA that follow below. *First*, adults understand that young
people have a desperate need to be loved, liked, admired, and acknowledged;
therefore, the NEA maintains, "US teens and young people may turn to

extremist groups when they feel excluded or deprived, or when they lack a sense of belonging and purpose."[62] *Second*, adults should definitely monitor their children's social media and internet use. The NEA admits that far too often "the process of radicalization happens online in mainstream sites like YouTube and TikTok, where teens spend hours every day."[63] *Third*, according to the NEA, if educators are serious about preventing student radicalization, they "need to understand why teenagers go in that direction, and how to use their classrooms to build resiliency to hate and empathy and critical thinking skills."[64]

There should be a fourth statement in the prevention of student radicalization. That is about the roles teachers play in indoctrinating students, advancing personal interests in radical ideas, and sharing these with their students. No teacher should ever use their classroom privilege as a platform for ploying for affirmation from students. School is not the place (1) to disguise personal advocacy as civic activity, (2) to use a captive audience for instructor catharsis, (3) to insert race or gender exclusivity, or (4) for teachers to bypass parent knowledge about accepting and using student alternate pronoun use.

The NEA has built the assumption that radicalization comes primarily from the right and that battling it in schools is progress, not its own form of radicalization. The true threat identified by the NEA, and the current Biden administration through the Department of Justice, appears to be from those questioning what schools are teaching children.

Recently, parents were investigated and placed on lists and it was alleged that rowdy parents were labeled as possible domestic terrorists for voicing their disapproval of what they saw as blatant indoctrination of their children against the values they held dear.[65] During the 2021 gubernatorial election in Virginia, parents who heard statements like those from former Virginia governor Terry McAuliffe, became acutely aware of the progressive game plan for the control over their children's education.

During his failed 2021 campaign to recapture the governor's office, progressive Democrat McAuliffe stated in a debate, "I'm not going to let parents come into schools and actually take books out and make their own decisions . . . I don't think parents should be telling schools what they should teach."[66] The progressive game plan to indoctrinate children had been exposed for all to hear.

In an interview after the debate with then Virginia Republican candidate for governor, Glenn Youngkin, McAuliffe reiterated, "You don't want parents coming in in every different school jurisdiction saying, 'This is what should be taught here' and, 'This is what should be taught here.'"[67]

Avoiding some of the radicalization that currently takes place in America's schools could be dealt with by electing officials who do not share the same radical ideology or secular worldview as those in power. Parents must continue speaking up and exposing the true nature of some of the radical positions of those in power, as a means of resisting radicalization on behalf of their children

PREDICTABLE OUTCOMES FOR GEN Z

Radical ideologies lead to some predictable outcomes. What follows are several predictable outcomes that coincide with Gen Z's exposure to radical ideas.[68] *First*, there is a general zombie-like lack of interest in truth, and along with that there is a confused sense of moral direction. This usually occurs when students are taught to feel their way through experiences rather than use reason and logic.[69]

Some researchers tie this to the fact that Gen Z are the first to truly focus on social-emotional learning. Thinking with one's emotions is to rely on feelings as one's guide. Gen Z displays quite radical emotions when there are misuses of gender pronouns,[70] and they are easily triggered by their indoctrination over microaggressions and red baseball caps that contain Trump slogans.

Second, Gen Z has become attached to another group as a larger therapy generation, the millennials, and some from both generations are out in the workforce while others remain in school. Some from Gen Z are having difficulty adjusting to the pressures of the workplace, so they have set about demanding their recognition of ideologies, and some refuse to accept employment without established DEIO offices upon which to rely and to report microaggressions.[71]

Third, the axiom is true that what students learn by emotions they internalize. A distinct characteristic of Gen Z, aside from their training in activism in social science classes, is that they were taught woke-ness ideology by a smattering of millennials as their mentors. This is primarily observed in college humanities departments, where all sorts of ideological majors have garnered academic interest over the past several years.

The shift in K–12 schooling has resulted in attempts to shatter so many of the values that have previously characterized what it meant to be American and what a true education entails. Favoring more radical actions over peaceful protests, for example, will only lead to more radicalization over exercises of rights. This realization has led to the formation and burgeoning success of "classical Christian" schools.[72]

In the recent past, many students were proud to be Americans and demonstrated this by their civic actions. The new reality is that identifying as an American usually brings with it accusations of racism and microaggressions pinned to a reputation of dangerous white supremacy and nationalism. The contrast could not be any clearer.

Gen Z Characteristics

Observe the following characteristics that describe and define Gen Z today:

- Gen Z has walked away from the faith they owned while young children, or teenagers.
- Their beliefs in God and absolutes have tanked, which is why, coming out of college, they view the world subjectively and fluidly.
- There is confusion over who and what they are, to the extent they have acquiesced to a system that provides answers that do not comport with traditional science and biology.
- They are more impressed with grievances and canceling people than they are about solutions.[73]
- They do not know the history, conditions, and qualifications associated with socialism.
- Gen Z are inclined to participate in capitalism, while badmouthing the capitalists that provide goods and services to them. For example, computers, the internet, automobiles, college privilege, and zip codes apply to Gen Z. Radicals also possess and utilize smart technology devices.
- When asked if they would give up their material goods, Gen Z would decline—while pointing to excesses in which many others participate.
- Gen Z has no problem with breaking from traditional marriage and living together, as well as having children out of wedlock.
- They enjoy complaining about racial issues and that some form of white racism is systemic and discriminatory; they claim these things while participating in those systems for personal gain.
- The popular cult of woke-ness ideology and its outreach organization, BLM, have a stronghold on many in Gen Z.
- Some in Gen Z are breaking free of their indoctrination and are questioning whether woke fanaticism has peaked.[74]

The Bodily Experiments and Outcomes

Child abuse, chemical castration, and genital mutilation are escalating among Gen Z. More and more children's hospitals are signing on to this money-making venture, under the moniker of gender affirming care.[75] At the same time, more and more of them are scrubbing any mention of the controversial procedures from their websites.[76] The slippage of morality over the years has contributed to the mainstreaming of a practice that removes children's sex organs with impunity and for a profit. This occurs knowing that chemical castration and puberty blockers have serious side effects and that the long-term effects are unknown. Gen Z are the modern experimental creatures on behalf of psychology and sociology.

The fields of psychology and sociology have invaded education to the point where education as a discipline is taking a back seat to ideologies that have little-to-no basis in science. Even brain research has been tainted by ideology, and that which clearly demonstrates the differences between boys and girls is now interpreted through the lens of radical ideologies resulting in life-altering experiments.

So as to complicate matters, physicians and parents are now described as mere "guessers" as to the gender and sex of a baby, because gender is regarded as an expression, even if the sex organs remain intact. In other words, a guess is overridden by feelings about their identity. These feelings are required to be accepted as fact, even in the face of biology and science. They are accepted, that is, until a person decides to change their identity a second or third time, becoming new all over again. The time will come when a very high percentage of transgendered individuals will de-transition back to their birth gender.[77] The only question at this juncture will be, "What then?"

ALINSKY'S RADICAL APPEAL TO GEN Z

Saul Alinsky acknowledges Lucifer, the original radical and rebel, as he writes:

"Lest we forget at least an over-the-shoulder acknowledgment to the very first radical: from all our legends, mythology, and history (and who is to know where mythology leaves off and history begins—or which is which), the first radical known to man who rebelled against the establishment and did it so effectively that he at least won his own kingdom—Lucifer."[78]

Alinsky's twisted attribution to Lucifer is an indication of the radical's ethic: the ends justify the means. The application of this in society-in-general is best demonstrated in athletics and politics, or as Alinsky refers to these: the establishment. Cheating and cutting corners are sometimes celebrated if a person advances his cause without getting caught.

Alinsky's words of exhortation and challenge seem to resonate across the decades and are highly relevant for Gen Z. As if privy to knowledge about Gen Z, he pronounces "What the present generation wants is what all genera-tions have always wanted—a meaning, a sense of what the world and life are—a chance to strive for some sort of order."[79]

In order to achieve this order, Alinsky takes his followers on a bizarre jour-ney into his belief system. In the following tables below are segments of (4.1) the radicals' instructions and doctrines, (4.2) radicals' rules of ethics of means and ends, (4.3) radicals' tactics for radical organizers, and (4.4) radicals' rules for the radical organizers.

In an effort to come across with an ethical foundation for his radicalism, Alinsky shares his rules of ethics as some sort of guide to his approach. These are based on the premises that there exists a common "series of rules pertaining to the ethics of means and ends: first, that one's concern with the ethics of means and ends varies inversely with one's personal interest in the issue."[80] The following is an abridged, selected list of Alinsky's rules of ethics of means and ends that remains quite pervasive across American society.[81]

The first realization an organizer of radicals must consider is that "the power of the human mind can also devise philosophies and ways of life that are most destructive for the future of mankind. Either way, power is the

Table 4.1. Radical Instructions and Doctrine*

Instructions	*Doctrines*
Revolution, not Revelation	"Remember we are talking about revolution, not revelation. . . . First, there are no rules for revolution any more than there are rules for love or rules for happiness, but there are rules for radicals who want to change their world."
Work Inside the System	"The present generation wants to go right into the third act, skipping the first two, in which case there is no play, nothing but confrontation for confrontation's sake—a flare-up and back to darkness. To build a powerful organization takes time. . . . What is the alternative to working 'inside' the system? A mess of rhetorical garbage about 'burn the system down.'"
Reform before Revolt	"Revolution must be preceded by reformation. To assume that a political revolution can survive without the supporting base of a people of a popular reformation is to ask for the impossible in politics. A revolution without a prior reformation would collapse or become a totalitarian tyranny."
Understand the Way Things Are	"The basic requirement for understanding of politics of change is to recognize the world as it is."
Common Good is Really Common Greed	"In this world laws are written for the lofty aim of the 'common good' and then acted out in life on the basis of the common greed."
Angles Are Not Angels	"It is a world not of angels but of angles, where men speak of moral principles but act of power principles . . . organized religion is materially solvent and spiritually bankrupt."
Movement and Friction	"Change means movement. Movement means friction."
Use of Unethical Means	"The most unethical of all means is the non-use of any means."

*Excerpts from Saul Alinsky. *Rules for radicals.* 1971. New York: Random House, Inc., pp. xviii, xx, xxi, xxii, 12–14, 21, 26.

Table 4.2. Radical Rules of Ethics of Means and Ends*

The second rule of the ethics of means and ends is:	"that the judgment of the ethics of means and ends is the political position of those sitting in judgment."
The third rule of the ethics of means and ends is:	"that in war the end justifies the means."
The sixth rule of the ethics of means and ends is:	"that the less important the end to be desired, the more one can afford to engage in ethical evaluations of means."
The eighth rule of the ethics of means and ends is:	"that the morality of a means depends upon whether the means is being employed at a time of imminent defeat or imminent victory."
The ninth rule of the ethics of means and ends is:	"that any effective means is automatically judged by the opposition as being unethical."
The tenth rule of the ethics of means and ends is:	"that you do what you can with what you have and clothe it in moral garments."
The eleventh rule of the ethics of means and ends is:	"that goals must be phrased in general terms like, 'Liberty, Equality, Fraternity,' 'Of the Common Welfare,' 'Pursuit of Happiness,' or 'Bread and Peace.'"

*Excerpts from Alinsky. *Rules for radicals*, pp. 26, 29, 34–36, 45.

dynamo of life."[82] Radicals must use power effectively to accomplish their goals—and to do so, at times, by any means necessary.

Community organizers and organizers of radicals are encouraged to follow Alinsky's radical tactics and follow his radical rules, in order to achieve maximum benefit from his experience in group dynamics. These rules are what both Presidents Obama and Biden utilized in stirring up their political base, while running for president and while in office. These tactics (see tables 4.3 and 4.4) and rules can be used for and against any group that fashions itself empowered toward a cause.

Alinsky adds the following caveat as clarification. When radical organizers focus on a target, after "this focus comes a polarization . . . all issues must be polarized if action is to follow. The classic statement on polarization comes from Christ: 'He that is not with me is against me' (Luke 11:23). He allowed no middle ground to the money changers in the Temple."[83]

Alinsky reminds his followers about the ultimate rule in developing the appearance of hypocrisy as a tactic to diminish opposition. He quips, "No organization, including organized religion, can live up to the letter of its own book. You can club them to death with their 'book' of rules and regulations. This is what the great revolutionary Paul of Tarsus knew when he wrote to the Corinthians: 'Who also hath made us able ministers of the New Testament; not of the letter, but of the spirit, for the letter killeth.'"[84] Radicals are also good at misreading Scripture to support their indoctrination.

Table 4.3. Radical Tactics of Radical Organizers*

Tactic of Disorganization	Tactic of Dissatisfaction	Tactic of Development
"All change means disorganization of the old and organization of the new."	"An organizer must stir up dissatisfaction and discontent; provide a channel into which the people can angrily pour their frustrations."	"The job then is getting the people to move, to act, to participate; in short, to develop and harness the necessary power to effectively conflict with the prevailing patterns and change them."

* Excerpts from Alinsky. *Rules for radicals*, pp. 116–117.

Table 4.4. Radical Rules for Radical Organizers*

The Fourth and Fifth Radical Rules	"The fourth rule is: Make the enemy live up to their own book of rules. You can kill them with this, for they can no more obey their own rules than the Christian church can live up to Christianity. The fourth rule carries within it the fifth rule: Ridicule is man's most potent weapon. It is almost impossible to counterattack ridicule. It also infuriates the opposition, who then react to your advantage."
The Eighth Radical Rule	"Keep the pressure on, with different tactics, actions, and utilize all events of the period for your purpose."
The Ninth Radical Rule	"The threat is usually more terrifying than the thing itself."
The Twelfth Radical Rule	"The price of a successful attack is a constructive alternative. You cannot risk being trapped by the enemy in his sudden agreement with your demand and saying 'You're right—we don't know what to do about this issue. Now you tell us.'"
The Thirteenth Radical Rule	"Pick the target, freeze it, personalize it, and polarize it . . . the problem that threatens to loom more and more is that of identifying the enemy. Obviously there is no point to tactics unless one has a target upon which to center the attacks."

*Excerpts from Alinsky. *Rules for radicals*, pp. 128–131.

Author Jeremy S. Adams addresses Gen Zs in his book *Hollowed Out*: "We assume many of our students are broken and thus completely incapable of filling in what our society and their background has hollowed out. This belief—this scourge of low expectation, moral complacency, and an utter failure to appreciate and pass on what a . . . well-rounded liberal education really is—is why we have hollowed out schools."[85]

In the hollow of their souls there is hope—the hope of maturity and rejection of ideologies based on erroneous theories. There is hope in the rejection of medical procedures that solve absolutely nothing in the lives of the confused. Squarely in the middle of these hopes is the baggage that is accumulating and the wreckage of souls unfulfilled.

It remains ever-so-important for Gen Z to understand their vulnerabilities and to be discouraged from transitioning into divisive radicalism. This discouragement must take place with love and concern before an ultimate decision is made by them, which then makes any notion of de-transitioning impossible.

NOTES

1. Saul Alinsky. *Rules for radicals*. 1971. New York: Random House, p. 5.

2. Kim Parker and Ruth Igielnik. "On the cusp of adulthood and facing an uncertain future: What we know about Gen Z so far." Pew Research Center. May 14, 2020. Retrieved November 1, 2022, from https://www.pewresearch.org/social-trends/2020/05/14/on-the-cusp-of-adulthood-and-facing-an-uncertain-future-what-we-know-about-gen-z-so-far-2/.

3. Calla Walsh. "The democratic socialists of America can mobilize Gen Z'ers like me." *Teen Vogue*. August 5, 2021. Retrieved November 3, 2022, from https://www.teenvogue.com/story/democratic-socialists-of-america-gen-z.

4. Andrew Deichler. "Though socially conscious, Generation Z remains practical." Society for Human Resource Management. July 16, 2021. Retrieved November 3, 2022, from https://www.shrm.org/resourcesandtools/hr-topics/behavioral-competencies/global-and-cultural-effectiveness/pages/though-socially-conscious-generation-z-remains-practical.aspx.

5. Rebekah Cohen Morris. "Teachers feel afraid to speak up." *Georgian Educator*. December 6, 2015. Retrieved November 1, 2022, from https://georgianeducator.org/2015/12/06/teachers-feel-afraid-to-speak-up/.

6. Florene Earle Ledger. "Gen Z: Proudly the most sensitive generation." *Luxiders Magazine*. 2022. Retrieved October 31, 2022, from https://luxiders.com/gen-z-the-most-sensitive-generation-2/.

7. Joe Gillespie. "The fame trap: Gen Z, TikTok and the influencer culture." *Areo*. April 22, 2022. Retrieved October 5, 2022, from https://areomagazine.com/2022/04/22/the-fame-trap-gen-z-tiktok-and-influencer-culture/.

8. Luke Gentile. "Brainwashed: Young conservatives say leftist indoctrination is crippling their generation." *The Washington Examiner*. March 1, 2022. Retrieved November 1, 2022, from https://www.washingtonexaminer.com/restoring-america/faith-freedom-self-reliance/brainwashed-young-conservatives-say-leftist-indoctrination-is-crippling-their-generation.

9. John Patrick Leary. "Activism isn't a coherent ideology." *The New Republic*. November 26, 2021. Retrieved June 16, 2022, from https://newrepublic.com/article/164412/activism-isnt-coherent-ideology.

10. Paul Mason. "How the covid shock has radicalized Generation Z." *The Guardian.* June 2, 2021. Retrieved September 4, 2022, from https://www.theguardian.com/world/2021/jun/02/how-the-covid-shock-has-radicalised-generation-z.

11. Nicole Neily. "Toxic ideologies are spreading in our schools." *Parents Defending Education Newsletter.* August 31, 2022. Retrieved September 4, 2022, from https://www.DefendingEd.org. Cf. Ernest J. Zarra, III. *Detoxing American schools.* 2020. Lanham, MD: Rowman & Littlefield Publishers.

12. Brian Mountford. "Why is Generation Z leaving the church?" *Premier Christianity.* July 26, 2022. Retrieved October 4, 2022, from https://www.premierchristianity.com/opinion/why-is-generation-z-leaving-the-church/13492.article.

13. Kristy Bleizeffer. "Survey: Most college students believe political views influenced by professors." Poets & Quants for Undergrads. September 6, 2022. Retrieved September 8, 2022 from https://poetsandquantsforundergrads.com/news/survey-most-college-students-believe-political-views-influenced-by-professors/.

14. Dana Kennedy. "Mount Holyoke grad deprogrammed from women-only woke culture." *New York Post.* November 26, 2022. Retrieved November 27, 2022, from https://nypost.com/2022/11/26/mount-holyoke-grad-deprogrammed-from-women-only-woke-culture/?fbclid=IwAR29kSODTLek_e9-WwO8QN_-l-lQXM-c5LE7b59UnAtBbgtOoJIQP3EqOXk.

15. Ibid.

16. Michael Torres. "Parents must stop letting woke colleges indoctrinate their children (opinion)." *Newsweek.* July 19, 2020. Retrieved August 18, 2022, from https://www.newsweek.com/parents-must-stop-letting-woke-colleges-indoctrinate-their-children-opinion-1518780.

17. Paul Bond. "Nearly 40 percent of US Gen Zs, 30 percent of young Christians identify as LGBTQ, poll shows." *Newsweek.* October 20, 2021. Retrieved November 25, 2022, from https://www.newsweek.com/nearly-40-percent-us-gen-zs-30-percent-christians-identify-lgbtq-poll-shows-1641085.

18. Sarah Pulliam Bailey. "Church membership in the US has fallen below the majority for the first time in nearly a century." *Washington Post.* March 29, 2021. Retrieved May 3, 2022, from https://www.washingtonpost.com/religion/2021/03/29/church-membership-fallen-below-majority/. Cf. Dale Hudson. "Why Generation Z's distorted view of God matters." *Church Plants.* December 27, 2021. Retrieved November 25, 2022, from https://churchplants.com/articles/13840-generation-zs-distorted-view-god-matters-dale-hudson.html.

19. Samuel Blumenfeld and Alex Newman. *Crimes of the educators: How utopians are using government schools to destroy America's children.* 2021. Nashville, TN: Post Hill Press, p. 157.

20. Alinsky. *Rules for radicals,* p. 185.

21. Ashley Stahl. "How Gen-Z is bringing a fresh perspective to the world of work." *Forbes.* May 4, 2021. Retrieved June 16, 2022, from https://www.forbes.com/sites/ashleystahl/2021/05/04/how-gen-z-is-bringing-a-fresh-perspective-to-the-world-of-work/?sh=3bb7eae210c2.

22. Tanu Biswas. "Letting Teach: Gen Z as socio-political educators in an over-heated world." *Frontiers in Political Science*. April 28, 2021. Retrieved June 16, 2022, from https://www.frontiersin.org/articles/10.3389/fpos.2021.641609/full.

23. Hannah Grossman. "Texas teacher bragging about indoctrinating the youth interviews middle school kids on non-binary identity." Fox News. November 25, 2022. Retrieved November 26, 2022, from https://www.foxnews.com/media/texas-teacher-bragging-indoctrinating-youth-interrogates-middle-school-kids-nonbinary-identity. Cf. Hannah Grossman. "New Jersey teacher interviews 4th graders on they/them pronouns on TikTok: Indoctrinating my students." October 10, 2022. Fox News. Retrieved November 26, 2022, from https://www.foxnews.com/media/new-jersey-teacher-interviews-4th-graders-they-them-pronouns-tiktok-indoctrinating-students.

24. Ryan Andrew Brown, Todd C. Helmus, Rajeev Ramchand et. al. "Violent extremism in America: Interviews with former extremists and their families on radicalization and deradicalization." 2021. RAND Corporation. Retrieved September 12, 2022, from https://www.rand.org/pubs/research_briefs/RBA1071-1.html.

25. Ibid.

26. Ibid.

27. Andrea Peyser. "Parents and the left are in an all-out war, and the kids are collateral damage." *New York Post*. October 31, 2022. Retrieved November 1, 2022, from https://nypost.com/2022/08/21/collateral-damage-in-war-on-parents-kids-caught-in-the-middle/.

28. Julia Dandoy. "Parents are going on the offensive to fight indoctrination in education." Intellectual Takeout. May 2, 2022. Retrieved October 31, 2022, from https://intellectualtakeout.org/2022/05/parents-are-going-on-the-offensive-to-fight-indoctrination-in-education/. Cf. Adrianna Kezar. "Consequences of radical change in governance: A grounded theory approach." *The Journal of Higher Education*. November–December 2005. 76(6): pp. 634–668. Retrieved October 17, 2022, from https://www.jstor.org/stable/3838781.

29. Brian O'Leary. "Backgrounds and beliefs of college freshmen." *The Chronicle of Higher Education*. August 12, 2020. Retrieved October 31, 2022, from https://www.chronicle.com/article/backgrounds-and-beliefs-of-college-freshmen/.

30. Bonnie Kerrigan Snyder. *Undoctrinate: How politicized classrooms harm kids and ruin our schools—and what we can do about it*. 2021. Nashville, TN: Post Hill Press, p. 115.

31. Ibid., p. 119.

32. Ibid., p. 26.

33. BBC Newsnight. "Detransitioning: Reversing a gender transition." British Broadcasting Corporation. Posted November 26, 2019. YouTube video. 2020. Retrieved October 31, 2022, from https://www.youtube.com/watch?v=fDi-jFVBLA8.

34. Staff. "Gender ideology 101." *Parents Defending Education*. 2022. Retrieved September 5, 2022, from https://defendinged.org/resources/gender-ideology-101/.

35. Women's Liberation Radio News. "The indoctrination of children into gender ideology." Edition 74. Posted on June 5, 2022. YouTube video. 2022. Retrieved October 21, 2022, from https://www.youtube.com/watch?v=YC1YVQQQqwU.

36. Thomas Koenig. "Tribalism is anti-American." *National Review*. July 24, 2021. Retrieved August 2, 2022, from https://www.nationalreview.com/2021/07/tribalism -is-anti-american/.

37. Farah Pandith. "Teen terrorism inspired by social media is on the rise. Here's what we need to do." *THINK*. March 22, 2021. Retrieved May 9. 2022, from https: //www.nbcnews.com/think/opinion/teen-terrorism-inspired-social-media-rise-here-s -what-we-ncna1261307.

38. David Brooks. "The nuclear family was a mistake." *The Atlantic*. March 2020. Retrieved August 8, 2022, from https://www.theatlantic.com/magazine/archive/2020 /03/the-nuclear-family-was-a-mistake/605536/.

39. Julie Compton. "Trans dads tell doctors: 'You can be a man and have a baby.'" NBC News. May 18, 2019. Retrieved June 14, 2022, from https://www.nbcnews.com /feature/nbc-out/trans-dads-tell-doctors-you-can-be-man-have-baby-n1006906.

40. Snyder. *Undoctrinate, p.* 63.

41. Christopher Rufo. "The child soldiers of Portland." *City Journal*. Spring 2021. Retrieved June 2, 2022, from https://www.city-journal.org/critical-race-theory -portland-public-schools.

42. Bob Bland. *The little book of little activists*. 2017. New York: Viking Press. Cf. Robin Stevenson. *Kid Activists: True champions of childhood from champions of change*. 2019. Philadelphia, PA: Quick Books.

43. Ernest J. Zarra III. *When the secular becomes sacred: Religious secular humanism and its effects upon America's public learning institutions*. 2021. Lanham, MD: Rowman & Littlefield Publishers.

44. Stephen Sawchuk. "What is critical race theory, and why is it under attack." *EdWeek*. May 18, 2021, p. 6. Retrieved May 20, 2021, from https://www.edweek.org /leadership/what-is-critical-race-theory-and-why-is-it-under-attack/2021/05.

45. Snyder. *Undoctrinate*, p. 20.

46. Adam Sabes. "Harvard University student newspaper survey of graduates finds very few lean conservative." Fox News. May 29, 2022. Retrieved Amy 20, 2022 from https://www.foxnews.com/us/harvard-university-student-newspaper-survey -graduates-finds-results.

47. Sawchuk. "What is critical race theory," p. 7.

48. Ibid.

49. Snyder. *Undoctrinate*, p. 25.

50. Staff. "Grooming: Know the warning signs." Rape, Abuse, and Incest National Network (RAINN). July 10, 2020. Retrieved May 30, 2022, from https://www.rainn .org/news/grooming-know-warning-signs.

51. Adam Jowett. "The gay community should stop attacking anyone who dares suggest sexuality is a choice." *The Conversation*. July 17, 2014. Retrieved November 27, 2022, from https://theconversation.com/the-gay-community-should-stop -attacking-anyone-who-dares-suggest-sexuality-is-a-choice-29297.

52. Staff. "Body image, sexual orientation and gender identity." Mental Health Foundation. 2022. Retrieved November 27, 2022, from https://www.mentalhealth.org .uk/our-work/research/body-image-how-we-think-and-feel-about-our-bodies/body -image-sexual-orientation-and-gender-identity.

53. Steve Brown. "Paedophiles want to be accepted by the LGBT community claiming they are minorities." *Attitude*. July 11, 2018. Retrieved October 7, 2022, from https://www.attitude.co.uk/news/world/paedophiles-want-to-be-accepted-by -the-lgbt-community-claiming-they-are-minorities-296424/.

54. Melissa Block. "Accusations of grooming are the latest political attack— with homophobic origins." NPR. May 11, 2022. Retrieved October 12, 2022, from https://www.npr.org/2022/05/11/1096623939/accusations-grooming-political-attack -homophobic-origins. Cf. Staff. "Gays against groomers." Instagram. Retrieved November 18, 2022, from https://www.instagram.com/gaysagainstgroomers/?hl=en.

55. Blumenfeld and Newman. *Crimes of the educators*, p. 139.

56. Ibid., p. 141.

57. Aimee Hart. "All of the LGBTQ inclusive things coming to Disney Plus in August 2022." *Gayming Magazine*. August 5, 2022. Retrieved October 21, 2022, from https://gaymingmag.com/2022/08/all-of-the-lgbtq-inclusive-things-coming-to -disney-plus-in-august-2022/.

58. Daniel Deme. "Disney embraces woke political activism designed to destroy families." *ReMix*. April 6, 2022. Retrieved June 16, 2022, from https://rmx.news/ united-states/disney-embraces-woke-political-activism-designed-to-destroy-families /.

59. Ernest J. Zarra III. *America's sex culture: Its impact on teacher-student relationships today*. 2020. Lanham, MD: Rowman & Littlefield Publishers. Cf. Ernest J. Zarra III. *Teacher-student relationships: Crossing into the emotional, physical, and sexual realms*. 2013. Lanham, MD: Rowman & Littlefield Publishers.

60. Mary Ellen Flannery. "Is QAnon radicalizing your school board?" *NEA Today*. June 6, 2021. Retrieved November 12, 2022, from https://www.nea.org/advocating -for-change/new-from-nea/qanon-radicalizing-your-school-board.

61. Ibid.

62. Ibid.

63. Mary Ellen Flannery. "How educators can prevent student radicalization." *NEAToday*. July 6, 2021. Retrieved September 4, 2022, from https://www .nea.org/advocating-for-change/new-from-nea/how-educators-can-prevent-student -radicalization.

64. Ibid.

65. Senator Charles Grassley. "Judiciary Republicans to Garland: Are concerned parents domestic terrorists or not?" US Senate Judiciary Committee. December 6, 2021. Retrieved September 5, 2022, from https://www.grassley.senate.gov/news /news-releases/judiciary-republicans-to-garland-are-concerned-parents-domestic -terrorists-or-not.

66. Staff. "Terry McAuliffe's war on parents." *National Review*. October 1, 2021. Retrieved September 22, 2022, from https://www.nationalreview.com/2021/10/terry -mcauliffes-war-on-parents/. Cf. Brittany Bernstein. "McAuliffe argues parents shouldn't have control over public school curriculum." *National Review*. September 29, 2021. Retrieved May 24, 2022, from https://www.nationalreview.com/news/ mcauliffe-argues-parents-shouldnt-have-control-over-public-school-curriculum/.

67. Staff. "Terry McAuliffe's war on parents."

68. Laura Meckler. "In social-emotional learning, right sees more critical race theory." *Washington Post*. March 28, 2022. Retrieved November 2, 2022, from https://www.washingtonpost.com/education/2022/03/28/social-emotional-learning-critical -race-theory/.

69. Todd Farley. "Gen Z is made of zombies—less educated, more depressed, without values." *New York Post*. August 21, 2021. Retrieved November 2, 2022, from https://nypost.com/2021/08/21/gen-z-students-are-less-educated-more-depressed-and -lack-values/. Cf. Jeremy S. Adams. *Hollowed out: A warning about America's next generation*. 2021. Washington, DC: Regnery Publishing.

70. Chan Tov McNamarah. "Misgendering." *California Law Review*. 109(6): n.p. September 2021. Retrieved November 3, 2022, from https://www.californialawreview .org/print/misgendering/.

71. Jennifer Miller. "For young job seekers, diversity and inclusion in the work-place aren't a preference. They're a requirement." *Washington Post*. February 18, 2021. Retrieved October 19, 2022, from https://www.washingtonpost.com/business /2021/02/18/millennial-genz-workplace-diversity-equity-inclusion/.

72. "Classical Christian Schools." https://classicalchristian.org/.

73. Avani Raj. "All about Gen Z and their toxic culture." *EdTimes*. June 13, 2021. Retrieved June 2, 2022, from https://edtimes.in/all-about-gen-z-and-their-toxic -cancel-culture/.

74. Daniel Roman. "Has the woke wave peaked? Show poll reveals Generation Z rejects cancel culture." Association of Mature American Citizens. August 19, 2021. Retrieved June 5, 2022, from https://amac.us/has-the-woke-wave-peaked-shock-poll -reveals-generation-z-rejects-cancel-culture/.

75. Tamara Bannow. "Harassment prompts children's hospitals to strip websites, threatening access to gender-affirming care." *STAT*. October 3, 2022. Retrieved, October 21, 2022, from https://www.statnews.com/2022/10/03/childrens-hospitals-strip -websites-gender-affirming-care/.

76. Ibid.

77. Rikki Schlott. "I literally lost organs: Why detransitioned teens regret changing genders." *New York Post*. June 18, 2022. Retrieved November 1, 2022, from https://nypost.com/2022/06/18/detransitioned-teens-explain-why-they-regret-changing -genders/.

78. Alinsky. *Rules for radicals*, p. ix.

79. Ibid., p. xvii.

80. Ibid., p. 26.

81. Al Fuller. "Left wing morality, part II: The ends justifies the means." *The Other Half of History*. August 22, 2010. Retrieved November 2, 2022, from https://historyhalf.com/liberal-morality-part-ii-the-end-justifies-the-means/.

82. Alinsky. *Rules for radicals*, pp. 52–53.

83. Ibid., pp. 133–134.

84. Ibid., p. 152.

85. Adams. *Hollowed out*, p. 71.

Chapter 5

Top-Down Radicalism

Is it any wonder that socialist societies lose their economic vitality and creativity because the individual is negated in favor of the group?

— Samuel Blumenfeld and Alex Newman, *Crimes of the Educators*[1]

In short, the Communists everywhere support every revolutionary movement against the existing social and political order of things. . . . They openly declare that their ends can be attained only by this forcible overthrow of all existing social conditions.

— Karl Marx and Friedrich Engels, *The Communist Manifesto*[2]

When radicals gain power at the highest levels of government, either by vote or revolutionary coup, change happens quickly. What radicals promise the general population, in order to gain power, is short-lived. Soon after power is seized, they make claims of democracy and promises of protections for rights and freedom for all, and use social issues as ploys to gain support. However, as history demonstrates, these claims largely amount to propaganda, and the most gullible among the population are quick to act at a level equivalent to that of the propaganda they digest.

The propaganda that is set out from the highest of government levels is found to be in collusion with media and technology companies.[3] Recent revelations coinciding with the 2022 purchase of Twitter by Elon Musk[4] and congressional hearings with Mark Zuckerberg of Facebook[5] have demonstrated how radicalized large media platforms have become.

The radicals that gain governmental control make every effort to point to its opposition as the real problems with society. As a result, radical government entities engage in operations at any cost, in order to guarantee their retaining of power. Sometimes this is ensured by use of the legal system.

Other times fraudulent means are undertaken to thwart any attempts to unseat the radicals in power. Still, at other times, perceptions are crafted to cause disarray among the electorate.

In extreme cases, the radical government speaks of weapon confiscation, implying that oppositional forces want to ban certain books,[6] and selectively prosecuting oppositional groups, while allowing supportive groups leeway when committing similar questionable actions. Radical governments round up people who are branded as trouble to the regime and heavy-handedness toward citizens emerges as a new form of governmental enforcement.[7] This type of bullying by governments is a common tactic of political radicalism, and all of it comes down from the top levels.[8]

RADICALISM FROM THE TOP

Throughout the history of the world, including into the third century of the United States, governments have come and gone due to top-down heavy-handedness playing out in real time. Some would argue that under the Biden administration, radicalism is moving the United States in a frighteningly familiar historical direction.[9] For example, Matthew Continetti of the American Enterprise Institute wrote the following at the beginning of the Biden administration: "you see the outlines of an administration committed to the same technocratic principles and top-down, uniform, centralized style of governance as its Democratic precursor (Obama)."[10]

Extremes make good conversation in political science classes, where students can analyze pendulum swings. More often than not, one extreme seems to set off others, and then all sorts of political and cultural battles begin. The embattlements tend to originate from two entities. The first group represents those not in political power at the time. The second group represents those in power seeking to remain in power.

Radicalism Makes Its Mark

Radicalism made its mark in the United States from the nation's inception. The American War for Independence was viewed by England as a revolution. It was actually both. From the Southern Democrats who wanted to continue slavery, to the rebels who fought the abolitionist Northern Lincoln supporters, radicalism had divided our nation just seventy years after the formation of the United States.

Over time, groups like the Ku Klux Klan were formed in the South to enforce Jim Crow laws and to keep racial separation as part of American culture, as evidenced from the *Dred Scott v. Sanford* (1857) and *Plessy v.*

Ferguson (1896) Supreme Court cases. This changed with *Brown v. Board of Education of Topeka Kansas* (1955) case, when the Supreme Court ruled that separate was not equal and ordered courts to enforce desegregation.

American presidents like Woodrow Wilson, Franklin Delano Roosevelt, and Lyndon Johnson demonstrated racial animosity toward blacks. History is not kind to Wilson and his record on race issues. To many, Wilson was a racist. Even though Johnson signed civil rights acts and voting rights acts into law, Lyndon Johnson was allegedly a racist Democrat from the South. America has had its radicals, including Martin Luther King Jr. (1960s), whose work was cut short by an assassin's bullet in 1968. King blazed a peaceful civil rights trail, and his efforts still resonate in the twenty-first century. Malcolm X, the Black Panthers, and Louis Farrakhan took somewhat different approaches. During the tumultuous 1960s, radicalism was party to a family of concerns.

From Africa to Asia, and certainly in the Americas, wherever humans pursue and gain power, there is the strong desire to hold onto that power. Radicals, as we have read in earlier chapters, resort to self-fulfilling justification while practicing an *end justifies the means* ethic. Removal of such radicals from power results in massive upheavals of society and pits citizens against each other. This is the case in a constitutional republic, such as the United States, or even in nations with a life-long dictator. The former relies on elections, while the latter relies mostly on military or political coups.

Table 5.1 illustrates a sample of seven of the more infamous radicals of the past, their brief bios, years in power, and how their reigns ended. A comprehensive list of radicals is not possible within the space of this book. However, one commonality is that each leader that is listed had used schools to propagandize and indoctrinate students. Additional examples of this,[11] and ways to guard children from indoctrination, are found during the mid-twentieth century, as well as in more modern times in many other nations.[12] One example is during the Cold War with the former Soviet Union (USSR). Many children were indoctrinated in the United States and the USSR to be mindful that a nuclear attack could occur at any moment.

Although the characters below are extremists and notorious for their twentieth-century propaganda, their acts of radical terrorism and aggression against their own people are horrendous. Beneath the surface, these leaders suffered from narcissism and were members of the cult of personalities. In their thirst for power, each leader presented a populism, where messages contrary to the status quo consisted of promises for better lives for each nation's citizens. Given what humans are capable of, and the traits common to megalomaniacs lusting for power, the possibilities of past evils occurring in our day are actually quite frightening.

Table 5.1. Seven Infamous Radicals Who Became Political Leaders

Radical Leader	Brief Biographical Sketches	Years in Power	How Regime Ended
Vladimir Lenin	Marxist radical leader of the Bolsheviks that murdered Czar Nicholas and his family. Promised the Russian people "Peace, bread, and land."	1917 to 1924	Lenin died in 1924, at age 53, of a stroke.
Joseph Stalin	Named Josef Jughashvili at birth, the Georgian dictator of Soviet Union that led the nation from peasantry to military power, while purging millions of Russians. Known for the phrase: "Death is the solution to all problems. No man—no problem." Nicknamed Stalin, the Russian word for steel, as a result of his exploits in the Bolshevik Revolution.	1929 to 1953	Stalin died in 1953, at age 74, of a stroke.
Adolf Hitler	Chancellor/Fuhrer/dictator of Germany. Hitler's favorite term was the promise of *Arbeitsschlacht* (the end of unemployment). Convinced the German people with the propaganda that "The fruits of victory are tumbling into our mouths too quickly." Leader of the Nazi Party that directed and carried out propaganda campaigns in schools, and one of many responsible for the Jewish Holocaust.	1933 to 1945	Hitler died in 1945, at age 56, of a self-inflicted gunshot wound.
Benito Mussolini	Nicknamed "Il Duce" (The Leader). Founder of Fascism in Italy and is credited with the rise of fascism in other parts of the world. Famous propaganda slogan: "Everything in the state, nothing outside the state, nothing against the state." Mussolini believed society should organize itself based on a strong national identity, rather than according to class or social status.	1922 to 1943	Mussolini died in 1945, at age 61, by firing squad execution.
Mao Tse-tung	Radical cultural-revolution communist dictator of Red China. Chairman Mao's purpose was to develop and preserve communism by defeating capitalist and traditional Chinese living. There was a power struggle between Communist Maoists and Chinese cultural pragmatists. Propaganda was Mao's *Little Red Book*. While purging millions of Chinese, Mao claimed that: • to read too many books is harmful; • politics is war without bloodshed while war is politics with bloodshed; and • political power grows out of the barrel of a gun.	1949 to 1976	Mao died in 1976, at age 82, after a series of heart attacks.

Pol Pot	Cambodian revolutionary Saloth Sar was a dictator who transformed Cambodia into a one-party state, hoping it would evolve into a communist state. The dictator and his government killed nearly 2 million of its own citizens and forcibly relocated the majority of the nation's urban population to the countryside to work on collective farms. Later became leader of the Khmer Rouge and used the name Pol Pot, which means "original Cambodian." Pol Pot's propaganda statements included: • Exterminate the 50 million Vietnamese and purify the masses of the Cambodian people. • Better to kill an innocent by mistake than spare an enemy by mistake.	1975 to 1979	Pot died in 1998, at age 72, of heart failure while under arrest by a Khmer Rouge splinter group.
Fidel Castro	Cuban revolutionary and politician who was the prime minister of Cuba from 1959 to 1976, and served as president of Cuba from 1976 to 2008. Castro proclaimed himself to be a socialist and Marxist–Leninist seeking to develop a socialist economic system in which the means of production are owned by the workers. He regularly used the media to assist in propaganda campaigns to control his people. Castro's propaganda: • A revolution is a struggle to the death between the future and the past. • The revolution is a dictatorship of the exploited against the exploiters.	1959 to 2008	Castro died in 2016, at age 90, from natural causes.

AMERICAN RADICALISM

At this juncture, it is important to point out that the radical ideologies faced by the United States—those that are addressed in the earlier chapters of this book—have much in common with the radical ideologies that remain as challenges for other nations of the world. Many are driven by the same or similar political ideologies. Whether socialism or communism, there really is nothing new under the sun. The propaganda packaging may change, but the underlying radicalism that spans the breadth of each culture remains.

Anti-government groups and individuals sprang up during the 1960s and 1970s. Weather Underground, Black Panthers, Chicago 7, SDS, hippies, MOVE 9, Abbie Hoffman, Tom Hayden, Jerry Rubin, the Manson Family, the Youth International Party, Bill Ayers, Bernardine Dohrn, Symbionese Liberation Army, Nation of Islam, and a raft of other group and individual names remain familiar to Baby Boomers. Battles against the US government over civil rights, the nation's involvement in the Vietnam War, and against capitalism were the hallmarks of the emerging Marxism that was taking hold on college campuses while Boomers were adolescents.

Some of the battles just mentioned are still being fought—and then there are the K–12 schools and institutions of higher education. There is no secret that colleges aggressively pass on ideologies stressing Marxism. Activists and influencers impact the young, and violent battles on the streets occur.

After the killing of George Floyd, there were more than five hundred riots in cities all across America by groups capitalizing on Floyd's killing. Each of these riots ended with little-to-no accountability for the radicals who caused billions of dollars in damage to property and the deaths and injuries of multiple law enforcement officers.

Bureaucrats that want to push a certain narrative will fund that narrative, and for those that want or need government money, they play along. Teachers' unions supportive of radical policies use the weight of votes and money to sway policy in their favor. A good example is all of the DEI/DEIO (diversity, equity, inclusion, and opportunity) offices that have popped up all over college campuses and within K–12 schools.

Across the nation, for every one hundred tenured faculty on college campuses, there are 3.4 DEI positions.[13] When reports are made on school campuses about perceived hate language, or because a person was offended by something, such microaggressions are reported to the DEI office. There are always strings of false accusations that find their ways into these offices, and the jury is out as to their effectiveness—outside the appeasement and window dressing for antiracists.[14] Fortunately, there are some states fighting back against race radicalism.

In many public schools, indoctrination runs deep. Even in states where indoctrination of race ideology is illegal, people are violating the law because they think it is their civic duty to promote what had been previously allowed. Again, the end justifies the means ethic comes into play, and the thinking is that a higher ideal legitimizes breaking the law. Parents from all walks of life are stepping up and being heard on a large number of issues affecting their children. Race radicalism is no exception.[15]

The Place of Race

Race is still an issue in America. The late journalist Mike Wallace, then working for the program *60 Minutes*, asked actor Morgan Freeman a question some years ago. Wallace asked, "How are we going to get rid of racism?" Freeman replied, "Stop talking about it. I am going to stop calling you a white man, and I am going to ask you to stop calling me a black man."[16]

Sage advice. Focusing on differences and blaming others for issues that have no current context is not healthy and teaches children to hold other people's grudges. What people focus their full attention on becomes their reality, whether it is real or not.

Sufficient is the fact that antiracism is incorporated into the highest levels of government, politics, and bureaucracy. Its ideology has spread to the US military, healthcare industry, major and minor league sports, and has been pushed politically throughout education while being supported by the NEA and the AFT teacher unions. The rapid spread of this ideology illustrates just how quickly top-down radicalism spreads when it is a part of a federal government's agenda.

Be that as it may, all one needs to do is follow the money flow. In twenty-first-century America, without money, ideologies die a pauper's death. Ironically, the very capitalism that is decried by the radical left is the very privileged resource that is used to keep their radicalism sustained.

Americans agree there is no doubt that "Black lives matter. But in the United States, black lives are not valued equally to white lives. Not in the streets, not in the courts, not in our work places, not in the halls of our government, not in our schools, not even in our progressive movements for change."[17] Some would argue that black lives do not matter on the city's streets or in the wombs of women, given that the highest percentage of aborted babies are black.[18]

Michael Gavin thinks that the race issue should be viewed from the perspective of change. But in the process, he presents this change by continuing to focus on race. He writes, "Making change requires more from white people than simply saying 'black lives matter,' though that's an important start."[19] Gavin, in the *Inside Higher Education* piece titled "Uncloaking the Hidden Force of Whiteness," writes, "Indeed, whiteness is so baked into our norms it is easy to overlook the ways in which it exerts itself, even as we implement initiatives aimed to antiracism. To manifest a liberative education system, though, we must grapple with the uncomfortable truth that in our work on antiracism, we have generally focused our lens on only the effects of systemic racism and often overlooked the cause."[20]

The reader should note that it appears Gavin wants to use schools for indoctrination and social activism. Gavin explains his approach: "One of the effects of whiteness is marginalization. While we must eliminate marginalization, we often focus our efforts on doing so without working to disrupt the normative and powerful center of whiteness upon which systemic oppressions are built. We must, therefore, look at both whiteness as a cause and marginalization as an effect in our antiracist work."[21] Furthermore, Gavin insists there must be a simultaneous commitment to intersectionality and address how whiteness and "higher education systems are a complex web of practices, policies and procedures steeped in White normativity,"[22] and how these continue to marginalize. He concludes by saying "whiteness protects its own power by often presenting itself as an invisible force."[23] How can something *invisible* be presented as any kind of force? Is whiteness God?

Certainly, since the 1950s, there has been "an overall decline in civic and social organization—documented by academics such as Theda Skocpol and Robert Putnam. It is true we have seen some surges in the big organizing—immigration activists fighting and winning deportation relief for Dreamers, the climate defenders stopping infrastructure like the Keystone XL pipeline and pushing to keep fossil fuels in the ground, and the movement to defend black lives fighting to hold cops accountable for murdering black people with impunity and un-electing some county prosecutors in the process."[24] Most would agree that the mission of education has changed and student indoctrination is coming home to roost in schools and among students at all levels.

SHIFTING OF THE MISSION OF EDUCATION

The mission of education has shifted from teaching and learning and traditional civic involvement to social justice and equity. However, civics of old are not the civics being recommended today. Conservative scholars perceive that the Civics Secures Democracy Act does not promote "true instruction for young people"[25] but "serves as a vehicle to promote Critical Race Theory and anti-American indoctrination in the nation's schools."[26] This represents a massive change from learning the Constitution and the three branches of government.

The equity-based and social justice civics programs are celebrated as the true modern purposes of education. Researchers are writing that without them as the foundation of educational institutions, true teaching and learning cannot be maximized.[27] This is another shift, and as an example of what is present in public school policies, appendix 1 includes excerpts from a sample of school board statements addressing social justice and equity policies.

Some of the policies contained in the appendix address race and racism issues, while others address antiracism. The reader should ask the question as to whether focusing on race, equity, and social justice amount to guaranteed outcomes for people of color and are just forms of affirmative action racism-in-disguise. These certainly are not civics or citizenship education. Consider also how any of the guaranteed equity outcomes make for a greater or lesser united American society.

A RETURN TO SANITY?

Some states that rushed into the social justice arena, prompted by the death of George Floyd, quickly passed resolutions to support the sociopolitically charged antiracism. These states had local politicians calling for the defunding of police and the adoption of policies that promoted and funded the organization Black Lives Matter. Some of these states have sobered a bit from the emotionally-driven legislative actions taken at the time, and several have now restructured their policies.[28] The state of Ohio is one example.

Near the end of 2021, "The Ohio State Board of Education rescinded an antiracism and equity resolution that it passed . . . in the wake of the George Floyd murder, replacing it . . . with a statement that seeks to promote academic excellence without respect to race, ethnicity or creed."[29] The resolution passed by the Ohio State Board of Education appears more balanced and fair for all students because it "condemns any standards, curriculum, or training programs for students, teachers, or staff that seek to divide or to ascribe circumstances or qualities, such as collective guilt, moral deficiency, or racial bias, to a whole race or group of people."[30] Furthermore, "in practical terms, the new resolution ends implicit bias training that the Ohio Department of Education employees had to take. The former resolution also required Department of Education contractors to undergo implicit bias training."[31]

Ohio seems to be bucking up against the tenets of woke ideology and succeeding. They are attempting to bring some balance back, as the state returns to more sane and sensible policies. This demonstrates how quickly a narrative can spread among the population, especially given the duplicity of social media. Another example of borderline paranoia, this time spun out by mandates and narratives from the top levels of government, were the COVID-19 pandemic responses.

ATTEMPTS TO RADICALIZE THE SUPREME COURT OF THE UNITED STATES

Radicals continue to pressure the Supreme Court of the United States (SCOTUS) to adjudicate in favor of their policies and laws. This pressure has become much more than lobbying. There have been activist threats, a leak of a significant case on an abortion decision, and protesters illegally camping outside the homes of conservative justices. In some ways, the recent confirmations of SCOTUS appointments by former president Donald Trump have angered the political left, and protest was not enough.

The Court now leans conservative, and this is unacceptable to the radical leftists. But the radicals on the left are not content with protesting the conservative status quo. Their desire is either to dismantle the Court, or to add to it, in order to guarantee political outcomes in their favor.[32] Remember, radicals favor quick, radical changes.

The SCOTUS is charged under Article III of the US Constitution to interpret laws for the United States. Congress is tasked with making law under Article II of the Constitution. In a nutshell, it is the SCOTUS that considers congressional laws as constitutional, or not. At least, that is the traditional constitutional role. The political right and political left have criticized the Court in the past for acting like legislators and legislating from the bench, rather than as interpreters of the US Constitution and the nation's laws. Both sides have valid justifications for their claims. Nevertheless, what are the methods used by the Court to interpret America's legal documents?

Methods of Interpretation

The methods of interpreting the Constitution usually fall into one of four category types, each of which reflects both literary and personal preferences toward determining the meanings of words. Interpretational methodology is extremely important, in terms of the cultural direction of American society. For example, the SCOTUS is responsible for signaling the legalization of same-sex marriage in the *Obergefell v. Hodges* (2015) case,[33] while at the same time allowing for religious freedom for artisans and bakers to choose not to use their artistic and culinary skills against their religious convictions.[34] Also, another example is the *Dobbs v. Jackson Women's Health Organization* (2022) case, overturning nearly fifty years of federal abortion law, established under the *Roe v. Wade* (1973) case. The Court returned the issue of abortion back to the states.

Decisions by the SCOTUS can be culture-shaping and responsible for the validation of ideologies that either are representative of the American populace or representative of a fringe set of Americans. Sometimes cases are decided without precedent, as was realized in the *Roe* case. These cases are considered landmark decisions, often viewed by the losing parties as radical departures from the Court's charge and hailed by the winning parties as progressive and forward-thinking.

Application of any of the four basic methods of constitutional interpretation affects how laws are interpreted. Therefore, it is imperative that members of the Court begin with the Constitution and not a worldview that is counter to the founding document of our nation.[35]

Textualism. The first method of interpreting the Constitution is *textualism, literalism,* or *strict construction.* This method examines each word of the

Constitution and allows words to have plain and ordinary meanings. This allows a high level of *predictability* on behalf of those receiving the interpretation of the document by the SCOTUS.

Originalism. The second method of interpreting the Constitution is that of determining *original intent*, or using the *originalism method*. Those in favor of this method seek to determine what the Framers of the Constitution and the Founders of our nation meant by their specific uses of words and phrases. The use of this method allows for *stability* of interpretation and a standard by which to judge future interpretations. For example, when Congress "shall make no law infringing on the right to bear arms" is interpreted, the Second Amendment is interpreted in terms of what the Founders meant by their original intent.

Fundamentalism. The third method of interpreting the Constitution is referred to as the *fundamental principles*, or *fundamentalist approach*. Advocates of this method apply the *general principles* derived from the Constitution to the words and phrases used in the document, especially where the clarity of the meaning of these terms may be in question. For example, beginning with the principle of natural rights or limited government power would shape the way that a justice might view a case and affect the decision by the overall Court. For example, if the right to life is a fundamental right, it could be used to argue the limitation of abortion.

Modernist. The fourth and last method used by justices to interpret the Constitution is the *modernism method*, or also what is referred to as *instrumentalism*. This method allows for the Constitution to be *fluid*, adapting to modern times and to modern social circumstances. For example, this method would be used if the Court decided that every American was required to have a COVID-19 vaccine for the cause of *common good*, or whether members of an LGBTQ+ group are determined as a minority group by law thereby determining them to be a protected class of people.

The results of SCOTUS cases impact American culture. The ideological makeup of the Court has much to do with its decisions and how the justices interpret the law. On the one hand, the Court can be criticized for being too conservative by sticking to precedent and the foundational documents of the nation. On the other hand, the Court can be criticized as too liberal for finding rights that do not exist in any of the nation's founding documents.

It is important to remember that the Court's role in American society is critical, that losing parties in cases brought before the Court will criticize the Court as being too radical. Nevertheless, losing parties then understand the weakness of their case and petition the Court under another case at a later time. The SCOTUS is the ultimate top-down arbiter of legal decisions in the United States, and its purpose is not the seeking of truth. Rather, its purpose is to interpret law.

SYSTEMIC IMPACT OF RADICALISM

The systemic impact of radicalism on American education, students, and families is significant and can be pinpointed to decisions made by those in power. Some of the points are the speculative writings and radical activities supported by psychologists, sociologist, politicians, community organizers, and educators. Each of these can contribute to the intensive indoctrination of children's minds and subsequent radical actions. Blumenfeld agrees that the system we have now "is anti-Christian, pro-socialist, and owned lock, stock, and barrel by the progressives and behavioral psychologists."[36] Some would disagree with Blumenfeld's conclusion. They would see hope in parents rising up in support of conservative social values.[37]

In the following section, there are brief examinations of some of the principal progressive and Marxist contributors to the systemic radicalization of today's teachers. If a person wants to be a teacher, most states' teacher training programs incorporate into their classes the writings of the following: Vygotsky, Skinner, Dewey, and Freire, among others.

Lev Vygotsky (1896–1934)

Lev Vygotsky was an early Soviet-Russian psychologist who was best known for developing his concept of the *Zone of Proximal Development* (ZPD).[38] This concept remains as a sociocultural theory that states that there are some tasks assigned to children that are too difficult for them, but with the assistance of others, the difficult tasks can remain in the zone of accomplishment.

Vygotsky believed that communication is key for both the psychological development of children and the accomplishment of tasks. Some theorists point to the interest in group work or pairing of students to tackle difficult work as an offshoot of Vygotsky's ideas.

Aside from the educational attributions and contributions of Vygotsky to sociology, Vygotsky's biographer, James Wertsch writes, Vygotsky "was a staunch advocate of dialectical and historical materialism. He was one of the creators of Marxist psychology. . . . People such as Vygotsky and his followers devoted every hour of their lives to making certain that the new socialist state, the first grand experiment based on Marxist-Leninist principles, would survive."[39]

Burrhus F. Skinner (1904–1990)

B. F. Skinner is probably the most *influential of American behavioral psychologists*. Cognitive development and aspects of the life of the mind were of "no interest to the behaviorist. . . . Skinner's theories of education removed any last vestige of spirit from the student, who . . . [became] totally deprived of any spiritual life or soul."[40] He "reduced all of learning to conditioning [and] . . . believed that, like animals, humans acted only in response to consequences good or bad, of the same action performed previously."[41]

Skinner's theories of operant and classical conditioning remain "important theories in . . . understanding . . . how humans and other animals learn new forms of behavior."[42] Furthermore, "Skinner was among the signers of the controversial *Humanist Manifesto II,* written in 1973 . . . [he] called his brand of behaviorism *radical behaviorism.*"[43]

John Dewey (1859–1952)

All of Skinner's behaviorism fit in nicely with Dewey's progressive "plan to change America,"[44] which he said "must come gradually."[45] If America is forced to change radically and quickly, "it unduly would compromise its final success by favoring a violent reaction."[46] Dewey was right. It is true that "John Dewey provided the educational philosophy and the dumbing-down plan that justified the shift from intellectual training to socialization."[47] Progressives with utopian ideas ruined education. Over the course of decades, their actions "have led to the creation of millions of functional illiterates and a nation of dummies."[48] Students of history are quick to point out that Dewey's dummies bear a resemblance to what is being produced in American schools today.

Paolo Freire (1921–1997)

Brazilian educator and philosopher, Paolo Freire, favored political socialization of children in the shaping of their knowledge and attitudes. He emphasized that early childhood educators help to shape children in their social and political development from the very beginning. "Freire developed an approach to education that links the identification of issues to positive action for change and development,"[49] and that it is "essential that people link knowledge to action so that they actively work to change their societies at a local level and beyond."[50]

In reference to Freire, Blumenfeld writes, "early childhood education should include political indoctrination by way of vocabulary development, which is very much in line with Freire's methodology."[51] "Cooperative learning . . . is indeed a good example of communist ideology in the classroom. The student is not judged by his individual effort but as a member of a group."[52]

On a wider scale, communism by way of Karl Marx and Friedrich Engels emphasized intent "to do away with . . . property"[53] and the "abolition of the family,"[54] and "communism abolishes eternal truths, it abolishes all religion, and all morality."[55] Race-radical groups are today focused on the same outcomes.

TAKING A STAND

Educators of previous generations are aware that their training informed them that "each student is an individual responsible for his own achievement. And since each student is different in his learning abilities and the amount of efforts he puts into his work, the outcome for each student would be different."[56] According to modern socialists, "individualism creates a competitive spirit that is opposed to a collectivist spirit, which is needed in a socialist society. Competition, of course, is the hallmark of a capitalist, individualistic society. Socialist philosophers from the late 1930s and 1940s believed in cooperative learning."[57] The influx of radical Marxist American psychology and philosophy of education changed the focus of many teacher training institutions. The United States is now more commonly known as a collection of *tribal fringe groups*, allied in seeking power.

Across America, "more and more parents are opposed to what is going on in the public schools. Activist parents are labeled 'extremists,' 'troublemakers,' 'censors,' 'religious bigots,' 'fanatics,' 'fascists,' and so on. This is done to neutralize the vast majority of parents who don't want to get involved, who don't like controversy, or who go along to get along. The good news is that the homeschool movement continues to grow. . . . But lurking in the wings are those socialist educators who would like to outlaw homeschooling."[58] This is an example of the power hungry at the top levels of government seeking avenues to punch down at those looking to alternative modes of education for their children.

Nevertheless, parents must continue to take stands against the forces of radicalism that compete for the minds and hearts of their children. One good way is to remove them from the environment that is indoctrinating them.

KENDI AND IVORY TOWER
ANTIRACIST RADICALISM

At first take, the term antiracism seems a reasonable and certainly an admirable goal. However, in order to understand the term, one must delve deeper etymologically. As with all terms that emerge from the social sciences, there is often more to the story beyond the definition. For a good discussion on this term, readers should turn to a leading African American studies antiracist named Ibram X. Kendi. At present, Kendi is the *go to* person setting the tone for African American antiracist studies in the humanities.

How to Be an Antiracist, by Ibram X. Kendi, is a book that proposes definitions to terms such as racism, racial inequity, racist policies, and institutional, structural, and systemic racism. Kendi writes: "racial inequity is when two or more racial groups are not standing on approximately equal footing."[59]

The first point to be made here is that Kendi switches terms on the reader. There is first the supposed inequity, and this inequity is the result of not being equal in terms of melanin. Equity has very little to do with equality, and inequity has less to do with inequality. Equity is being given opportunities that others either do not have, do not want, or are not allowed, in order to level the playing field.

Kendi believes that because members of certain races do not occupy homes at the same percentage rates as whites, some sort of systemic white supremacy controls the differential. Kendi cherry-picks numbers and wishes that the decades of the "forties, seventies, or . . . nineties"[60] could have demonstrated more racial equity. But Kendi misses a very important point.

According to the world's largest individual-level population database, the IPUMS (Integrated Public Use Microdata Series), percentage increases among demographics, in terms of home ownership, changed significantly over the decades of the twentieth century. William J. Collins and Robert A. Margo authored a white paper for the National Bureau of Economic Research. They examined data correlated between race and home ownership for the years 1900 to 1990. The following is a summary of their findings.[61]

> The historical evolution of racial differences in income in the 20th century United States has been examined intensively by economists, but the evolution of racial differences in wealth has been examined far less. This paper uses IPUMS data to study trends in racial differences in home ownership since 1900. At the turn of the century approximately 20 percent of Black adult males (ages 20 to 64) owned their homes, compared with 46 percent of White men, a gap of 26 percentage points. By 1990, the Black home ownership rate had increased to 52 percent and the racial gap had fallen to 19.5 percentage points. All of the long-term rise in the rate of Black home ownership, and almost all of the corresponding long-term decline in the racial gap, occurred after 1940, with the majority of both changes concentrated in the 1960 to 1980 period.[62]

Kendi overlooks statistics like these. But he does not miss a beat and continues by defining *racist policy* as "any measure that produces or sustains racial inequity between racial groups. An antiracist policy is any measure that produces or sustains racial equity between racial groups. . . . There is no such thing as a nonracist or race-neutral policy. Every policy in every institution in every community in every nation is producing or sustaining racial inequity or equity between racial groups."[63] Observe the effort put into dichotomizing the issue. One is either racist or antiracist, and there is no in between. When this kind of approach is brought to students, it is a top-down radical false binary. Furthermore, according to antiracist scholars, a person can be racist and not even know of his or her racism.

Radical racist policies have been described using other terms, according to Kendi. Three of these terms are "institutional racism, structural racism, and systemic racism, all three of which Kendi concludes is present in America."[64]

Discrimination

For those seeking to end racial discrimination, the race radical claims, "The only remedy to racist discrimination is antiracist discrimination. The only remedy to past discrimination is present discrimination. The only remedy to present discrimination is future discrimination. . . . As US Supreme Court Justice Harry Blackmun wrote in 1978, 'In order to get beyond racism, we must first take account of race. There is no other way. And in order to treat some persons equally, we must treat them differently.'"[65]

Being equal today is not any major concern. People understand they are equal across and between races. The real question is equity, which Blackmun clearly articulates in his last line of the quote.[66] Not only is Kendi using false dichotomies but he is also attempting to delineate between ideas that are racist and ideas that are antiracist. He sets himself apart as the arbiter of race theory, as he contends, "A racist idea is any idea that suggests one racial group is inferior or superior to another racial group in any way. Racist ideas argue that the inferiorities and superiorities of racial groups explain racial inequities in society."[67] One cannot help but think that Kendi implicates himself by his own terms.

Kendi's ideas impact education in several ways, not the least of which might occur in a second grade classroom. If a student refers to another student as better at math, or is a faster runner, or whose hair is different. Would Kendi declare this as racist? Some students are inferior in certain academics. Asians do not always like to hear they are good at math, because everyone understands this is not the case. According to Kendi, this "idea" is racist, and so too would be generalizations about racial groups. Kendi's antiracism has radicalized people to assume things that are not accurate.

Kendi has invested much into keeping racism alive. To him, "Racist ideas have defined our society since its beginning and can feel so natural and obvious as to be banal, but antiracist ideas remain difficult to comprehend, in part because they go against the flow of this country's history."[68] Kendi indicts an entire nation of whites at the nation's beginning, yet claims this is not racist. He extrapolates his assertions upon all present whites and claims this is also not racist. Only a radical would use such convoluted logic to arrive at such erroneous conclusions.

In an effort to bolster his antiracism, Kendi asserts, "to call women as a group stupid is sexism. To call Black people as a group stupid is racism. To call Black women as a group stupid is gender racism. Such intersections have also led to articulations of class racism (demeaning the Black poor and Black elites), queer racism (demeaning Black lesbians, gays, bisexuals, transgender, and queer people) and ethnic racism (concocting a hierarchy of Black ethnic groups), to name a few."[69]

Classifying all whites as racists, implicitly biased, supremacists, and nationalists, is demeaning an entire race and is racist. Taken to its logical conclusion, calling others racist is racist also. Kendi says nothing about intra-racial slurs, as to whether those who use them are to be held to his standard of racism.

Antiracist teams have spread their ideologies and have infected colleges, universities, and K–12 public schools across the nation. Even private schools have fallen prey to the propaganda of race radicalism.

Teacher education departments are now required to be trained in critical race theory (CRT) and antiracism as part of their state's credentialing. Some states are thankfully restricting this training and have banned the ideas from K–16 classrooms throughout their states.[70]

Not all states are on the same page, though, when it comes to dealing with antiracism. At some colleges, there are even snitch teams designed to catch and remove professors who do not fall into compliance with DEI mandates. This is reminiscent of fascist and socialist revolutionaries bent on purifying their ranks for their *cause celebre*. Antiracist activists have invaded elite post-secondary learning institutions, such as Bryn Mawr College, New York City's elite Dalton School, Northwestern University, Princeton University, Mount Holyoke, and hundreds of others across America.

John McWhorter recognizes this phenomenon: "American universities have long been more committed to antiracism than almost any other institutions."[71] The addition of offices of DEIO make it easier for people to be anonymously accused of racism. Radicals understand that when some accusations are made there are seldom ways out of them for the accused.

At Bryn Mawr, *woke ideals* are largely unquestioned. Dalton has made inroads to establish a substantially non-white student body, and at Northwestern the debate still rages as to what percentage of black students should matriculate, in order to be considered representative of the remedy of past discrimination.[72] Mount Holyoke was exposed for its indoctrination of students.[73]

The reasons given by McWhorter as to why institutions should not yield to CRT and antiracism are worth addressing. He declares,

They must resist destructive demands, even by self-proclaimed representatives of people of color, and even in a society where racism is real. To give in to anti-intellectual, under-considered, disproportionate, or hostile demands is condescending to the signatories (of the university letter to the Princeton administration) and the protesters. It implies that they can do no better, and that authorities must suspend their sense of logic, civility, and progress as some kind of penance for slavery, Jim Crow, redlining, and the deaths of people such as Floyd. That 'penance' would hurt only the community in the end, through lower educational quality.[74]

McWhorter claims that the "writers of manifestos might classify resistance as racist, denialist backlash. But the civil, firm dismissal of irrational demands is, rather, a kind of civic valor."[75] Therefore, no one should be surprised when (1) schools indoctrinate children, (2) provide for them avenues in which to express activism, and (3) require their activities as credit for graduation. When students are molded and then emboldened, is there any mystery as to why teenagers and young adults hit the streets of Portland, or Seattle, and cause mayhem?

As an example, not only have teenagers taken the revolutionary mantle upon themselves, but so too have their teachers. As Christopher Rufo records, "teachers . . . have immersed themselves in the destruction. Over the course of the summer unrest [2020], police arrested at least five school teachers for riot-related crimes."[76]

Teachers Arrested

Some of the crimes for which the teachers were arrested included felony riot, disorderly conduct, attempting to steal an officer's baton, interfering with a police officer, and assaulting a police officer.[77] The arrested teachers ranged from preschool through high school.

Some of the very teachers instructing in CRT fought toe-to-toe with police in the streets of Portland. CRT does not present itself as a peaceful course of study if radicals find its theory most practical in violent protests. The theory is based on disruption, destruction, and revolution—the kinds of actions that spin directly from the annals of Marxist revolutions of the past. Basically, with CRT, race warfare has now replaced class warfare.[78]

Bonnie Kerrigan Snyder writes:

> Critical theory is having a cultural moment. . . . As a philosophy that interprets events, culture, politics, and art primarily through the lens of power relationships between participants, it tends to reach certain conclusions and seeks to redress perceived imbalances in society. One of the ways it does this is by silencing voices it associates with power and privileging (giving more space to)

those it considers to be or to have been disadvantaged. When this plays out in the classroom, we get the chilling effect on free speech that sometimes actively seeks to shut down unwelcome discussions and otherwise encourages some students to voluntarily self-censor. This, then, can run up against students' rights, as spelled out in school handbooks and as enshrined in established case law. Now we have a conflict.[79]

RADICALISM AND MISPLACED ACCOUNTABILITY

An example of a *worldview gone badly* can be observed in schools that have reduced codes of discipline to little more than conversations and periods of time out. For example, the San Francisco leftist progressive organization Pacific Education Group "promotes the theory that white privilege is the cause of academic underachievement and misbehavior among African American students. The organization recommends stopping suspensions and expulsions for bad behavior."[80] This type of progressive ideology has been extended far beyond classrooms in San Francisco.

In major cities where progressives are positioned in leadership, the result is often no cash-bail requirements for criminals who are rearrested. There are less and less punishments for crimes, both misdemeanor and serious. Add to the criminal *intersectionality* the rampant homelessness and drug concerns. The permissive ideology that does not hold people accountable in schools results in much less stringent accountability on the streets.

The unfortunate part of this is the decisions to reduce accountability for violence in schools and on the streets is based on race. Most often, whites and whiteness are saddled with being accountable, by their whiteness, for some of the criminal actions taken by BIPOC (black, indigenous, and people of color). The individual might be held liable, but the white culture becomes overly indicted.[81]

Another aspect of the ideology of permissiveness based on race includes the accusation that traits such as punctuality and promptness, excellence, work ethic, respect, and so forth, are actually cultural and racial. It is declared that white supremacy is the reason for the expectation that all people living in the United States should develop white practices and display white traits.

School principals have been found lacking in dealing with students that need discipline. School leaders minimize events of violence and attribute them to cultural misunderstandings and socioeconomics. In fact, some teachers are blamed for creating or tolerating classroom environments that lead to incitement of student actions against them, as well as to fellow students.[82]

Radicals do not come into their radicalism in isolation. Leaders at the top of any radical group have gone through a radicalization process. Some of the leaders set expectations for those whom they intend to radicalize, while not adhering to the expectations for themselves. Black Lives Matter is an excellent example. In the fight for black lives, leaders of the movement have enriched themselves far beyond levels of the average black life.[83] Black lives may matter, but blacks living well in capitalist and white supremacist America seem to circumvent the very ideology of the origination of BLM.

While not the first BLM leader to become enriched, the allegation is that "Shalomyah Bowers, the leader of Black Lives Matter Global Network Foundation (BLMGNF), defrauded the local chapters for unjust enrichment and used their funds as his personal piggy bank."[84] A lawsuit was filed against Bowers on behalf of twenty-six grassroots BLM chapters, alleging the BLM leader siphoned the money from "charitable contributions to pay for his own personal expenses."[85]

Radicalism has made its mark on American society. From the Ivory Towers of academe to the halls of government—and on into the local school board meetings—radical ideologies have been accepted. This does not occur without orchestration of top-down decision-makers.

The time is now for those who are concerned by what they see taking place in American schools—and within culture at-large—to unite their voices and fight against indoctrination and radicalization of the children of America. As far as children are concerned, whether they recognize it or not, this type of top-down parent and family involvement is of the greatest of importance.

NOTES

1. Samuel Blumenfeld and Alex Newman. *Crimes of the educators: How utopians are using government schools to destroy America's children.* 2021. Nashville, TN: Post Hill Press, p. 120.

2. Karl Marx and Friedrich Engels. *The communist manifesto.* 2019. Independently published: Zwrihander Press, pp. 63–64.

3. Andrew Stiles. "Collusion: Media outlets meet with White House to reshape coverage of Biden Administration." *Washington Free Beacon.* December 7, 2021. Retrieved November 4, 2022, from https://freebeacon.com/media/white-house-media -collusion/. Cf. Jacob Sullum. "These emails show how the Biden Administration's crusade against misinformation imposes censorship by proxy." *Reason.* September 1, 2022. Retrieved October 26, 2022, from https://reason.com/2022/09/01/these-emails -show-how-the-biden-administrations-crusade-against-misinformation-imposes -censorship-by-proxy/.

4. Todd Olmstead. "Twitter purchased by Elon Musk: A timelines of how it happened." *Wall Street Journal.* October 28, 2022. Retrieved October 29, 2022, from https://www.wsj.com/story/twitter-purchased-by-elon-musk-how-it-went-down -72a07de3.

5. Jessica Guynn. "Facebook throttled Hunter Biden article after being warned by FBI of hack and leak operations, Mark Zuckerberg says." *USA Today*. October 28, 2020. Retrieved November 13, 2022, from https://www.usatoday.com/story/tech/2020/10/28/zuckerberg-facebook-throttled-ny-post-article-after-fbi-warning/3755249001/. Cf. Daniel Henninger. "The Zuckerberg collusion." *Wall Street Journal*. April 11, 2018. Retrieved November 13, 2022, from https://www.wsj.com/articles/the-zuckerberg-collusion-1523487173.

6. Ernest J. Zarra, III. "Graphic content restrictions are not book bans." *Minding the Campus*. National Association of Scholars. February 2, 2022. Retrieved March 4, 2022, from https://www.mindingthecampus.org/2022/02/02/graphic-content-restrictions-are-not-book-bans/.

7. Katie Lobosco. "The IRS is set to get billions for audit enforcement: Here's what it means for taxpayers." CNN. August 11, 2022. Retrieved October 27, 2022, from https://www.cnn.com/2022/08/11/politics/irs-inflation-act-funding-audit-enforcement/index.html.

8. Jessie Yeung. "China's lockdown protests: What you need to know." CNN. November 28, 2022. Retrieved November 29, 2022, from https://www.cnn.com/2022/11/28/china/china-lockdown-protests-covid-explainer-intl-hnk.

9. Matthew Continetti. "Heavy-handed bureaucracy is set for a comeback under Biden." American Enterprise Institute. November 13, 2020. Retrieved November 28, 2022, from https://www.aei.org/op-eds/heavy-handed-bureaucracy-is-set-for-a-comeback-under-biden/.

10. Ibid.

11. Staff. "The power of propaganda." *Facing History & Ourselves*. July 14, 2022. Retrieved November 4, 2022, from https://www.facinghistory.org/resource-library/power-propaganda-1.

12. Ashley Berner. "Many countries use exposure to guard against indoctrination in education." United Press International. November 4, 2021. Retrieved November 2, 2022, from https://www.upi.com/Voices/2021/11/04/public-education-indoctrination/1521636031533/.

13. Jay Greene and James Paul. "Diversity University: DEI bloat in the academy." *The Heritage Foundation*. July 27, 2021. Retrieved November 1, 2022, from https://www.heritage.org/education/report/diversity-university-dei-bloat-the-academy.

14. Candice Bristow. "Why DEI programs are failing." *Tech Crunch*. November 16, 2021. Retrieved November 20, 2022, from https://techcrunch.com/2021/11/16/why-dei-programs-are-failing/.

15. Brian Jones. "Furious parents at school board meetings have a right to speak. We should listen to them." *Washington Post*. October 13, 2021. Retrieved November 5, 2022, from https://www.washingtonpost.com/opinions/2021/10/13/angry-parents-school-board-meetings-dissent-free-speech/. Cf. Ernest J. Zarra III. *From character to color: The impact of critical race theory on American education*. 2022. Lanham, MD: Rowman & Littlefield Publishers.

16. The Rubin Report. "Morgan Freeman silences *60 minutes* host by insulting black history month." Posted February 3, 2022. YouTube video. Retrieved November 4, 2022, from https://www.youtube.com/watch?v=RosCZkH5uTI. Cf. B. V. Polito.

"Letters: Take Morgan Freeman's advice about allegations of racism." *The Advocate.* March 29, 2021. Retrieved November 2, 2022, from https://www.theadvocate.com/baton_rouge/opinion/letters/article_2fe0ad80-8f18-11eb-affc-9bacbec5a896.html.

17. Becky Bond and Zack Exley. *Rules for revolutionaries: How big organizing can change everything.* 2016. White River Junction, VT: Chelsea Green Publishing, p. 38.

18. Staff. "Reported legal abortions by race of women who obtained abortion by the state of occurrence." Kaiser Family Foundation. 2019. Retrieved November 3, 2022, from https://www.kff.org/womens-health-policy/state-indicator/abortions-by-race/?currentTimeframe=0&selectedDistributions=white--black&selectedRows=%7B%22wrapups%22:%7B%22united-states%22:%7B%7D%7D%7D&sortModel=%7B%22colId%22:%22Location%22,%22sort%22:%22asc%22%7D.

19. Bond and Exley. *Rules for revolutionaries*, p. 38.

20. Michael H. Gavin. "Uncloaking the hidden force of whiteness." *Inside Higher Education.* September 2, 2022. Retrieved September 3, 2022, from https://www.insidehighered.com/advice/2022/09/02/campuses-must-examine-how-systemic-whiteness-protects-itself-opinion.

21. Ibid.

22. Staff. "A framework for advancing antiracism strategy on campus." National Association of Diversity Officers in Higher Education (NADOHE). 2021, pp. –9–11 Retrieved September 8, 2022, from https://nadohe.memberclicks.net/assets/2021/Framework/National%20Association%20of%20Diversity%20Officers%20in%20Higher%20Education%20-%20Framework%20for%20Advancing%20Ant-Racism%20on%20Campus%20-%20first%20edition.pdf.

23. Gavin. "Uncloaking the hidden force of whiteness."

24. Bond and Exley. *Rules for revolutionaries*, p. 84.

25. Peter Wood. "Monthly Newsletter." *National Association of Scholars.* August 2022, p. 7.

26. Ibid.

27. Brenda Alvarez. "Why social justice in school matters." *NEA Today.* January 22, 2019. Retrieved November 5, 2022, from https://www.nea.org/advocating-for-change/new-from-nea/why-social-justice-school-matters.

28. Hannah Natanson, Clara Ence Morse, Anu Narayansamy, and Christina Brause. "An explosion of culture-war laws is changing schools. Here's how." *The Washington Post.* October 18, 2022. Retrieved October 20, 2022, from https://www.washingtonpost.com/education/2022/10/18/education-laws-culture-war/.

29. Laura Hancock. "Ohio state board of education abolishes antiracism and equity resolution passed in the wake of George Floyd murder." *Advance Local.* October 14, 2021. Retrieved October 17, 2022, from https://www.cleveland.com/open/2021/10/ohio-state-board-of-education-abolishes-antiracism-and-equity-resolution-passed-in-wake-of-george-floyds-murder.html.

30. Ibid.

31. Ibid.

32. Julia Mueller. "House Democrats tout bill to add four seats to Supreme Court." *The Hill.* July 18, 2022. Retrieved November 13, 2022, from https://thehill.com/

homenews/house/3564588-house-democrats-offer-bill-to-add-four-seats-to-supreme
-court/. Cf. Giulia Carbonaro. "Can Democrats expand the Supreme Court and how
likely is it? *Newsweek.* June 29, 2022. Retrieved November 13, 2022, from https://
www.newsweek.com/can-democrats-expand-supreme-court-how-likely-it-1720256.

33. *Obergefell v. Hodges.* June 26, 2015. *Justia Supreme Court Center.* Retrieved
October 25, 2022, from https://www.oyez.org/cases/2014/14-556.

34. Staff. *Masterpiece Cakeshop, Ltd., et al. v. Colorado Civil Rights Commis-
sion* et. al. *Supreme Court of the United States.* June 4, 2018. Retrieved October 25,
2022, from https://www.supremecourt.gov/opinions/17pdf/16-111_j4el.pdf. Cf. Eliza
Green. "Tastries owner prevails in lawsuit alleging discrimination." *The Bakersfield Californian.* October 21, 2022. Retrieved October 25, 2022, from https://www
.bakersfield.com/news/tastries-owner-prevails-in-lawsuit-alleging-discrimination/
article_94ffbe00-51a3-11ed-919d-f324ed63040f.html.

35. Staff. *We the people: The citizen and the Constitution.* 2009. Calabasas, California: Center for Civic Education, pp. 180–181.

36. Blumenfeld and Newman. *Crimes of the educators,* p. 24.

37. Eric W. Dolan. "Study finds parents tend to be more socially conservative and
judgmental than non-parents." *PsyPost.* August 27, 2018. Retrieved November 18,
2022, from https://www.psypost.org/2018/08/study-finds-parents-tend-to-be-more
-socially-conservative-and-judgmental-than-non-parents-52061.

38. Saul McLeod. "Vygotsky's sociocultural theory of cognitive development."
Simple Psychology. August 18, 2022. Retrieved September 4, 2022, from https://www
.simplypsychology.org/vygotsky.html.

39. James V. Wertsch. *Vygotsky and the social formation of mind.* 1985. Cambridge,
Massachusetts: Harvard University Press, p. ix. Wertsch quote excerpted from Blumenfeld and Newman. *Crimes of the educators,* p. 103.

40. Blumenfeld and Newman. *Crimes of educators,* p. 193.

41. Ibid., p. 192.

42. Staff. "Operant conditioning." *Psychologist World.* 2022. Retrieved October
26, 2022, from https://www.psychologistworld.com/behavior/operant-conditioning.

43. Blumenfeld and Newman. *Crimes of the educators,* p. 193.

44. Ibid., p. 194.

45. John Dewey. *The early works of John Dewey.* Vol. 5. *1882–1898.* 2008. Car-
bondale, IL: Southern Illinois University Press, pp. 254–269.

46. Ibid.

47. Blumenfeld and Newman. *Crimes of the educators,* p. 188.

48. Ibid.

49. Staff. "Who is Paolo Freire?" *Freire Institute.* 2022. Retrieved September 27,
2022, from https://www.freire.org/paulo-freire https://www.freire.org/paulo-freire.

50. Ibid.

51. Blumenfeld and Newman. *Crimes of the educators,* p. 108.

52. Ibid., p. 119.

53. Marx and Engels. *The communist manifesto,* p. 37.

54. Ibid., pp. 39–40.

55. Ibid., p. 43.

56. Blumenfeld and Newman. *Crimes of the educators*, p. 120.

57. Ibid.

58. Ibid., p. 121.

59. Ibram X. Kendi. *How to be an Antiracist*. 2019. New York: One World, Random House, p. 18.

60. Ibid.

61. William J. Collins and Robert A. Margo. "Race and home ownership, 1900 to 1990." August 1999. National Bureau of Economic Research. Retrieved May 20, 2021 from http://www.nber.org/papers/w7277.

62. Ibid.

63. Kendi. *How to be an Antiracist*, p. 18.

64. Ibid.

65. Ibid.

66. Ibid., p. 19.

67. Ibid., p. 20.

68. Ibid., p. 21.

69. Ibram X. Kendi. *Stamped from the beginning: The definitive history of racist ideas in America*. New York: Bold Type Books, p. 6.

70. Ellie Bufkin. "States push back against critical race theory in education." *Sinclair Broadcast Group*. May 6, 2021. Retrieved May 21, 2021, from https://foxbaltimore.com/news/nation-world/states-push-back-against-critical-race-theory-in-education.

71. John McWhorter. "Schools must resist destructive antiracist demands." *The Atlantic*. January 29, 2021. Retrieved May 21, 2021, from https://www.theatlantic.com/ideas/archive/2021/01/when-antiracist-manifestos-become-antiracist-wrecking-balls/617841/.

72. Ibid.

73. Dana Kennedy. "Mount Holyoke grad deprogrammed from women-only woke culture." *New York Post*. November 26, 2022. Retrieved November 28, 2022, from https://nypost.com/2022/11/26/mount-holyoke-grad-deprogrammed-from-women-only-woke-culture/.

74. McWhorter, "Schools must resist destructive antiracist demands."

75. Ibid.

76. Christopher F. Rufo. "The child soldiers of Portland." *City Journal*. Spring 2021. Retrieved May 22, 2021, from https://www.city-journal.org/critical-race-theory-portland-public-schools?mc_cid=9ddf5edee7&mc_eid=dd2cd80aa4.

77. Ibid.

78. Staff. "Ben Domenech on Bill Barr speech: Critical race theory is public schools pushing religion." *The Federalist*. May 20, 2021. Retrieved, May 22, 2021, from https://thefederalist.com/2021/05/20/ben-domenech-on-bill-barr-speech-critical-race-theory-is-public-schools-pushing-religion/.

79. Bonnie Kerrigan Snyder. *Undoctrinate: How politicized classrooms harm kids and ruin our schools—and what we can do about it*. 2021. Nashville, TN: Post Hill Press, , p. 18.

80. Lance Izumi, Cassidy Syftestad, and Christie Syftestad. *The corrupt classroom: Bias, indoctrination, violence, and social engineering show why America needs school choice.* 2017. San Francisco, CA: Pacific Research Institute, p. 51.

81. Savala Nolan. "Black and brown people have been protesting for centuries. It's white people who are responsible for what happens next." *Time.* June 1, 2020. Retrieved October 26, 2022, from https://time.com/5846072/black-people-protesting -white-people-responsible-what-happens-next/. Cf. Izumi, Syftestad, and Syftestad. *The corrupt classroom,* p. 51.

82. Ernest J. Zarra III. *Assaulted: Violence in schools and what needs to be done.* 2018. Lanham, MD: Rowman & Littlefield Publishers, pp. 61–70. Cf. Izumi, Syftestad, and Syftestad. *The corrupt classroom,* pp. 52–53.

83. John Brown. "Black lives matter leader accused of stealing $10M from organization: Unjust enrichment." Fox News. September 4, 2022. Retrieved September 9, 2022, from https://www.foxnews.com/us/black-lives-matter -leader-accused-stealing-ten-million-organization-unjust-enrichment?fbclid =IwAR10um2jlTLtGopQB6olrIglY3LU-x1uG3beNiDkQu2P-7EtyAcVCwKkz-8.

84. Ibid.

85. Ibid.

Chapter 6

The Battle against Radicalism

Ego must be so all-pervading that the personality of the organizer is contagious, that it converts the people from despair to defiance, creating a mass ego.

—Saul Alinsky, *Rules for Radicals*[1]

The media in the United States has been labeled as the fourth estate, fourth rail, or fourth branch of the federal government. The term implies that the press in America, and the news media—both in print and online—have explicit and implicit capacities to frame political discourse. Some would even argue the fourth estate has the power to even sway election results.[2] This argument has taken on even greater meaning with the advent of smart technology, manipulated algorithms, and detailed analytics used by giant technology companies.

By all accounts, the ultimate pushback against big tech was the recent blockbuster purchase and acquisition of Twitter by billionaire Elon Musk, in October 2022.[3] Musk's purchase is significant, because in the past, the news media were hailed as watchdogs, calling out governmental actions and holding elected officials accountable for their words and actions.[4] However, around 2010, when social media sites began to explode in popularity, something had changed.

A newer generation was accessing social media for its news and information. The media watchdog morphed into a well-trained bloodhound, sniffing out opposition. Progressive, woke millennials and Gen Z began exercising control over some of the messaging and worked with federal agencies of the US government to develop and disseminate political narratives.[5] To date, the media has become a safe space for radicals and their messaging.[6] That is, until Musk's purchase of Twitter brought some semblance of free speech.

More recently, giant media platforms have become apologists for politicians on the left and the right. Media giants CNN, Fox, MSNBC, and the broadcast networks of ABC, CBS, and NBC were pushing their own narratives in support of the political parties and candidates they favored. This partisanship all came to a head in 2020.

People began accepting the majority of their newsfeeds from sources other than major media sources. They began to read their news through the lenses of the media platforms, such as Facebook, Google, AOL, Twitter, Yahoo, and others.[7] Always seeking an edge, politicians and their political parties have sought to take advantage of this direct form of communication and personal information feeds. Now, with smart phones and 24/7 access, narrative messaging has become ubiquitous. Add to this a large voting bloc in Gen Z and their impact can turn an election.

Recently, as suspected by a large group of Americans, it was announced that entities and agencies of the federal government had worked together to withhold information about the son of President Joseph Biden, which could have impacted the election results of 2020. This relationship led to serious, impactful economic and political fallout.

More than halfway into his term as forty-sixth president, Biden's apologists have been jumping ship,[8] and doing so for many reasons. Midterm elections are often excellent opportunities for changes within administrations. However, as it turns out, this was not the case in the election of 2022. What did happen was many employed at the social media giant Twitter had been ousted, or pushed overboard.[9] Any battle against indoctrination today has to now include social media and technology giants.

MEDIA DISINFORMATION AND POLITICS

The term *disinformation* is used regularly to distract from reality and truth. Both of these can be shaped by indoctrination. Indoctrination not only occurs when false information and narratives are spread. Indoctrination also occurs by withholding information and creating narratives that what is being withheld is disinformation or conspiracy theory.

Arbiters of the gateway of information use the term *disinformation* and apply it to anyone in government calling for investigations into events that might implicate officials in wrongdoing. Mark Zuckerberg's explosive revelations[10] about direct communications with the FBI over alleged matters of disinformation, along with narrative messaging about Russian influences in the election of 2020, became all the chatter. Congressional hearings were held. Labels were placed upon those whose actions were described as collusion, in efforts toward harming Donald Trump's 2020 reelection campaign and protecting Joe Biden and his family.[11]

However, after taking a serious blow in cable news ratings, some media outlets began to reconfigure and shift their focus away from partisan political news castings. For example, "Since being named the new president of CNN, Chris Licht has been vocal about his ambition of shifting the network away from being anti-Trump TV in order to restore the journalistic credibility CNN once had. . . . At first, his personnel and programming changes seemed to signal his seriousness. Licht fired Brian Stelter, Jeffrey Toobin and John Harwood, all three were known for their hostile commentary towards former President Trump."[12]

Licht even demoted CNN partisans Don Lemon and Brianna Keilar, because they "became . . . CNN's biggest critics of Republicans [and] almost never targeted Democrats."[13] However, a radical progressive ideology remains ingrained at CNN. To exemplify, just a few weeks prior to the 2022 midterm elections, CNN advocacy reporter Jake Tapper gave a lecture on "extremism" and how Republicans have been using the label against their Democratic opponents leading up to the midterms, specifically when it comes to crime and the "defund the police" movement.

Tapper defended Democrats, arguing, "there's a difference between extremists who are exiled to the outer fringes of their party and extremists who are embraced by their party,"[14] and quickly pointing to Representative Marjorie Taylor Greene's (R-GA) history of peddling conspiracy theories and "openly, hideously, shamelessly racist" comments. Tapper implied that Trump "invited all of these extremists into the Grand Old Party."[15]

Tapper went on to say, "These extremist views are making the American experiment difficult to achieve. How can you work on legislation with someone who pushes messaging and seems to subscribe to QAnon, a group that accuses Democrats of being part of a satanic, pedophilic cult that eats babies? They cast their political opponents not just as wrong, but as evil."[16] Tapper made these accusations prior to showing footage from the Capitol riot, which occurred on January 6, 2021. Now, a few years after the fact, Tapper still holds to a provocative narrative. He declares, "Forget defunding the police. . . . Trump is promising the insurrectionists full pardons if he gets re-elected [in 2024]. He's embracing that extremism, he's embracing that extremist violence."[17]

Joseph Wulfsohn describes Tapper's incessant preoccupation with all things Trump. He writes, "Since Biden took office, Tapper has doubled down on his animosity toward Trump and his followers, and even expanded it to a large swath of the general Republican Party. There has been no justification as to why he was 'waging war' on GOP lawmakers who challenged the results of the 2020 election and banning such *election deniers* from his CNN programs despite making exceptions for Democrats like Stacey Abrams, who famously did not concede her 2018 defeat in the Georgia gubernatorial race against Brian Kemp."[18]

Why is the battle between politics and the media so important? The principles used by radicals to shut down dissent and those that would critique leftist narratives have been taken up, in practice, within America's classrooms.

Schools Learned from Media

Schools have taken a page from media partisanship. Snyder explains, "Unfortunately, we've also seen situations where innocent students have been presumed guilty of offensive acts in sweeping statements used by groups of educators, in which students were singled out by race by the school district and/or held presumptively responsible for acts they hadn't committed."[19]

Paul Valone asserts, "It's nice to be nice, and it's good to be right. But alas, public policy is generally driven by neither."[20] Snyder agrees: "Rather than engaging in fault-finding and blame-fixing, how much better we would all be if we learned to count blessings and to cultivate a garden of gratitude rather than grievances?"[21] Excellent intentions. But where does this lead?

Radicals of all types have drawn attention to their ideologies by their words and often by their actions. Regardless of the radical and the ideology to which their radicalism is affixed, there is a common goal. This goal is change. The methodology used to bring about the change, they expect, may vary. Nevertheless, the object is change—and by revolution, if necessary!

The argument is that change needs to occur across education in America. Others argue this change must begin with teacher training programs. Disagreement over who to blame and where to start can be a political roadblock. The reason is if you do not know who to blame, then you cannot change or fix a problem.[22]

American students, especially those in upper secondary and higher education, today have been complaining about their inability to assemble a society more akin to their progressive beliefs and practice. If one is to believe what we read from professors and students, there is great desire to incorporate socialist Marxism into all facets of life. This is a departure from the traditional America known by older citizens.

Society Fractured

As a result of a fractured society, unwilling to assimilate or honor traditional American culture, several things occur. *First*, protest and violence mark some of those who wish to destroy an entire system, so that that those on the margins and fringes of society may establish one they believe to be more equitable and less like their grandmother's America. *Second*, political efforts on college campuses and in society in general are employed to censor, or cancel, anyone with views that challenge the prevailing progressive-liberal views on social matters, particularly pertaining to race, gender, and sex.

Third, drug usage, suicides, criminal and gang activity, as well as homelessness have increased exponentially among Gen Z and the millennials. Lawfulness and a moral compass seem to be lost on so many twenty- and thirtysomethings. *Fourth*, the younger generations are fast becoming known as the therapy generation, due to their inability to handle who and what they are as people.

Even before the pandemic, mental and emotional health issues had risen sharply over the past few years among the younger generations.[23] The unwillingness to fit into established society and the inability to create another has frustrated a growing contingent of younger Americans.

WHAT HAPPENED TO CIVIL DISAGREEMENT?

Whatever happened to the art of disagreement? The old adage, *agree to disagree agreeably* is no longer in play. The gloves are off and people are divided by so many things that a group's willingness to fight and become violent appears to the indoctrinated as a radical's virtue. People are willing to throw away relationships,[24] shut down debate, and shame others over divergent political views.

Incivility involves parents of school-age children who boisterously and vehemently disagree with school board positions and decisions on issues. Confrontations occur and arrests are made over disagreements at these meetings. As a result, relationships with friends, family, neighbors, and even co-workers are lost. Teachers and parents are also finding themselves at odds with each other. Each side has lost trust in the other. Such confrontations and rage spill over onto social media and emotions spill out online for the world to see.

Much, but not all, of this heat is a reaction to the political left and radicalized students, to teachers and professors who simply want the world to change to fit their ideas. But radicals on the right bear their share of the blame for incivility. Refusal to change is a radical's entrenchment. Many parents and grandparents fear the America they knew as children, and as adults, is slipping away into a crime-ridden, racialized and radicalized sexual, angry vortex. Thus, for them, schools are ground zero in the battle against indoctrination and radicalism.

THE GOOD OLD DAYS

Hard work and ethics mean less today than in the past. The strategy for radicals is to make almost everything political. What matters today is winning at all cost. Doing unto others before they do unto you, and doing unto others worse than they have done unto you, are perverse reversals of the Golden Rule. What is also reversed is the relational ethic between people, which had been a mainstay of the American culture.

Far too many people—including radicals of all stripes—hold to an ethic that states the end they wish to achieve is the justification of the means by which they intend to attain it. For example, even when elections are certified in states by those of their own political party, there are cries of foul, fraud, and cheating by those in political parties. Trust has diminished greatly in America and this not only applies to politics. Distrust cuts across all parts of culture and has found residence in our nation's schools.

Americans who long for the good old days, where "basic tolerance for student ideological diversity [was] a longstanding cultural expectation in American schools,"[25] are finding it difficult to teach values at home while, at the same time, these values are overridden by teachers and professors at the schools and colleges their children attend. Snyder claims, preserving these values "involves upholding normative social agreements and certain implicit assumptions that govern how we treat one another in civil society. . . . These practices are based in common sense, wisdom, and mutual respect,"[26] much of which is sorely lacking in American society.

One of the better elements of the good old days was the respect and trust forged between teachers and the parents. Teachers and professors were not as bold and presumptuous as to "dictate to students what values they should hold, beyond insisting upon adherence to established school rules. Responsible educators refrained from using their access to impressionable children in order to exert influence upon them, but instead respected the sanctity of each child's individual free will and emerging understanding of the world."[27]

As Snyder explains, "For so many decades, the trust between parents and teachers was unspoken and well deserved. Good faith and shared aims were presumed. Educators were revered as some of the most selfless, sacrificing, hard-working public servants in the community, upholding high standards and molding responsible, dutiful, informed citizens. Parents relied on them not to subvert their authority, undermine their values, or, worse, mislead them about their intentions under the guise that they somehow know better. Tragically, this trust has eroded."[28]

The desires regarding public schools, in terms of government actors, means they "must refrain from attempts to enforce belief systems upon students."[29] And yet, schools continue pressing their progressive agenda forward and meddling with the fundamentals upon which traditional American education is based. Students always seem to be in the crosshairs of cultural changes and the battles that ensue over these changes.

CHILDREN BELONG TO PARENTS

There must be no question about who is responsible for children that attend public school. "The final authority over the education of children has long been settled: it is the parents—not the schools or the teachers. . . . National educational organizations readily concede this long-established legal fact, even if they don't always appear to be following it."[30] This may be "because this fundamental point is so well established, activist educators inclined to opposing parental wishes or to teaching outside the established curricular guardrails appear to be resorting to covert means and dissembled terminology to accomplish their aims without going through open, democratic channels where they have to face and overcome opposition. This is obviously unacceptable and must be actively exposed and opposed by those who know and understand their rights and natural authority."[31] Saying one thing in public and doing the opposite in private is a way to avoid immediate transparency. Such practices are also called hypocritical.

Teachers who are concerned about the direction of their schools and are sensing the changes in the soul of their profession should take note of the following steps. Snyder shares five significant steps parents and sympathetic teachers can take.

1. "First, educate yourself and others on the ideologies behind curriculum changes. Don't take seemingly innocuous terminology like equity, anti-racism, or ethnic studies at face value, but instead take a dive into the literature which unpacks enthusiastically promoted concepts so that you can equip yourself with the knowledge required to understand and discuss these topics circumspectly."[32]
2. "Second, speak up. If you are a tenured teacher, now is not the time to sit back and shut up. Do what you can to help and defend the untenured, who may find they have much more on the line than you do."[33]
3. "Third, be hypervigilant about diversity consultants. Unpacking deceptive terminology will provide you valuable insight into the minds and motivation of those who work to narrow the opinion corridor. Oftentimes, questionable ideology is smuggled into schools through

diversity, equity, and inclusion consultants who use such concealing terminology. Once you are well versed in the ambiguous language they use, you will realize the tremendous amount of baggage that comes with accepting many of the recommended ideas and programs."[34]

4. Fourth, "What values are being promoted with DEI programs or initiatives?"[35]

5. "Fifth, be aware of complicit administrators. Insist that administrators uphold and enforce existing ethical standards among staff. Insist that teachers refrain from teaching outside their area of training/competence or in the private realm of values or dispositions. Reject the notion that a short training seminar by an outsides consulting group qualifies teachers to be instructing on complex and values-laden topics such as justice, equity, or social justice."[36]

DEVELOPING STRATEGIES TO BATTLE INDOCTRINATION

Developing strategies to prevent schools from exceeding their authority and establishing themselves as determined centers of indoctrination is important in dealing with radicalism. The sad reality is that in some cases parents might already consider it too late to make an impact. But it is not too late. This battle must involve parents and others concerned about what is being taught in their children's schools and who is teaching them.[37] Snyder agrees that, "The solution to classroom indoctrination . . . must be led by determined parents, grandparents, principled educators, concerned citizens, and legislators prepared to oppose unhealthy school degradation with sufficient energy and necessary stamina. Addressing the current problems requires transparency, organization, determination, and effort, but it can—and must—be done."[38]

Furthermore, because radicals in classrooms love to shift language and utilize word games "all terminology must be clearly defined. No confusion should exist about what anyone is talking about. . . . Already social justice has shifted to critical race theory, and anti-racism is being overtaken by ethnic studies and culturally responsive teaching."[39]

Parents should also understand that one of the very best tools they can provide for the children who attend public schools is to teach them to become advocacy partners and "to stand up for the isolated target of Alinsky-style ridicule, name calling tactics (Racist! Homophobe!). This is utterly terrorizing to a young person. It's ironic, indeed, that as anti-bullying programs have increased in the schools, public shaming has increased."[40] Like-minded parents and students should stand up to radical teachers and those bullied in classrooms, when a brave student refuses to be indoctrinated.[41]

Parents should teach their kids to disengage when horrible discussions, name calling, or debates marginalize people with views not held by the teacher. "It's perfectly fine for them to say, 'I'm not sure how I feel about that. I need some time to think about that.' They must be allowed to leave it at that. Pursuing them after such a final statement constitutes harassment. Values are a guiding star by which to evaluate competing ideas and ideologies,"[42] and these values are best taught by parents at home.[43]

HOPE ON THE HORIZON

Parents are rising up and taking stands all across America. Parents' advocacy groups, such as Parents Defending Education, No Left Turn in Education, National Parenting Education Network, Focus on the Family, Moms for Liberty, and others, are affecting legislation. What some on the left claim is that parent groups are the causes of legislative gag orders, which are implemented by legislators in order to stop indoctrination of students.

The left's tactics are similar each time. They freeze their target with a released narrative to media, then give the target a new moniker. After this, the modus operandi is to repeat the new moniker *ad nauseam*. A good example of this was the "Don't say gay" law in the state of Florida. The law has nothing to do with the term *gay*. It has everything to do with stopping the radical sexualization of children in grades K–3. But the media repeated the narrative in support of the radical LGBTQ+ members.

Without laws such as those in Florida, and other states, arrogant teachers will force children to listen to books that celebrate the teacher's own sex and gender, and expose them to more confusion. For example, in California, childhood development teacher Danita McCray currently works at an elementary school in the Sacramento City Unified District. At a 2021 California Teachers Association (CTA) conference, McCray gave a presentation on how to incorporate gender ideology into early childhood. The teacher told the attendees that if parents did not like what was being done they should go to another class.[44]

Parents must continue to lead the charge against radicalism in schools.[45] Those that receive their power from parental votes will either pay attention or they must be forced out by recall, or by the next election.[46] This is the true power of local politics and where radicalization can be stopped in its tracks. As stated earlier in this book, sometimes it takes a radical approach to standing for truth in order to remove a radical set of erroneous or harmful ideas and the people who support them.

Personal experience validates that "like most bullies, if you stand up to them, they will cave. They rest on an extremely shaky intellectual foundation as well, and will quickly topple under intelligent cross examination. They thrive using fear, intimidation, and the expectation of appeasement in the face of those tactics."[47]

FIGHTING RADICALISM THE PRACTICAL WAY

If parents see indoctrination occurring in classrooms, there are ways to combat the effects. Snyder, and others, list suggestions for parents[48] in the battle against indoctrination.[49] These are addressed in expanded form below.

1. *Ask for reasonable alternatives for unacceptable lesson plans.* Parents have every right to have access to the curriculum that is being taught to their children. Put in an in-person request to the local school principal to examine the curriculum frameworks for your children's teachers. Request also to have a tour of the school library to have a better understanding of the grade-level books accessible to your child's teachers.
2. *Go public.* If the school principal refuses to comply with parent requests to view curriculum, the school library, or to examine the adopted series of academics, then put in a request to speak at the next school board meeting and share the denial with the board. Additional steps to take would be to (a) engage other similarly minded parents in the requests, (b) file Freedom of Information Act (FOIA) lawsuits, (c) partner with support organizations promoting classical liberal education and fighting biased indoctrination, and (d) offer to create clubs that celebrate free thought but support common sense in education.
3. *Inoculate your kids* by discussing with them the truth about what is taking place at their schools. Standing against indoctrination means holding teachers, principals, and school boards accountable. Parents should not be fearful of using online groups and supportive media sites to bring the battle against indoctrination to others across the nation. Parents should remember there are those with moral compasses and who believe in truth. These should be used to evaluate what transpires in schools and what students learn in their classrooms.

In terms of inoculating children against indoctrination, families can model ways to combat indoctrination. Parents can teach their children skills, practice these skills, and provide confidence for their children to counteract many forms of indoctrination. Parents desire their children "to be able to cope with a certain appropriate amount of intellectual challenge,"[50] and also provide opportunities for them to challenge ideas, whereby providing stimuli for student growth in character. Moreover, "role modeling from parents is essential in well-functioning character education."[51] Most adults would recommend one major shift in the battle against radicalizing children. That is, students should put away their individual smart devices for periods of time.

Keeping Watchful Eyes

If you find that teachers are teaching material outside their licensing, or outside their credentialed areas, parents should reach out to the school and find out why this is happening. If it is discovered that a teacher is an activist in the BLM or Antifa movements, or any other radical groups, please note there will be a significant impact on your children. In fact, "a lot of what these teachers are doing in the realm of attitude adjustment is close to unlicensed therapy. Classroom teachers have absolutely no business engaging in unethical practices . . . teachers are not priests and are not tasked with instructing on moral values or character beyond lowest common denominator values, such as the Golden Rule."[52]

Any discussion on indoctrination must necessarily include information on those who indoctrinate. There are two major types of teachers that indoctrinate. These two types include "the misguided and the true believer."[53] A distinction between the two types of indoctrinating teachers rests in the following basic understanding: "A sincere but misguided teacher may simply be unaware and uninformed about hidden motives and political ideologies embedded in skillfully packaged materials helpfully offered by partisan actors. Such a teacher may be willing and able to correct errors and oversights when they're pointed out, but a true believer never will."[54]

If parents run across a teacher who ignores parental input and has made it clear that indoctrination is the aim, then this teacher is what Snyder calls "a bad faith educator."[55] In addition to being inflexible, the bad faith teacher also "sees nothing wrong with what he or she is doing. Radicals are often blinded to truth by their radicalism."[56] Parents' watchful eyes are necessary to hold teachers accountable.

Teachers blinded by radicalism have been indoctrinated to believe it is their duty to appropriate the classroom for personal partisan ends. These types of teachers are often unrepentant and unremorseful. "They will lie, dissemble, double down, and persist proudly."[57] Many parents are now having to contend with bad faith teachers, as well as bad faith school board members. To some extent, a national teacher shortage is not helping any. Even so, radical extremist adults should not be working with our children.[58]

The need for a stronger teacher force implies that the United States has a weak one.[59] There is little hope that teacher education programs will be moving away from preparing teachers to instruct students on race, sex, and gender any time soon.[60]

If reform is going to happen, it must pull rank on the unions to produce better teachers. That will not happen unless teacher education institutions consciously end indoctrination and focus on content instruction and assessment. Teachers should spend time on the basics, rather than kowtowing to political progressives and their social engineering programs. Public schools will be considered lost in the United States, unless this shift is made toward reform.[61]

THE BATTLE IS REAL

It has been established that America's schools have become ground zero for radicals as indoctrination centers. The system of education itself is a top-down bureaucracy that relies on compliance of those down the line and reaches all the way into the classrooms in America. No public school teacher ever escapes mandates that their district requires. No public school district escapes the mandates that come down from the state, through their state departments or offices of public instruction. The same goes for state education money that flows downward from both the federal and state levels.

As an educator, fighting against what is required because of funding is nearly impossible. Then there are teachers' unions and associations that supposedly represent teachers in times of conflict. The unions claim that teachers know better than anyone what children need in order "to learn and thrive."[62] And so it goes as it has gone for many decades. Parents are left to the side in the education process. They are left to the side, only and until they speak up and step up boldly to form parent boards to review curriculum and school policies.

The good news is that this type of involvement is still welcome in pockets of elementary schools. In addition, parent volunteer boards can often obtain a bit more of an impact by establishing fundraising, giving general advice about holiday parties, and the like. This just illustrates the importance of having elected the right school board members and turning out the radicals. But there is an issue that needs to be addressed.

As it stands, the involvement of parents at schools, especially in middle and secondary schools, is becoming more and more discouraged. The COVID-19 pandemic placed teachers, students, and parents in unique situations. Students were receiving their instruction. Parents were observing the instruction and their observations began to yield concerns about teachers and the curriculum. Parents' involvement in their children's education took a different form and every administrators' and school boards' nightmares started to become realities.

Changes in Norms

School counselors and teachers in some states are forbidden to tell parents if their children go by a different identifier at school than they use at home. Students who tell school counselors, or teachers, they are homosexual, or feel trapped in a body that does not match their feelings, are told their parents will be kept in the dark about such revelations.

Students of all ages are emotionally confused, and confusing them ever more at school is leading to drastic rises in mental health concerns. Radicals who claim to have endured confusion of their own view what children are experiencing as natural trauma in coming out sexually and emotionally. Schools are now places where children are counseled to consider their gender and sexuality as expressions against hetero-normativity and American patriarchy.[63]

Norms have changed in schools. The subtleties of indoctrination take time to root themselves and become obvious. As pushback to the changes in norms, legislators in several states have crafted bills and passed laws to slow radical trends that undercut families. States have legislated against the revisionist radicalization of American history, as well. The expectation is that more bills will be written and more laws passed that will continue to restrict schools and teachers from (1) circumventing parents' mores, (2) placing value on feelings over science, (3) mainstreaming politically correct sociological concepts, and (4) not supporting the nuclear family. Changes like these might be short-lived. In terms of politics, the more radicals that are elected from Gen Z, the greater the change of radicalization manifested in society.

Benjamin Bosman shares his perspective: "Leftists believe they are the mainstream. Even when their views are opposed by the people, they condescendingly sneer that the people don't know what is good for them. They believe they are so smart that they are ahead of the curve of intellectual thought and their purpose is to lead the people to accept their ideas of how the world should be."[64]

Politically-left watchdog groups are keeping their eyes on legislation that would restrict the direct teaching of race issues in America. They are also watching the limitations placed on LGBTQ+ issues unfold in states. Each of these is meant to protect children from being indoctrinated. The left watchdog groups complain that their rights are being infringed and limitations are being placed on free speech. They also complain that the right is indoctrinating their children to the values of right-wing extremists.

The irony involving radicals, whether on the left or right, is stark. The irony is also quite predictable. In this case, radical leftists had no problem indoctrinating students against whiteness and white privilege. They felt assured and secure in bombarding students with proclaimed LGBTQ+ claims, drag queen shows, and anti-conservative rhetoric. The left had little problem limiting dissent and free speech of those who are against their type of indoctrination. As with most things in culture, the loudest voices draw most of the attention.

Free speech advocates on the left are quick to make the claim that restricting conservative speech is protectionary and limits harm to the emotions of students. Leftist radicals paint those who disagree as troublesome and anti-democratic. In this current battle, the advocates on the right favor open dialogue and desire conversations about issues on all sides, as long as (1) what is being taught is not meant as indoctrination and (2) dissent is allowed. These desires appear radical to those on the left.

When leftists find their efforts to indoctrinate are being limited by law, they retreat to the claim of free speech violations. It would be wrong to radicalize students toward any issue or toward any political side. But it is more egregious when one side indoctrinates, disallows any contrarian efforts of dissent, and marginalizes dissenters as dangerous and semi-fascist. Again, this is a strategy straight from Alinsky's *Rules for Radicals*. Where does this battling over free speech leave our students?

The battle is on for more than the minds of America's students. It is also on for their bodies and their souls. Jeremy Young and Jonathan Friedman explain this battle: "There is a legislative war on education in America. At the heart of this war are educational gag orders—state legislative attempts to restrict teaching, training, and learning in K–12 schools and higher education. These bills, which generally target discussions of race, gender, sexuality, and US history, began to appear during the 2021 legislative session and quickly spread to statehouses throughout the country. By the year's end, fifty-four bills had been filed in twenty-two states, of which twelve became law."[65]

A New Radicalism

After COVID-19 lockdowns by states, the education mindset changed for millions of parents. These changes came as a result of what they saw through online instruction. When schools brought back live instruction, the winds of change had shifted many states' educational philosophies. As a result of the change in educational philosophies, the winds have blown a different political direction than parents could have ever expected. Presently, there are few limits on private conversations with children about gender transitioning, or that certain students are oppressed by other students in the classrooms. Race, gender, sex, and the environment are the prized themes of the radical left.

Leaders have taken their eyes off what is truly important in education and have instead adopted an approach that ensures post-COVID-19 radicalism is the status quo. Parents' understanding of this newly adopted educational approach did not exactly coincide with the reality of education prior to the pandemic. Parents saw this as an effort to indoctrinate their children.

Parents who refuse to go away and back into their *uninformed corners*, will do what is best for their children by fighting against the bureaucracy wherever they can. Others will simply continue to remove their children from public education, in order to avoid what they perceive as leftist indoctrination. School leaders must refocus on what matters and leave the social engineering aside. If they do not, then student outcomes will continue to decline, and the National Council on Teacher Quality, the American Federation of Teachers, and the National Education Association will still be blaming COVID-19 well into the 2030s.

Not only is leftist radicalism destroying the teaching *profession* but the same can also be said about America's military recruitment. This is also the case within the fields of heath care, especially in the fields of medicine and physicians' training. As was stated before, sometimes it takes a radical approach to thwart radicalism. Many parents nationwide have figured this out, but there is much more that needs to be accomplished,

THE BATTLE OVER FREE SPEECH AND CENSORSHIP

The liberal research organization, PEN America, released a report on censorship in America's classrooms. This report does not go deeply into the restriction of conservative speech in schools and at colleges. Rather, it is a comprehensive free speech complaint about the legislative limits placed on progressive indoctrination at schools and colleges by conservative lawmakers in primarily red states. In true spin, the report states, "Just a few years ago, Republican legislators were championing bills protecting free expression on college campuses, many are now focused on bills that censor the teaching of particular ideas. Meanwhile, conservative groups and education officials are working to broaden the interpretation of existing gag order laws. . . . In 2023, we anticipate that the assault on education will continue. . . . Based on current trends, we predict that other legislative attacks on education, such as curriculum transparency bills, anti-LGBTQ+ bills, and bills that mandate or facilitate book banning are also likely to increase."[66]

Prohibitions

There are three types of prohibitions that states have litigated. These include the prohibition of compulsion, the prohibition of promotion, and the prohibition of inclusion.[67]

Young and Friedman conclude that of the three types of prohibitions addressed by legislators, "the bills that prohibit inclusion are the most censorious."[68] The reason the authors make this claim is that such bills are written so that "it makes no difference how objectively a teacher discusses a given idea, or even whether they forcefully critique it. The mere fact of including that idea in the curriculum risks violating legislation in this category."[69]

The pendulum swing has caused those on the left to resort to the very arguments disallowed by the right when leftist indoctrination was deemed protected from objective analysis and critique. The interesting part about most free speech claims is that they are only brought up when the pendulum swing empowers the prevailing opposite position. Politicians rarely practice politics by the Golden Rule.

Bosman's insights are in contrast to PEN America. He declares, "Leftists will be the first to tell you that radicalism is something that is on the right. Republicans and conservatives are radical because they typically are against people ruining their lives."[70] As a result, radicals will resort to using ridicule as a tactic to shame and cancel those with whom there are disagreements. Particularly those on the left have no patience for dialogue and dissent. In fact, "ad hominem is part of the ridicule of the Left's opposition. It is difficult to prove a negative. How can one prove he is not a racist, or bigoted in some way? If one believes homosexuality is wrong according to his biblical beliefs, he is called a gay-basher or homophobe, though he may have sympathy for those who practice it, or even have a libertarian attitude of live-and-let-live."[71]

Legislation

Legislative orders that were introduced in 2022 "tended to be more expansive and to target a wider array of educational speech"[72] than the bills introduced in previous years. The bills for 2022, and going into 2023, seem to be targeting LGBTQ+ issues and identities . . . lawmakers . . . assert political control over everything from classroom speech to library content, from teachers' professional training to field trips and extracurricular activities."[73]

The use of words can often diminish the levels of concern people have about what affects their children. In this case, Young and Friedman tend to minimize what parents face in the battle against indoctrination and radicalization in American schools. *First*, the supposed targeting of LGBTQ+ issues and identities are not regarded by the authors as truly sex and gender groups that are targeting children. Lawmakers are merely providing legislative protectionary efforts meant to stop the targeting of captive audiences in grades K–12.

Second, gender identities have nothing to do with learning mathematics and proficiency in reading comprehension. Children do not need to have their minds confused about who they are to perform mathematical operations. So many of them are already struggling.

If girls claim to be good at language, and an introverted boy claims a female identity, he could then make the claim to be identified as a female introvert. At this point, because of the claim—or even biological changes—there is no sudden bursting forth of higher levels of miraculous language usage, or infused vocabulary, by the claimant's assertion. Such notions only cause greater confusion about what students are trying to learn.

Conversely, a student weak in mathematics will not somehow become a stellar mathematician by claiming a new race, gender, or sexual identity. It is a parent's responsibility to address the identity of the children they conceive and bring into this world. It is not the teachers' responsibility and certainly not the government's privilege.

Third, teachers have no right to free speech when they are teaching erroneous material, lying to students, or projecting bias. This is especially insidious when a teacher walks students into a biased belief system that disallows dissent and impugns those who dare step outside the teacher's narrative. For example, teaching the principles of antiracism as a topic from critical race theory, that a person is either a racist or an antiracist is wrong. Nevertheless, this did not stop the National Association of Diversity Offices in Higher Education from releasing their "Framework for Advancing Anti-Racism Strategy on Campus"[74] for colleges and universities.

Teaching that white children are born into privilege and must come to terms with deconstructing their oppressive whiteness is immoral, racist, and wrong. What is also wrong is teaching students that boys can be girls and girls can be boys and that men can be women, get pregnant, and have babies. Free speech to address issues from all vantage points is one thing. Teaching error as fact is just plain wrong and is not education. It is indoctrination.

If the errors just mentioned were allowed to be corrected in class, or opposed by facts, then there would be less argumentation about fairness, or even indoctrination. However, as it stands, any disagreement with the dominant erroneous narrative is somehow considered mean and creating a dangerous place for advocates of the error. The claim of free speech to indoctrinate students with error is specious and offensive—and it is immoral!

Teaching against established factual science is erroneous—regardless of one's feelings about the errors. Either teach the facts and truth, allow dissent of arguments and positions, or do not teach the controversial topics at all. If the warning is not heeded, the only resorts are to legislate against the indoctrination, mobilize student and parent protests, or vote out school board members.

Last, any organization that would imply that students being restricted from having literature in a library, taking field trips, or scheduling extra-curricular

activities is somehow punitive is merely playing a semantics game to minimize reality. Parents do not want descriptive and graphic sex in the books
their children are reading.

Those that do want these materials in schools for children to explore their
sex and gender are falling into a trap set by radical LGBTQ+ advocates. For
example, in reviewing some of the questionable material for this book, the
descriptions on how to perform homosexual sexual acts, and discovering
transgenderism are not fictional literature. Rather, they are *how to* books, with
drawings, dialogue, and graphic depictions, that leave nothing to the imagina-
tion. What is the purpose of instructing children on the how-to of homosexual
oral and anal sex?

Adults must stop sexualizing our nation's children in schools. These same
adults must cease the indoctrination of students toward an adult way of carnal
thinking. Recruiting children by means of sex exploration and gender curiosity—and exposing underdeveloped minds is perverse and amounts to child
abuse. This abuse extends to and includes inviting drag queens to schools for
assemblies and taking children on field trips, as extra-curriculars, to bars and
nightclubs to probably see the exposed breasts and genitalia of men dressed
as women.[75]

The only purpose for children to see sexualized transvestites is to break
down their natural wall of embarrassment and shame—essentially their innocence—and enable their own childhood curiosity to lean toward sexualization
as merely fun. Drafting and passing anti-radical and anti-indoctrination legislation, to protect children from these types of exposure in print and in person,
is the right and loving thing to do on behalf of the children and families of
our nation.

THE BEAT GOES ON

There are fewer things that anger parents than school teachers secretly
molding the minds and hearts of their children. When this occurs, instead of
learning academic content, children are unlearning home-taught values and
distorting facts. Parents have every right and moral obligation to step in.

For example, learning about race, racism, and the history of the South's Jim
Crow laws, the politics involved, and how skin color was used in the past to
segregate is appropriate. Placing blame on students in the present, because of
the past, is to saddle students with responsibility they do not deserve. This
is not appropriate. Such attributions may cause trauma and lead to serious
spirals downward in mental health. Teachers have no business causing students trauma.

More and more mental health cases are popping up. A good number of these cases are from Gen Zs and millennials. Parents are making their voices heard because of the fear that sex education, suicide prevention information, and social-emotional learning programs are adding ideas into the psyches of already confused children.[76]

Consider two examples. *First*, it is indoctrination to tell students that people that look like them are the reason for racism. It is also indoctrination to make the claims that racism can exist even without racists.[77] This is the kind of word-twisting that more than implies white students are racists without knowing or consciously doing things to demonstrate their racism. *Second*, it is indoctrination to tell students that their whiteness must be deconstructed, even as they have no idea how skin color implicates them in the first place. The following statement by Rashawn Ray and Alexandra Gibbons of the Brookings Institution illustrates the concerns about woke ideological indoctrination that accompanies critical race theory, and why many states, including Florida,[78] have restricted discussions on race.

CRT does not attribute racism to white people as individuals or even to entire groups of people. . . . Sociologists and other scholars have long noted that racism can exist without racists. However, many Americans are not able to separate their individual identity as an American from the social institutions that govern us—these people perceive themselves as the system. Consequently, they interpret calling social institutions racist as calling them racist personally. It speaks to how normative racial ideology is to American identity that some people just cannot separate the two. There are also people who may recognize America's racist past but have bought into the false narrative that the US is now an equitable democracy. They are simply unwilling to remove the blind spot obscuring the fact that America is still not great for everyone.[79]

The problem with Ray and Gibbons, and their statement from the Brookings Institution, is they somehow left out the sentiments of teachers from a variety of states. Hannah Grossman reports that many educators view critical race theory curriculum that is used in schools, even though not under the technical heading of CRT, as "going horribly wrong."[80] According to Erec Smith of *Free Black Thought*, "there should be a bipartisan push against CRT because it is adamantly opposed to the foundation of liberty—free speech, equality, individuality, and the concept of merit."[81]

Another example of indoctrination being fought by parents is found in the battles over sex, gender, and the LGBTQ+ pressure for widespread acceptance into all schools. Students who are exposed to ideologies that are beyond their understanding are being swayed by adults. Again, such actions of these types can lead to serious effects upon the mental health of children—all under the guise of gender-affirming care. Stephen Sawchuk notes these concerns and responds in *EdWeek*:

> Gender-affirming care includes a spectrum of services to validate students' gender identities. It can include counseling, supporting a child's choice to change names and pronouns, or supporting a child's choice to alter dress and presentation. For adolescents, it may eventually include the use of drugs to delay puberty or hormones, though these are rarer. Major US and international health organizations do not endorse gender-conforming surgery for minors. . . . An Education Week Research Center poll found that about half of teachers said they thought they should teach about LGBTQ topics. . . . LGBTQ organizations have raised the alarm in part because some youth aren't comfortable discussing feelings of gender dysphoria with their parents, fearing abuse or other consequences.[82]

Parents are angry that schools have taken upon themselves to indoctrinate children about topics unrelated to education. Social engineering and indoctrination have no place in public education. Students should not be taught about gender fluidity, or that doctors and parents make mistakes and mis-gender children at birth, and that some children feel born in the wrong bodies and that needs to be fixed.

Joy Pullman of *The Federalist* summarizes what schools say to parents who are angry over their preschool children being indoctrinated by LGBTQ+ radical ideologies. Pullman addresses what are "6 crazy responses" given to parents who complain about indoctrination.[83] These are listed below, including excerpts that demonstrate the reasoning for the indoctrination that parents battle in public school districts across America.

1. *Teaching transgenderism to preschoolers is age-appropriate.*
   - "Sometimes people use their bodies to help them know their gender, and some people know their gender in their heart."[84]
2. *Sex education isn't sex education.*
   - "There's nothing in the district's [LGBT curriculum] that overlaps with sexual education that would require any form of opt out that State law requires."[85]
3. *Religion has nothing to say about sex.*
   - "When people were talking about religious objections, it does become challenging, so we've been trying to help people understand that this is not a religious curriculum, this is not a curriculum that is advocating any form of sexuality."[86]
4. *Let's deliberately keep parents in the dark.*
   - "Not telling people the time of the curriculum is an option."[87]
5. *Differences of opinion make people fearful, unsafe.*

- "[Teachers'] names are linked to this curriculum, and there is real fear. . . . We didn't want to be out this weekend . . . because we are truly fearful. . . . We are now truly unsafe in this community in which some of us live and all of us teach in."[88]
6. *No opt-outs allowed.*
   - "Our administration has heard from a number of parents who want the ability to opt their children out of this curriculum. The District . . . Board of Education does not support allowing students to opt out of this or any curriculum that seeks to include a more complete account of the role of the historically marginalized people in our society."[89]

Yes, the beat goes on to capture the souls of America's children. The drumbeat is real. Many public school students are already ensnared. There are forces that are waging war against traditional American history, the nuclear family, quality of education, and the moral and spiritual cultural underpinnings of Judeo-Christianity in the United States.

Parents are doing the right thing by fighting back against the indoctrination of their children. But the battle on one front can be won, while watching the war slip into the loss column. People of faith and people of good conscience—along with those awakened from their woke stupor—must work together to recapture America's schools from the radicals. If the only option is to surrender, then teams of mental health practitioners and personal counselors had better reserve rooms for the multitude of patients. Let us pray it never comes to this.

As for the veteran teachers still in the trenches in American public schools, there are strong desires to pass along truth to the newly-trained. Veteran teachers, and those recently retired, will be here when the current generation begins to realize how their dissatisfaction with radical pursuits has left them with a sense of purposeless. We will be here when regrets begin to mount over choices to change identities. At those moments, feel free to call on us. We do not reject. We simply disagree. We do not cancel. We summarily provide time for maturity. We do not emote for the sake of emotion. We think critically. Above all, we love unconditionally.

But if you do not want veteran teachers around because of their age and ways of looking at life, they will still remain resourceful and "resource full." Moreover, if there is no tolerance for the worldviews of previous generations, and participation becomes limited because indoctrination is in the way, then the result will be that we shall all join together as rejected contingents. Veteran teachers know a lot about battling propaganda, indoctrination, and radicalism. After all, some of them came though the Cold War. They will no doubt overcome the cold shoulder.

NOTES

1. Saul Alinsky. *Rules for radicals.* 1971. New York: Random House, p. 61.

2. Katie Harbath and Collier Fernekes. "A brief history of tech and elections: A 26-year journey." Bipartisan Policy Center. September 28, 2022. Retrieved September 30, 2022, from https://bipartisanpolicy.org/report/history-tech-elections/.

3. Luke Winkie. "Posters aren't heroes." *SLATE.* October 28, 2022. Retrieved October 30, 2022, from https://slate.com/technology/2022/10/elon-musk-twitter -resistance-tweeters.html.

4. Jennifer Whitten Woodring and Patrick James. "Fourth estate or mouthpiece? A formal model of media, protest, and government repression." *Political Communication.* April 2012. 29(2):113–136. Retrieved October 21, 2022, from https://www .researchgate.net/publication/239798102_Fourth_Estate_or_Mouthpiece_A_Formal _Model_of_Media_Protest_and_Government_Repression.

5. Christopher Booker. "The idea of safe spaces has turned on itself to exclude everyone who dares to differ." *The Print.* March 4, 2020. Retrieved November 6, 2022, from https://theprint.in/pageturner/excerpt/idea-of-safe-spaces-has-turned-on -itself-to-exclude-everyone-who-differs/375545/.

6. Katherine J. Wu. "Radical ideas spread through social media. Are the algorithms to blame?" *NOVA.* March 28, 2019. Retrieved November 7, 2022, from https://www .pbs.org/wgbh/nova/article/radical-ideas-social-media-algorithms/.

7. Staff. "The news consumption habits of 16-to-40-year-olds." America Press Institute. August 31, 2022. Retrieved November 5, 2022, from https: //www.americanpressinstitute.org/publications/reports/survey-research/the-news -consumption-habits-of-16-to-40-year-olds/.

8. John Fund. "Biden Apologists are abandoning ship." *National Review.* April 13, 2022. Retrieved October 20, 2022, from https://www.nationalreview.com/corner/ biden-apologists-are-abandoning-ship/.

9. Mikael Thalen. "Elon Musk fanboys are jacked about his plan to fire 75% of Twitter employees." *Daily Dot.* October 26, 2022. Retrieved October 28, 2022, from https://www.dailydot.com/debug/elon-musk-fans-celebrate-twitter-layoff-plan/.

10. Joe Concha. "Joe Rogan Experience: Mark Zuckerberg interview." Fox News. Posted August 26, 2022. YouTube video. August 26, 2022. Retrieved October 4, 2022, from https://www.youtube.com/watch?v=Mg8PaSYCP5E.

11. Miranda Devine. *Laptop from hell: Hunter Biden, big tech, and the dirty secrets the president tried to hide.* 2021. Nashville, TN: Post Hill Press.

12. Joseph A. Wulfsohn. "Jake Tapper fuels GOP bashing in primetime despite CNN's newfound mission toward nonpartisanship." Fox News. October 21, 2022. Retrieved October 22, 2022, from https://www.foxnews.com/media/jake-tapper-fuels -gop-bashing-primetime-despite-cnns-newfound-mission-towards-nonpartisanship.

13. Ibid.

14. Ibid.

15. Ibid.

16. Ibid.

17. Ibid.

18. Ibid.

19. Bonnie Kerrigan Snyder. *Undoctrinate: How politicized classrooms harm kids and ruin our schools—and what we can do about it.* 2021. Nashville, TN: Post Hill Press, p. 187

20. F. Paul Valone. *Rules for antiradicals: A practical handbook for defeating leftism.* 2022. Bryson City, NC: Bacchus USA Publications, p. xxi.

21. Snyder. *Undoctrinate*, p. 148.

22. Staff. "Steep national declines and widening gaps in student math and reading performance reinforces urgent need for supporting a high-quality, diverse teacher workforce." National Council on Teacher Quality. October 24, 2022. Retrieved October 25, 2022, from https://www.nctq.org/publications/Steep-National-Declines -and-Widening-Gaps-in-Student-Math-and-Reading-Performance-Reinforces-Urgent -Need-for-Supporting-a-High--Quality,-Diverse-Teacher-Workforce?fbclid=IwAR0u ZRHaN76ZXT4HPFiN5chCKRscp2Vbj-vaGlvArpsxI8B3u9gfK2lMal0.

23. Alison M. Darcy and Timothy Mariano. "Mental health in America: A growing crisis." *Psychiatric Times.* August 6, 2021. Retrieved October 28, 2022.

24. Julian Adorney. "How to have political disagreements without ruining relationships." Foundation against Intolerance & Racism. November 7, 2022. Retrieved November 8, 2022, from https://fairforall.substack.com/p/political-disagreements ?utm_source=substack&utm_medium=email.

25. Snyder. *Undoctrinate*, p. 15.

26. Ibid.

27. Ibid., pp. 15–16.

28. Ibid., pp. 15–16.

29. Ibid., p. 187.

30. Ibid., pp. 192–193.

31. Ibid., p. 193

32. Ibid., p. 212.

33. Ibid., p. 212.

34. Ibid., pp. 212–213.

35. Ibid., p. 213.

36. Ibid., p. 213.

37. John Schoof and Julia Dandoy. "Parents are going on offensive to fight indoctrination in education." The Heritage Foundation. April 27, 2022. Retrieved November 2, 2022, from https://www.heritage.org/education/commentary/parents-are-going -offensive-fight-indoctrination-education.

38. Snyder. *Undoctrinate*, p. 214.

39. Ibid., p. 215.

40. Ibid., p. 216.

41. James Dobson. "Mother equips parents to fight against cultural indoctrination." Dr. James Dobson Family Institute. July 27, 2021. Retrieved November 7, 2022, from https://www.drjamesdobson.org/articles/mother-equips-parents-to-fight-against -cultural-indoctrination.

42. Snyder. *Undoctrinate*, p. 227.

43. Aruna Raghuram. "Values begin at home—your children are watching and learning from you." Parent Circle. 2022. Retrieved October 8, 2022, from https://www.parentcircle.com/values-begin-at-home/article. Cf. Tanja McIlroy. "10 values you should teach your preschool child." *Empowered Parents*. Blog. 2022. Retrieved November 6, 2022, from https://empoweredparents.co/values-to-teach-your-child/.

44. Hannah Grossman. "California early childhood teacher admits using gender unicorn to instruct kids on sexual attraction." Fox News. November 16, 2022. Retrieved November 17, 2022, from https://www.foxnews.com/media/california-early-childhood-teacher-admits-gender-unicorn-instruct-toddlers-sexuality.

45. Grace Chen. "Public school boards demystified: How parents can influence the board's decision." *Public School Review*. May 27, 2022. Retrieved November 3, 2022, from https://www.publicschoolreview.com/blog/public-school-boards-demystified-how-parents-can-influence-the-boards-decisions.

46. Eesha Pendharkar. "Parental rights poised to be hot issue in school board races." *Education Week*. October 5, 2022. Retrieved November 1, 2022, from https://www.edweek.org/leadership/parental-rights-poised-to-be-hot-issue-in-school-board-races/2022/10.

47. Snyder. *Undoctrinate*, p. 224.

48. Ibid., pp. 216–219.

49. Ibid., pp. 230–231.

50. Ibid., p. 218.

51. Staff. "Character education: Parents as partners." *Association for Supervision and Curriculum Development*. 63(1): n.p. September 1, 2005. Retrieved November 4, 2022, from https://www.ascd.org/el/articles/character-education-parents-as-partners.

52. Snyder. *Undoctrinate*, p. 220.

53. Ibid., p. 225.

54. Ibid.

55. Ibid., p. 226.

56. Bob Weir. "The blindness of the radical left." *Yonkers Tribune*. August 15, 2022. Retrieved November 3, 2022, from https://www.yonkerstribune.com/2022/08/the-blindness-of-the-radical-left-by-bob-weir.

57. Snyder. *Undoctrinate*, p. 226.

58. Ernest J. Zarra III. *America's sex culture: Its impact on teacher-student relationships today*. Lanham, Maryland: Rowman & Littlefield Publishers, pp. 91–118.

59. Daniel Buck. "Education schools have long been mediocre. Now they're woke too." *Wall Street Journal*. August 19, 2022. Retrieved November 4, 2022, from https://www.wsj.com/articles/education-schools-have-long-been-mediocre-now-theyre-woke-too-teachers-college-ideological-manipulation-propaganda-11660925293.

60. William Biagini. "Academic calls out colleges of education for prioritizing woke activism." *Campus Reform*. September 13, 2022. Retrieved October 9, 2022, from https://www.campusreform.org/article?id=20147. Cf. Gerard J. Tellis, Nitish Sood, and Ashish Sood. "Governors' lockdowns driven less by science than by political polarization, social learning, and information cascades, new study finds." *Business Wire*. April 22, 2020. Retrieved November 7, 2022, from https://www.businesswire.com/news/home/20200422006060/en/Governors%E2%80%99

-Lockdowns-driven-less-by-science-than-by-political-polarization-social-learning
-and-information-cascades-new-study-finds.

61. Laura Meckler. "Public education is facing a crisis of epic proportions." *Washington Post*. January 30, 2022. Retrieved November 29, 2022, from https://www.washingtonpost.com/education/2022/01/30/public-education-crisis-enrollment-violence/. Cf. John Persico. "Why public-school education is dying: Part 1 of 5 parts." *Aging Capriciously*. December 15, 2021. Retrieved November 25, 2022, from https://agingcapriciously.com/2021/12/15/why-public-school-education-is-dying-part-1-of-5-parts/.

62. Bradford Betz. "Teachers union tweet claims educators know better than anyone what kids need to learn and to thrive." Fox News. November 13, 2022. Retrieved November 14, 2022, from https://www.foxnews.com/us/teachers-union-tweet-claims-know-better-than-anyone-what-kids-need-learn-thrive.

63. Jason Flom. "Heteronormativity in schools." *Edutopia*. September 25, 2014. Retrieved November 29, 2022, from https://www.edutopia.org/blog/heteronormativity-in-schools-jason-flom.

64. Benjamin Bosman. *Leftist tactics, conservative solutions: A conservative analysis of Alinsky's rules and other tactics*. 2022. Monee, IL: self-published, p. 30.

65. Jeremy C. Young and Jonathan Friedman. "America's censored classrooms." PEN America 100. August 17, 2022. Retrieved August 18, 2022, from https://pen.org/report/americas-censored-classrooms/.

66. Ibid.

67. Ibid.

68. Ibid.

69. Ibid.

70. Bosman. *Leftist tactics, conservative solutions*, p. 30.

71. Ibid., p. 38.

72. Young and Friedman. "America's censored classrooms."

73. Ibid.

74. Staff. "A framework for advancing anti-racism strategy on campus." National Association of Diversity Offices in Higher Education (NADOHE). 2021. Retrieved January 24, 2022, from https://nadohe.memberclicks.net/assets/2021/Framework/National%20Association%20of%20Diversity%20Officers%20in%20Higher%20Education%20-%20Framework%20for%20Advancing%20Ant-Racism%20on%20Campus%20-%20first%20edition.pdf.

75. Laurel Duggan. "Pridefest hosts apologize after drag queen's fake breasts exposed to children at family-friendly event." *The Daily Caller*. September 1, 2022. Retrieved November 12, 2022, from https://dailycaller.com/2022/09/01/pridefest-castle-rock-drag-queen-exposes-breasts/.

76. Tyler Kinkade and Mike Hixenbaugh. "Parents protesting critical race theory identify another target: Mental health programs." NBC News. November 15, 2021. Retrieved November 4, 2022, from https://www.nbcnews.com/news/us-news/parents-protesting-critical-race-theory-identify-new-target-mental-hea-rcna4991.

77. Rashawn Ray and Alexandra Gibbons. "Why states are banning critical race theory." Brookings Institution. November 2021. Retrieved November 8, 2022, from

https://www.brookings.edu/blog/fixgov/2021/07/02/why-are-states-banning-critical
-race-theory/.

78. Staff. "Governor DeSantis announces legislative proposal to stop WOKE activism and critical race theory in schools and corporations." Office of Florida Governor Ron DeSantis. December 15, 2021. Retrieved November 9, 2022, from https://www
.flgov.com/2021/12/15/governor-desantis-announces-legislative-proposal-to-stop-w
-o-k-e-activism-and-critical-race-theory-in-schools-and-corporations/.

79. Ray and Gibbons. "Why states are banning critical race theory."

80. Hannah Grossman. "Critical race theory curriculum in K–12 school is going horribly wrong." Fox News. May 2, 2022. Retrieved November 25, 2022, from https://www.foxnews.com/media/critical-race-theory-curriculum-k12-schools-horribly
-wrong-teachers.

81. Ibid.

82. Stephen Sawchuk. "What's driving the push to restrict schools on LGBTQ issues?" *Education Week*. April 19, 2022. Retrieved November 9, 2022, from https://www.edweek.org/leadership/whats-driving-the-push-to-restrict-schools-on-lgbtq
-issues/2022/04.

83. Joy Pullman. "6 crazy school district responses to parents mad about LGBT indoctrination of preschoolers." *The Federalist*. October 18, 2019. Retrieved November 7, 2022, from https://thefederalist.com/2019/10/18/6-crazy-school-district
-responses-to-parents-mad-about-lgbt-indoctrination-of-preschoolers/.

84. Ibid.

85. Ibid.

86. Ibid.

87. Ibid.

88. Ibid.

89. Ibid.

Appendix

Excerpts of Equity and Social Justice Policies Adopted by School Boards*

School Board	Policy Excerpts
Orange County Schools, North Carolina Equity in Education Resolution September 14, 2020	• Ensure that the district creates, implements, and evaluates a yearly equity plan. • Naming actionable steps to work toward changing disparate outcomes and experiences in the school district and including performance metrics to evaluate progress. • Provide district-wide equity training on implicit bias, culturally responsive teaching strategies, and effective communication and family engagement. • Recognize the phrase "Black Lives Matter" not as a partisan or political statement, but as an affirmation of the inherent value of the lives of our black students, staff, and community members—and affirm that Black Lives Matter.
Knox County, Tennessee A resolution of the Board of Education, acknowledging Juneteenth and affirming black lives in Knox County schools June 19, 2020	• Systems of oppression have continued in the United States since June 19, 1865; such as segregated schools and communities, disparities in educational outcomes that include but are not limited to higher suspension rates among black students, over-policing of black students, and disproportionate representation of black students within Special Education. • The impact of inadequate representation of black educators in Knox County schools and inconsistency of culturally relevant practices affects the physical and mental health, safety, and the education of black students. • Acknowledging these forms of institutionalized racism is an imperative step to support the Knox County schools' 2019 to 2024 strategic plan. • An annual celebration of the past, present, and future of black liberation and those who work toward that liberation are to be highlighted.

(Continued)

179

School Board	Policy Excerpts
Bend, Louisiana Pine Schools Equity and Anti-Racism Resolution August 13, 2020	• Actively articulate the systemic and institutional inequities that undermine historically underserved and marginalized students in achieving this vision. • Adopt and uphold an equity lens in decision-making. • Antiracist and culturally responsive practices that put the assets of students and families at the core of instructional practices. • Nurture healthy relationships and create just and equitable learning environments. • Become actively antiracist. • Employ restorative justice to repair harm and transform conflict. • Professional development: develops and deepens awareness of personal and systemic bias and racism; empowers staff with the tools to interrupt systemic and historical patterns of oppression. • Establish and sustain equity-based accountability systems across the district.
Clayton County, Georgia Public Schools— Black Lives Matter Resolution March 2, 2021	• The arrival of the first enslaved peoples to America in 1619, black men and women have experienced the extraordinary trauma of dehumanization and extrajudicial murder. The system of white supremacy that once defined black bodies as property and persisted in the form of lynchings during the one hundred years of Jim Crow has been reincarnated by government. • The over-policing of our youth has proven to be ineffective in the reduction of discipline and has directly contributed to the criminalization of our children and directly enables the school-to-prison pipeline. • Restorative justice has proven to be a powerful tool in the reduction of disproportionate discipline and that the creation and implementation of a culturally responsive curriculum and an ethnic studies program is of critical importance to supporting the diversity of students. • Proclaiming loudly that "Black Lives Matter" does not negate our commitment to *all* of our students. In fact, we believe that challenging all of our students and colleagues to recognize the innate value of black lives will help them grow and that the quality of life for all who live in our communities will improve when we value the lives of everyone. • Will observe and facilitate the annual Black Lives Matter at School Week of Action. • Action plan: to challenge racism, oppression and to build safe and constructive conversations around systemic racism and the history of black and brown Americans that extend throughout the school year and the training of all staff, district-wide, in the implementation of quality restorative justice practices.

School Board	Policy Excerpts
New Orleans, Louisiana Parish School Board Racial Equity Resolution August 13, 2020	• We are outraged by the killing of George Floyd and deeply shaken by the persistent racial violence and systemic racism we continue to see across our country. • Many current inequities are sustained by historical legacies and structures and systems that repeat patterns of exclusion, and institutions and structures have continued to create and perpetuate inequities. • The city of New Orleans is not exempt from our country's racist history that is still pervasive in today's systems. • Because our efforts are hindered by an unjust systemic racist America, we intend to be proactive in dismantling the pillars of unequal justice, bigotry, and oppression. • Continue to do the work within our system to create a safe environment free of racism or social inequity for all of our students and staff. • Develop a racial equity plan for the district, within and across departments, inclusive of goals and vision rooted in an antiracist and equity lens. • Identify areas of disparities based on race in the hiring, retention, promotion, and compensation.
East Baton Rouge, Louisiana School Board Commitment to Equity and Eradicating Racism Resolution August 13, 2020	• Committed to actively interrupting systemic racism and eliminating inequities in our education system. • This racism and disregard of human dignity and life reflect and perpetuate a system within which students, families, and staff of color are hindered by both explicit actions as well as barriers caused by unintentional bias. • Commits to its own work as individuals and our collective work overseeing the district in continuing to become equitable in policies and practices that dismantle racism. • Commits to working with our local governmental agencies to strengthen the collective work of diversity, equity, and inclusion in our community.
Atlanta, Georgia Board of Education's Commitment to Equity and Antiracism August 3, 2020	• The recent incidents of violence against black Americans highlight the systemic bias and institutional racism in our society that has senselessly and atrociously devastated black lives throughout our country's history. • Committed to actively interrupting systemic racism and eliminating inequities in our education system. • Violence, racism, and disregard of human dignity and life reflect and perpetuate a system within which students, families, and staff of color and their families are oppressed and attacked, both through explicit racist actions as well as unconscious bias and microaggressions. • Commits to its own work as individuals and our collective work overseeing the district in continuing to become equitable and antiracist in behaviors, actions, and policies. • Commits to working with our local governmental agencies to strengthen the collective work of diversity, equity, and inclusion in our community.

(Continued)

School Board	Policy Excerpts
Indianapolis, Indiana IPS Board approves Racial Equity Policy and Black Lives Matter Resolution June 25, 2020	• Through the racial equity policy, along with the district-led racial equity initiative, IPS will implement several measures. • Approved the Black Lives Matter resolution. The resolution details not only the city, state, and country's history of systemic racism, but also the pervasive remnants of racial exclusion and the barriers to universal success. The resolution underscores the policy's intentional efforts to support legislation, advocacy and the culture of diversity throughout the district, including the targeted training and hiring of teachers and staff of color, and the restructuring of the IPS Police Department. • Black lives matter. Every student is capable of success, deserving of respect, and valuable to our community. To believe that black lives matter—and to put that belief into action—means to commit ourselves to a radical refusal to give up on any student, to hand them over to a criminal justice system that doesn't share our values, or return them to communities that lack the resources to support the realization of their fullest potential. The rise in zero tolerance discipline policies by school districts has contributed to reinforcing existing racial inequalities and limiting the opportunities for black students to achieve success.

*Excerpts from Staff. "Anti-racist policy and resolution exemplars." School Board Partners. 2022. Retrieved October 14, 2022, from https://schoolboardpartners.org/anti-racist-policy-making/anti-racist-policies/.

Index

About the Author

Ernest J. Zarra III, PhD, is retired assistant professor of teacher education at Lewis-Clark State College. Zarra has earned five degrees and holds a PhD. from the University of Southern California in teaching and learning theory with cognates in psychology and technology. He has a storied forty-two-year career in teaching at all levels, with most of his classroom experience being teaching seniors United States government and politics and economics.

Ernie is a former Christian College First Team All-American soccer player, high school and club soccer coach, former teacher of the year for a prestigious California public school, and was awarded as top student in graduate education from the California State University at Bakersfield, California. He is the father of two outstanding, professional, and accomplished adult children, a daughter and a son.

Dr. Zarra has written fifteen books, several of which earned awards, and is author of more than a dozen journal articles and several op-eds. His writings have appeared in *RealClear Education*, The *National Association of Scholars*, of which he is a member, and peer-reviewed professional journals of education. He has designed professional development programs, is a national conference presenter, has been interviewed by national and international media, is a former district professional development leader for the largest high school district in California, a full-time and adjunct university instructor, and a member of several national honor societies. He also participated as a speaker of the Idaho Speakers Bureau, as well as a presenter in the Lewis-Clark Presents program, bringing special topics to high school students.

Originally from New Jersey, he and his wife Suzi, also a retired California public school teacher, live in Washington State and enjoy spending time with family, cooking, participating in church ministry, yard work, and finding energy to keep up with their two grandchildren.

Other Works by this Author

Ernest J. Zarra III has authored fifteen books, including the additional Rowman & Littlefield titles:

- *From Character to Color: The Impact of Critical Race Theory on American Education* (Rowman & Littlefield, 2022)
- *When the Secular Becomes Sacred: Religious Secular Humanism and Its Effects upon American Public Learning Institutions* (Rowman & Littlefield, 2021)
- *Detoxing American Schools: From Social Agency to Academic Urgency* (Rowman & Littlefield, 2020)
- *America's Sex Culture: Its Impact upon Teacher Student Relationships Today* (Rowman & Littlefield, 2020)
- *The Age of Teacher Shortages: Reasons, Responsibilities, Reactions* (Rowman & Littlefield, 2019)
- *Generacion Z: La Generacion con Derechos* (Narcea/Rowman & Littlefield, 2019)
- *Assaulted: Violence in Schools and What Needs to Be Done* (Rowman & Littlefield, 2018)
- *The Teacher Exodus: Reversing the Trend and Keeping Teachers in the Classrooms* (Rowman & Littlefield, 2018)
- *The Entitled Generation: Helping Teachers Teach and Reach the Minds and Hearts of Generation Z* (Rowman & Littlefield, 2017)
- *Helping Parents Understand the Minds and Hearts of Generation Z* (Rowman & Littlefield 2017)
- *Common Sense Education: From Common Core to ESSA and Beyond* (Rowman & Littlefield, 2016)
- *The Wrong Direction for Today's School: The Impact of Common Core on American Education* (Rowman & Littlefield, 2015)
- *Teacher-Student Relationships: Crossing into the Emotional, Physical, and Sexual Realms* (Rowman & Littlefield, 2013)

www.ingramcontent.com/pod-product-compliance
Lightning Source LLC
Chambersburg PA
CBHW030649270326
41929CB00007B/274